Angus & the Mearns

A Historical Guide

Richard Oram

First published in Great Britain, 1996,
by Birlinn Ltd,
14 High Street,
Edinburgh EH1 1TE

British Library Cataloguing-in-Publication Data
A Catalogue record for this book is available from the British Library.

ISBN 1 874744 47 5

Typeset in Plantin Light

Printed and bound by Werner Söderström OY, Finland

ACKNOWLEDGEMENTS

There are many debts owed to friends and colleagues, built up over the time which it took to prepare this book. Especial thanks are owed to Davy Adams and Nicholas Bogdan for their generous assistance with tracking down information in their specialist areas. As usual, I find myself deeply indebted to Geoff Stell of the Royal Commission on the Ancient and Historical Monuments of Scotland, whose vast reservoir of knowledge has been mercilessly tapped.

Again, my greatest thanks must go to my wife, Justine, who has found herself a 'computer widow' as I disappear for many hours on end to input another section of text. Without her support, this book would never have appeared. And to Alasdair, my son, I owe thanks for his willingness to sleep and let me get on with work.

CONTENTS

FIGURES

MAPS

PLATES

PREFACE

There is something quintessentially Scottish about Angus and the Mearns. They are not rugged or mountainous territories, except in the far NW of the region where the land climbs steeply to the high plateau of the Grampians, but have a soft landscape of rolling hills and wide valleys, a well-watered land lying between the Highlands and the North Sea. Typified by its fields of plough-turned rich-red soils, or by expanses of wind-wafted golden grain, this is a land whose wealth has always lain in the soil.

The region, which is made up of the territories of the pre-1974 counties of Angus and Kincardine, falls into four main divisions. Its northernmost component lies beyond the great geological boundary that splits Scotland in two along a line between Stonehaven in the E and Helensburgh on the W. The Dee forms its furthest limit, except for the small salient N of that river around Banchory. Between the Mounth – the great mountainous barrier which separates north from south – and the Dee, lies a district that is quite Highland in character, composed of narrow strips of cultivated land extending in long, groping fingers up the narrow glens which fringe the high plateau. The high ground is a bleak, sub-arctic waste of wind-scarred rock and quaking bog, rising above the forestry-cloaked lower slopes. Much is now grouse-moor, but on the margins between this highland zone and the still-fertile lowlands can be traced the ghosts of communities who once eked a fragile existence in this inhospitable land.

S and E of the hill country the land drops swiftly into the broad Vale of Strathmore. This is the land which to most folk epitomises Angus and the Mearns, the softly-rounded countryside of arable lowlands and cattle-studded pastures, dotted with prosperous-looking farms and douce small towns of warm red and pink sandstone. At its N end lies the Howe of the Mearns, the spiritual home of the Scots' ploughman, of bothy chiels and the hard farming life of Lewis Grassic Gibbon's novels.

It is another world along the coast. Although the rich

farmlands come down to the very lip of the cliffs which rear from the North Sea, this is a land with its feet firmly in the water. The coast between the Tay and the Dee is undoubtedly one of the finest in all Britain, changing in character along the way from glorious expanses of golden sand to beetling, sea-gnawed cliffs of Old Red Sandstone and knobbly conglomerate. Small fishing villages cling to the steep slopes which rear from the reef-fouled shores, or sit perched on cliff-edges high above their storm-battered havens. Old ports preserve the memories of thriving trade in former days, across the North Sea to Scandinavia, the eastern shores of the Baltic, and south to the Low Countries.

And then there is Dundee. There is nowhere else in Scotland quite like this semi-detached city sandwiched between the Sidlaws and the Tay. Its isolation from the other major centres of Scotland has produced an independent character, coloured further by its place as the only centre of major industry in a region which is still predominantly agricultural in spirit. Battered by developers and scarred by shifting industrial fortunes, Dundee seemed almost in the 1960s and 1970s to be in risk of losing all links to its past. Recent years, however, have seen a reversal of this trend, and there is a new self-awareness which has restored something of the vibrancy and pride of the glory days of the 19th century.

It is advisable for anyone visiting the sites listed in this book to use Ordnance Survey maps. By far the best maps are the 1:25000 Pathfinder Series, but most of the sites are marked on the 1:50000 Landranger Series, of which six sheets are needed to cover the whole region (Series Nos 38, 43, 44, 45, 53 and 54).

The sites listed in the gazetteer section of the volume represent a wide, but far from exhaustive selection of the many monuments in this region. The wealth of archaeology in Angus and Mearns is quite outstanding, and for full coverage a much larger volume than this present offering would be required. For example, a Royal Commission survey of Central Angus alone produced a list of 314 Prehistoric and Roman period sites and 171 of the Medieval and Later

Periods. In general, greater detail has been accorded the pre-1600 era, with most sites which are marked on the 1:50000 OS maps being included. With the exception of very important excavated but destroyed sites, such as the Neolithic long barrow at Dalladies, or the numerous medieval religious buildings which were destroyed after the Reformation of 1560, no crop-mark or very fragmentary sites are included, although reference may be made to them in the introductory comments to each section. To have excluded the medieval religious houses would have created too great a distortion of the religious wealth of this region in the Middle Ages.

The greater selectivity of the post-Medieval period is determined by a number of factors. In part it is a reflection of the proliferation of surviving buildings from this era, and their detailed coverage elsewhere. For example, most post-1800 mansions are excluded, except where there is an earlier building at their core, or where they represent outstanding examples of their kind, or rare survivals of a once common form. Those in the 1700–1820 period are intended to offer only a representative sample to avoid creating too great an internal imbalance. Similar reasons govern selection of the bridges and communications, industry, commerce, agriculture and fishing sections. Most of the surviving structures connected with these areas belong to the later 19th century and after, and therefore lie beyond the scope of this present work.

It is essential to bear in mind that many of these sites are on private ground and inclusion in this book should not be taken as an automatic guarantee of any right of access. Only those marked with an asterisk (*) are in the guardianship of the Secretary of State for Scotland, the National Trust for Scotland, or are opened on a regular basis by their private owners. Most of the asterisk-marked sites are subject to standard Historic Scotland opening times and regulations. In most other cases, permission should be sought from the nearest farm, house, forestry or estate office before setting out across country.

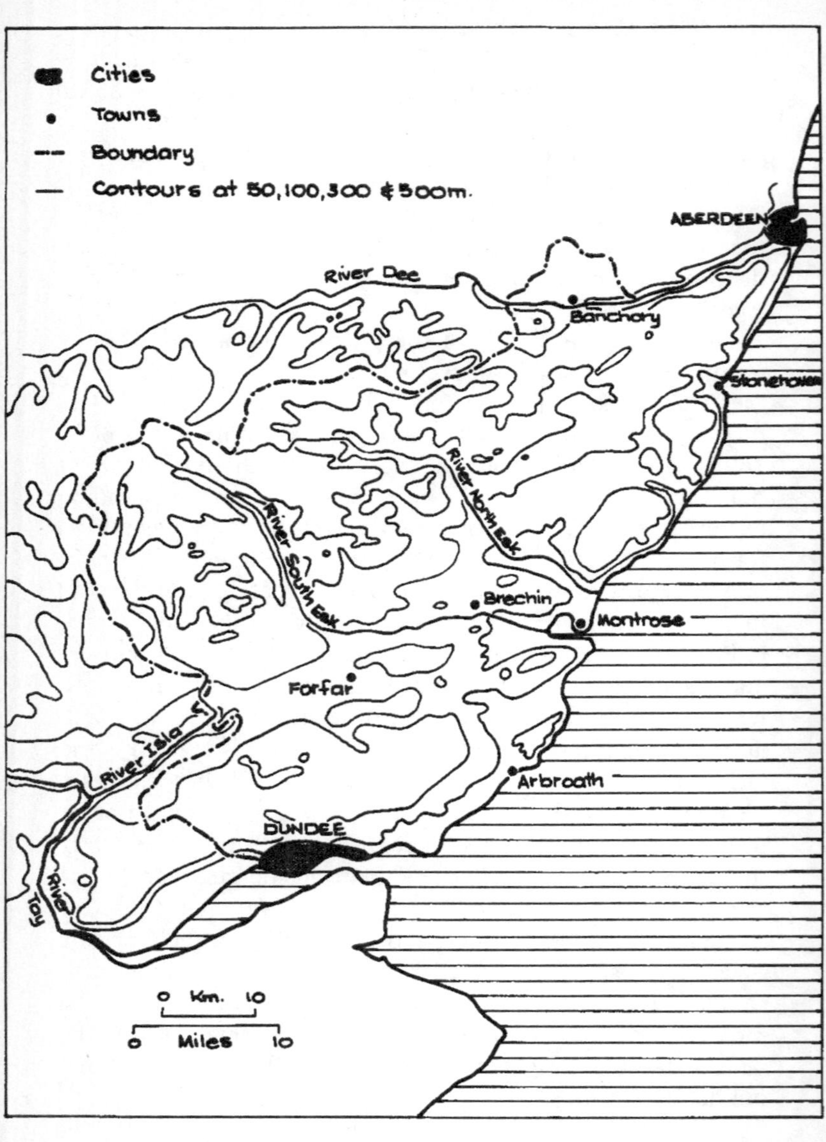

Cities
Towns
Boundary
Contours at 50,100,300 & 500m.
ABERDEEN
River Dee
Banchory
Stonehaven
River North Esk
River South Esk
Brechin
Montrose
Forfar
River Isla
Arbroath
DUNDEE
River Tay
0 Km. 10
0 Miles 10

INTRODUCTION

PALAEOLITHIC PERIOD

Before *c.*7000 BC

Summer in the rich arable lowlands of Strathmore, even when there is a snell wind off the North Sea to temper the warm sunshine, seems a far remove from the extremes of Nature which gripped Scotland during the most severe phases of the last Ice Age. Yet on the high plateau of the Grampian Mountains, deeply riven by the glacier-cut valleys of the rivers which water the fertile plain, and where snow can linger late in the N-facing corries, the world of the sub-arctic tundras is but a step away from the wheat-fields of Angus and the Mearns. It is sobering to think that only some 15,000 years ago, a comparatively short time in geological terms, this rich land was heavily mantled by a deep layer of glacial ice, or was at best a bleak, treeless tundra similar to that of northern Canada or Siberia. From about 13,000 BC the climate began to improve and the ice-sheet withdrew to the N, until by about 10,000 BC only some areas of the northern and western Highlands were under ice. Even then, though, small glaciers lingered in the northern corries of the Cairngorms and there were to be several occasions down to 8300 BC when the ice was to advance again out of these mountainous zones. Gradually, however, these climatic fluctuations stabilised and the sub-arctic wastes left in the wake of the retreating ice-cap were replaced by dense forests of birch and pine.

It is the general opinion that human settlement was impossible under such extremities of climate in the region which became Scotland. But some have argued, however, that the ice cover was never wholly complete, nor was it permanent for the whole of the so-called Ice Age, and occasional bands of hunters may have made their way N. This era is known to archaeologists as the Palaeolithic (Old Stone Age), when the first humans of physically 'modern' type (Homo sapiens sapiens) began to cross the low-lying valleys and alluvial plains which still connected Britain with northern Europe, to occupy the hunting-grounds on the margins of the ice. Archaeological evidence for human activity of this time, largely in the form of settlements found buried beneath the deposits on cave floors, is limited largely to parts of southern and S central England, and southern Wales which lay at the southernmost limit of the ice or beyond its greatest reach. In much of the remainder of these islands, where the landscape has been scoured repeatedly by the ice, or is cloaked with a deep layer of boulder clay, any such evidence has either been lost for ever, or lies concealed beneath this overburden.

MESOLITHIC PERIOD

*c.*7000 BC to *c.*4000 BC

Into the empty lands left in the wake of the retreating ice moved wandering bands of colonists. Archaeologists and anthropologists refer to these people as 'hunters and gatherers', nomads who lived a lifestyle very similar to that of the North American Plains Indians before the arrival of European colonists in the 18th and 19th centuries. Their culture, as can be seen especially in the stone tools and weapons which they fashioned and used, was markedly different from that of the older Palaeolithic types, and it is labelled Mesolithic, or Middle Stone Age. Their lifestyle was simple but hardly easy, based on the exploitation of the natural resources of the landscape through which they moved: hunting the abundant game and wildfowl; fishing in lakes and rivers swollen by ice melt-waters and in coastal waters; gathering nuts, berries and other edible plants. Their weapons and tools were fashioned from carefully-worked stone, usually flint. They dressed in the skins of the animals which they hunted, and lived a nomadic lifestyle, moving each season in pursuit of the migrant game on which they depended.

The routes which they followed into northern Britain can only be guessed at, but it is most likely that there were several favoured lines. Some bands moved by sea into the Hebrides. Others travelled N overland from the English lowlands, while some are believed to have crossed the wide plain which the North Sea now fills. The earliest Mesolithic settlement yet excavated in Scotland, at Loch Scresort in Rum in the Hebrides, is almost 9000 years old, but it is quite unlikely that it is actually the *oldest* human settlement in Scotland as the land had by then been suitable for colonisation for almost 1000 years. By about 8000 years ago there were Mesolithic encampments in the coastal areas around Oban, on Arran, and on the Hebridean islands of Islay, Jura and Ulva, while a site discovered at Inverness has been dated only slightly later. Still more sites of only slightly younger date are known from many parts of Scotland, with particular concentrations in the coastal districts and river valleys of Galloway, in the central Tweed basin, and along the valley of the Forth. Between the important sites of Morton in Tentsmuir in N E Fife and those at Banchory and Nethermills on the Dee in N Kincardineshire, however, there is as yet little evidence for Mesolithic settlement. This is not to say that it is not there – and middens unearthed in Broughty Ferry and the Stannergate in Dundee in the 19th century and now lost under the spread of the city show that it was – for it is unlikely that the N side of the Tay estuary and the great wildfowl over-wintering sites in Montrose Basin would not have found favour with these early hunters.

One of the greatest difficulties facing the archaeologist who would seek to chart the spread of Mesolithic settlement is the slightness of the traces left in the soil. Occupation sites of this period are often betrayed only by scatterings of tiny flint flakes uncovered through ploughing or erosion of the soil, or by irregularly shaped mounds of debris, mainly sea-shells, representing the remains of refuse middens. There are no structural remains as such, for shelters were light-weight and left little more than traces of stakeholes in the ground. Most of the sites yet discovered are located near to the sea or along the edges of important river valleys, sited to exploit the natural resources of food and raw materials.

NEOLITHIC

c.4000 BC to *c*.2500 BC

About 6000 years ago, new waves of colonists began to cross from NW Europe into Britain, bringing new ideas and new technologies. Their culture was markedly different from that of the nomadic Mesolithic hunter-gatherers, being based on settled communities supported by agriculture, growing both cereal crops (primitive types of wheat and barley) and rearing cattle and sheep. They used new types of tools and weapons, still of stone and flint, but shaped differently to those of the Mesolithic people, and they knew how to make pottery. This new culture is called Neolithic (New Stone Age) by archaeologists, and with it come the oldest surviving man-made monuments in the Scottish landscape.

As with the Mesolithic people, the Neolithic colonists arrived in Britain via several routes: from the S across the English Channel and up through England; by sea from Ireland into western Scotland, the Hebrides and the Northern Isles; and across the North Sea into the eastern coastlands. They entered a land still largely mantled by forest, where the soil had never been broken by the plough. Their arrival did not bring an overnight transformation – the Mesolithic folk did not just put down roots and take up farming – and both cultures probably lived side by side for several centuries before the Neolithic way of life swallowed up the older peoples: clearance for fields, and expansion of the cultivated area to compensate for the gradual exhaustion of the soil through repeated cropping and over-cultivation, was incompatible with the free-roaming lifestyle of the hunter-gatherers.

The biggest difference between the Mesolithic and Neolithic peoples was the settled existence of the latter and the communal lifestyle to which the label society can be attached. Cultivation of cereals and stock-rearing, coupled with the older traditions of hunting and fishing, allowed larger settlements to evolve. Few of the earliest Neolithic settlement sites in Scotland have been identified, and fewer

1. Neolithic – ritual sites and burials.

yet have been excavated. Instead, it is mainly from the communal tombs which they built and used over periods of perhaps several centuries that most of our knowledge of these people is derived. One of the earliest settlements yet identified and excavated lies within the region covered by this book, but there is now nothing to see there on the ground. This is at Balbridie in Kincardineshire, where aerial photographs revealed the presence of what was at first believed to be a massive timber-built hall dating from early medieval times. Excavation in 1977 produced the pits in which the massive timber uprights of a structure measuring 24.5m by 13m had stood. Confidence in its Dark Age date was shattered by the discovery of unmistakably Neolithic pottery, and radiocarbon dating of organic material from the dig produced a date of *c.*3500 BC. Rather than forming the hall of a Pictish warlord, Balbridie was the imposing communal residence of an extended family of Neolithic farmers.

Balbridie is as yet a unique site, but it has forced archaeologists to acknowledge that the old, traditional view of Neolithic communities as clusters of small, dark and squalid huts was overly simplistic. In the absence of excavation at similar sites, however, it is on the better-known and better-preserved settlement sites found further N in Scotland that our main ideas about Neolithic life are founded. Sites such as Knap of Howar and Skara Brae in Orkney, where groups of stone-built houses survived, do indeed give a unique insight into the daily life of these first farmers. There, fashioned from stone, can be seen furnishings such as box-beds and 'dressers' for storage and display of pottery, which would presumably have been made from perishable wood at other sites. Together with fragments of pottery, tools and utensils of stone and bone, items of personal adornment, and the debris of their food and craft activities preserved in the middens and under the sand dunes which eventually engulfed the abandoned settlement, these allow the reconstruction of a remarkably detailed image of past life.

Throughout the Mearns and down into Angus, there is a remarkable dearth of identified Neolithic settlement sites.

Aerial photography has identified sites of similar type to that excavated at Balbridie near Crathes and at Monboddo, but there are also sufficient dissimilarities to render any firm identification impossible without excavation. The distribution of recognised ritual and burial sites in the region, however, make it clear that this was an important area of settlement for early farmers, to whom the light soils would have been very attractive. Indeed, it is this very attractiveness to farmers that is probably most to blame for the comparative scarcity of known Neolithic settlement sites, more recent agricultural practices and the spread of larger communities having obliterated traces of less substantial structures.

Where there are no surviving structural remains of settlement above ground, the burial places of these early farming communities often still bulk large on the skyline. Throughout most of the region under coverage here, however, there are few burial sites of instantly-identifiable Neolithic form. This does not mean that they do not exist, it means simply that most probably take a form and use materials quite different to those of the great stone-built, cairn-covered chambered tombs more common further to the N and W with which we are more familiar. Such variation in type, moreover, is clear evidence for the striking diversity of the local cultures within Neolithic Scotland. A group of impressive stone-built tombs does survive in the extreme NE of the region, in the district between Aberdeen and Stonehaven, with good examples at *Raedykes*, *Clune Hill* and *Cairnwell*. These so-called 'ring-cairns' are outliers of a tradition of tomb-building more common in S Banffshire, E Inverness-shire and Nairnshire, related to the Clava Cairn class of monuments, where several burials were deposited in a central area – sometimes a roofed chamber – over a period of many years before the tomb was deliberately infilled. Few of this type of cairn lies S of the Mounth in Strathmore, where instead fieldwork is showing that burial sites were constructed in a different manner, often using different materials. Typified by the great earth and gravel long barrows of *Capo* and *Dalladies*, or the stone-built long cairns such as that at *Gourdon*, these provide striking evidence of the scale of the communal effort involved in constructing these huge monuments. It is estimated that the barrow at *Dalladies* took some 6000 man-hours to raise.

Alongside the cairns and barrows – often quite literally alongside – the ritual sites erected by the Neolithic peoples often survive where the settlement sites do not. As with the tombs, there is a clear division within the region in the distribution of the best-known types of site, the stone circles. The majority of these lie in the northern part of Kincardineshire, thinning markedly S of the Mounth. The change in burial practice S of that line, moreover, is also paralleled by a change in the type of stone circle. To the N of the Mounth, in the river systems which feed into the Dee from the S, we are on the fringes of the territory of one of the most striking Neolithic cultures in Britain, the heart of whose territory appears to have lain in the Garioch district of Aberdeenshire. Unique to this culture is the so-called recumbent stone circle. These, in short, are circles of uprights between 18.2 and 24.4m in diameter, with two particularly tall stones (the flankers) placed in the SW arc on either side of a massive slab – averaging 24 tons in weight – laid on its side and levelled with chocking stones (the recumbent). The dating of these circles is still debated, but they are generally assigned to the later 3rd millennium BC. Most are usually sited on hill crests or terraces which command wide southerly prospects, as at the *Nine Stanes*, Mulloch, or the nearby *Eslie the Greater*, and in some cases it is clear that the location has been levelled or terraced prior to the erection of the circles. Some of the circles, such as *Clune Hill* near Durris, or *Aquhorthies* near Portlethen, enclose low burial mounds of ring-cairn type, but it cannot be proven that the recumbent stone circles were built primarily as burial sites, indeed, it seems rather that the construction of the cairns often marked the end of the 'life' of the ritual sites. Common sense, moreover, dictates that for the circles to have had a ritual function, the interior space would have had to have been clear from the obstruction of the cairns. What is clear is that the recumbent stones formed the ritual focus of the stone circles. It has been shown that, to folk standing within the circle, the flankers and recumbent will frame the rising or setting of the moon in the southern sky. It has been suggested from this that the circles formed the communal – and seasonal – ritual sites of fertility cults associated with moon-worship.

S of the southernmost limit of the area of recumbent stone circle building, the stone circles of the Mearns and Angus are simpler and smaller. This may indicate that the circles of these areas are later in date, for it has been demonstrated that towards the end of the 3rd millennium and into the 2nd millennium the diameters of stone circles reduced considerably and the number of stones in the ring declined. It is possible, then, that sites such as *Balgarthno* on the outskirts of Dundee, measuring only 6m in diameter, or the larger *Colmeallie* in Glen Esk, may date from the early Bronze Age and represent the lingering and decadent remnant of the mature NE Scottish tradition. A tradition of stone circle building, moreover, may have been a late introduction into this area, influenced by the Aberdeenshire examples. This is supported by evidence for a different form of major ritual site in Angus in the late Neolithic, suggesting that the local barrow-building culture was also building ritual monuments of a strikingly different form to those of the recumbent circle and ring-cairn builders further N.

At Douglasmuir near Friockheim a complex of sites identified from the air was excavated in the late 1970s and early 1980s in advance of the development of the site for a gas pumping station. To the W of a group of later Bronze Age houses, the excavation revealed a large, post-defined enclosure measuring 65m by 19m, divided internally into two compounds. A radiocarbon date of 2900 ± 55 BC was recovered from the fill of one of the pits which had held the posts of the enclosure. The Douglasmuir site belongs to a class of monuments described as 'mortuary enclosures', ritual areas within which the dead were perhaps exposed to the elements to accelerate the decay process before the selection of parts of the corpse for burial. Excavation and analysis of English sites of this type has stressed the close relationship which this class of monument has with phases in the development of long barrows – for example, the large timber structure which was the earliest feature beneath the barrow at *Dalladies*.

Neolithic Sites

Ritual

1. Aquhorthies, Portlethen
NO 901 963

Positioned on a low knoll in agricultural land rising from the SE ridge of Hill of Aquhorthies, 150m NE of Aquhorthies farm, are the remains of a recumbent stone circle enclosing a ring-cairn. The cairn measures 15.4m in diameter, its outer kerb being graded in height towards the S and with one exceptionally large boulder in the ESE. The inner kerb is fragmentary, only five of its stones remaining *in situ*, and measures some 3.2m in diameter. The recumbent of the enclosing circles lies to the S of the cairn, its flankers – of which only the W survives – being linked to its kerb by smaller kerbstones. The circle is in fact an oval measuring 23.7m by 22m, and consists of twelve surviving stones and the stump of a possible thirteenth. It appears that the original setting consisted of ten large stones (two now being missing) with smaller pillars set between them. This arrangement survives on the N and E only. There are records of the discovery of a cist on the E side of the circle between the cairn and the standing stones in the late 18th century, and in 1858 excavation of the cairn chamber revealed the remains of a cremation burial and a broken pottery vessel.

2. Auchlee, Maryculter
NO 890 968

This severely damaged recumbent stone circle enclosing a disturbed ring-cairn lies on a low knoll 220m WNW of Auchlee farm, on the unclassified road between the A92(T) at Portlethen and Kirkton of Maryculter. The inner kerb of the cairn has been badly disturbed, leaving only one stone in position, but the central area appears to have measured 3m in diameter. The outer kerb, 14m in diameter, has eleven stones remaining, and encloses a robbed cairn structure which rises no more than 0.40m. The circle is even more severely damaged, the toppled recumbent now lies 2m beyond the outer kerb of the cairn, both flankers have been removed and only four other stones – all fallen – now remain. A second, yet more ruinous recumbent circle lies on a knoll 220m NNE of the farm at NO 893 970.

3. Balgarthno, Dundee
NO 353 316

On the edge of the football playing field between the Kingsway and South Road, at the western end of the suburbs of Dundee. Rather overgrown, neglected and used as a rubbish dump, it is difficult to appreciate the once open aspect to the W and SW over the Carse of Gowrie formerly enjoyed by this stone circle. Measuring about 6m in diameter, it consists of a ring of nine stones, only one of which is upright, and old accounts of the site mention that the stones occupied a platform within an encircling ditch.

4. Clune Hill (Rees of Clune), Durris
NO 794 949

Occupying a clearing in Clune Wood on the spine of Clune Hill, formerly enjoying fine views N over the Dee valley, 1.5 miles SE of Kirkton of Durris. Lying immediately to the W of one ring-cairn (see below p.20), this recumbent stone circle encloses a second, more ruinous, cairn. This measures 14.5m in diameter and rises some 1m in height, but shows signs of having been dug into in the past. The recumbent, which measures 2.8m by 0.7m by 1.2m in height, with both flankers surviving, lies on the S arc of both the cairn and circle. The latter measures 16.5m by 13.8m, and comprises six uprights in addition to the main setting.

5. Colmeallie, Glen Esk
NO 565 781

This superbly-positioned little stone circle stands on a slight knoll on the S side of the farm road leading to Colmeallie farm, 4.5 miles E of Tarfside, on the N side of the Glenesk road. Its position, overlooking the gentler lower slopes and gravel terrace above the valley floor, commands fine views over the lower half of the glen to E and W. The circle measures approximately 13m in diameter and may originally have consisted of twelve stones. Three stones on the SE side are still upright, the westernmost having been re-erected at some recent date to the N of its original position, while the stumps of five more stones and several fallen monoliths can be traced. The large depression containing irregular slabs lying to the S of the centre of the circle, appears to mark the position of a cist burial, but some of the slabs appear to have been dumped here as part of a field-clearance operation.

6. Crossroads, Durris
NO 754 940

In agricultural land 100m NE of Cairnfauld, to the E of the A957 immediately to the S of Crossroads school. The remains of this circle stand on the shoulder of the ridge between the Burn of Sheeoch and the River Dee. It measures 21.2m in diameter, but only three of the five remaining stones are in their original position. The stones on the E and S – in the thickness of the consumption dyke – and that on the SW are undisturbed. The circle may have enclosed a cairn, its stones removed and incorporated in the dyke, for remains of a burial were uncovered in the centre of the circle in the 19th century.

7. Eslie the Greater, Mulloch
NO 717 915

In grazing land approximately 0.5 miles S of Eslie farm, 2.5 miles S of Banchory. This is one of the finest recumbent stone circles in Kincardineshire. Positioned just below the crest of a wide saddle to the W of Mulloch Hill, it possesses fine views to the W. When complete it consisted of a pair of flankers to either side of a 2.9m-long recumbent, and eight other uprights, of which five remain in position. The uprights range from 1.5m to 0.8m and are graded in height with the lowest towards the NW. The 'circle' is more strictly an ellipse, 26.5m by 23.2m, and encloses a ring-cairn which has been used as a field dump. The cairn is 18m in diameter around a central area 6.3m in diameter. From the ends of the recumbent, two lines of stones run towards the perimeter of the cairn, an arrangement to be seen also at Aquhorthies near Portlethen (1).

8. Eslie the Lesser, Mulloch NO 722 921

This recumbent circle lies 800m to the NE – and is intervisible with – the circle at Eslie the Greater. It is situated slightly higher than its neighbour on a hill shoulder to the W of West Mulloch farm. The circle measures 15.3m in diameter.

9. Nine Stanes, Mulloch* NO 723 912

Signposted, in a clearing amongst forestry 3.25 miles SE of Banchory, off the unclassified road between the B974 S of Strachan and the A957 at Blairydryne. One of the better-preserved of the recumbent stone circles lying to the S of the Dee, the Nine Stanes occupies a typical position for monuments of this type on a broad shelf at the western end of Garrol Hill, from which it commanded fine views to the S and W. Its plan departs from the more strictly circular earlier sites in Aberdeenshire to the N, such as East Aquhorthies near Inverurie, in that it is a 'flattened circle' which measures 18m by 14.6m. The recumbent, which weighs over 16 tons, and its flankers, one of which has fallen, lie on the S side. Six uprights remain out of a total of eight, the seventh being reduced to a stump and the eighth having been removed at some time in the past.

Some time after the building of the stone circle a large ring-cairn was constructed within it, its southern kerb flattened by the need to follow the line of the earlier monument. The outer kerb encloses an area 12m in diameter, within which is a central setting approximately 5.5m in diameter. In no place does the ring of cairn material stand higher than 0.4m. Excavation in 1904 revealed a funnel-shaped pit within the central setting which contained a mass of charcoal and cremated bone. Around this lay four other deposits of cremated bone, charcoal and pottery.

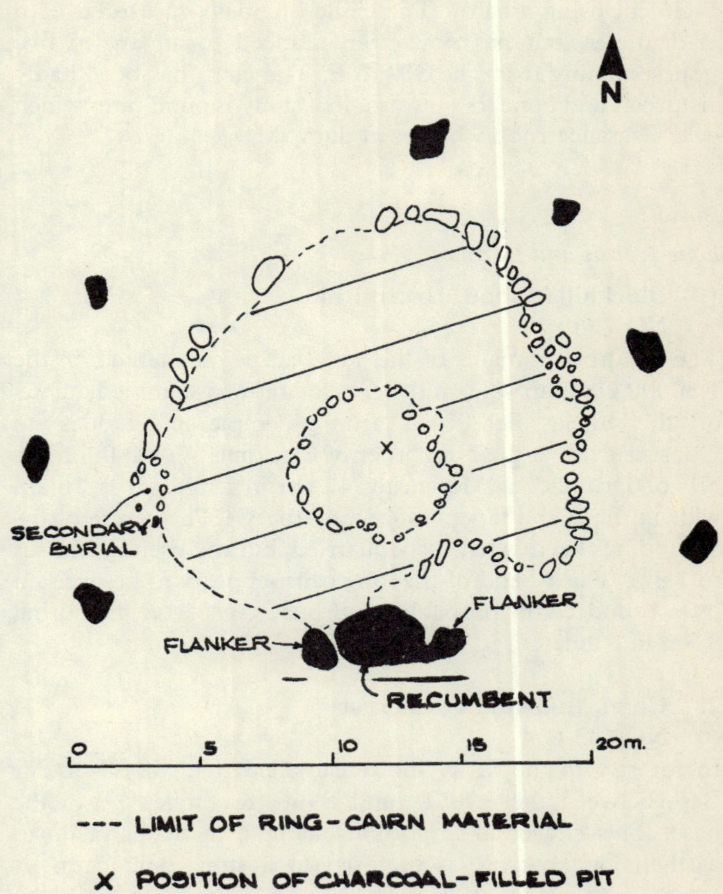

Figure 1. The Nine Stanes, Mulloch, recumbent stone circle and ring cairn.

10. Old Bourtreebush, Portlethen NO 903 960

In agricultural land on the crest of a low rise 240m W of Old Bourtreebush farm and some 300m SE of the recumbent stone circle at Aquhorthies (1) is a non-recumbent stone circle enclosing a cairn. The circle originally measured 26m in diameter, but has now been reduced to an arc of five stones running from the SW to E. The cairn has been badly disturbed and appears now as a low stony mound onto which field clearance rubble has been dumped.

Burial

Long Cairns and Barrows

1. Blackhills Wood, Drumlithie NO 796 817

The disturbed remains of this long cairn – unmarked on the 1:50000 OS map – lie on the crest of a low rise immediately S of the unclassified road from Temple of Fiddes to Goosecruives, at the NE corner of Blackhills Wood, 0.6 miles NE of Drumlithie. Measuring 47.6m in length, it is 16.2m wide at the E and tapers to 4.8m at the W. The centre of the mound has been extensively quarried, but the E end still rises to 1.8m. The W end of the long cairn appears to be overlain by a round cairn, probably of Bronze Age date, measuring 8.5m in diameter.

2. Capo, Inglismaldie Forest NO 633 664

In forestry to the W of the unclassified road to Edzell Air Base between the A90(T) and B966, two miles SE of the base. This site is an important example in Scotland of an earthen long barrow as opposed to a stone-built cairn. It stands on the edge of the gravel terrace on the E bank of the River North Esk, the fine material of the terrace having been used in its construction. Built from turf and scraped-up soil, it measures 80m long by 28m wide at its eastern end, rising to 2.5m in height. It does not appear to have been disturbed in antiquity. Analogy with similar sites suggest that the remains of a timber-built mortuary structure lie beneath the eastern end of the barrow.

3. Dalladies (Lost)
NO 627 673

This earthen long barrow was excavated in 1971 before destruction through gravel quarrying. Excavation showed a complex evolution commencing with the construction of a wooden building aligned NW-SE, supported by massive upright timbers. This was left to decay, whereupon a space within its site 3m wide by 7.5m long was enclosed with stone walls standing 1m high, within which was a flimsy wooden structure roofed with sheets of birch bark. Around this structure, forming the lowest part of the barrow mound, turfs were piled within a stone revetment. To the E of the timber building, used as a mortuary structure, the eastern end of the barrow was defined by a curved façade of stones, 1m high.

It has been suggested that the corpses of the dead were kept elsewhere and, after the flesh had rotted away, token bones were brought in to the mortuary structure. Alternatively, the corpses were placed in the mortuary, which was cleared of the bone remains from time to time. During the excavation only one small fragment of skull was unearthed within it.

At the expiry of its life, the mortuary house was deliberately burned down and turfs heaped over its position. More turfs were added, cut from an area of some 1.5 acres, to form the complete barrow mound. It is estimated that this stage of the work took some 6000 man-hours. After completion, the barrow remained a centre of ritual activity and further burials were inserted into the mound until well into the Bronze Age.

4. Gourdon
NO 818 706

On the SE top of the long ridge of Knox Hill, overlooking the A92, 0.5 miles WSW of Gourdon. Still substantial despite robbing for stone, this long cairn is a prominent skyline feature and commands extensive views along the coast in

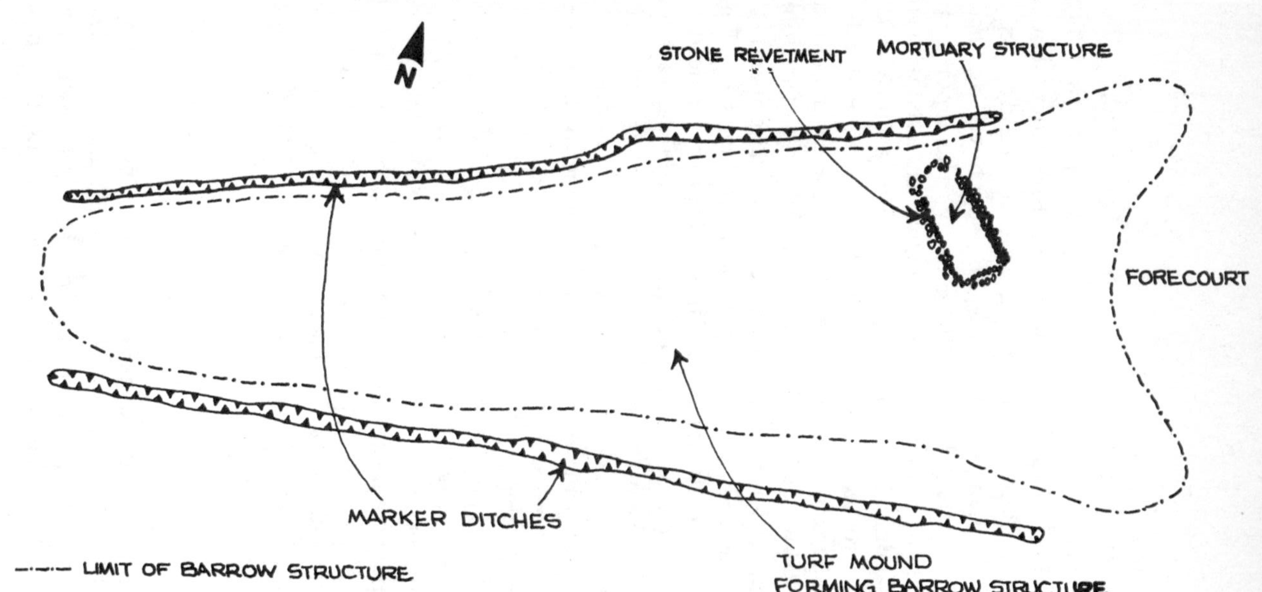

Figure 2. Dalladies long barrow

both directions. Measuring some 47.2m along its main axis (which runs ENE to WSW), it is 12.2m wide at its eastern end and tapers to 7.6m at the W. Both ends are rounded with no indication of forecourts or ceremonial areas. The cairn structure, which rises to 2.75m for most of its length, is composed of small boulders, stones and earth, and is now shrouded with turf and whins.

5. Upper Craighill (Hillhead Plantation), Arbuthnott NO 795 768

This long cairn occupies the summit of the isolated hill which rises due N of Arbuthnott House, lying between the unclassified roads from the B967 at Parkneuk to the A90(T) at Mondynes, and the B967 at Kirkton of Arbuthnott and the A90(T) at Meikle Fiddes. It measures 52m in length, is 22m wide at the ENE tapering to 9m at the WSW, and rises to a maximum of 2.7m in height.

Ring-Cairns and Clava-type Cairns

1. Cairnwell (Kingcausie), Banchory-Devenick NO 907 973

In farmland 400m SW of Craighead farm, to the W of the A90(T) six miles S of Aberdeen. This inconspicuous and ruinous ring-cairn of Clava type occupies a low-lying position in a shallow valley. Its structure has been disturbed badly, partly a consequence of its excavation in 1862–3, and it has been further obscured by use as a dump for field stones. The outer kerb, which can be traced intermittently, has a diameter of 6.7m. The inner setting of stones – slabs set on their long sides – has a diameter of 4.5m, producing a remarkably thin ring of cairn material only some 0.9m to 1.2m wide. Approximately 1m beyond the outer kerb are the remains of a stone circle, 9m in diameter, which once enclosed the cairn. Three monoliths of the thirteen noted in 1862 remain on the SE. The poorly-conducted and ill-recorded excavations yielded only some fragments of pottery and human bone, all now lost.

2. Clune Hill, Durris

NO 794 949

In a clearing in forestry roughly 2.5 miles SE of Kirkton of Durris. This ring-cairn occupies an elevated position on a headland which projects N into the Dee valley and would formerly have commanded clear prospects to the N, E and W. It stands immediately to the N of a recumbent stone-circle known as the Rees of Clune (see above p.12). Between 12.5m and 13.7m in diameter, the cairn has no apparent outer kerb and has a rather indistinct outline. The inner setting of stones is exposed, forming an area 2.75m in diameter inside the rather overgrown cairn mound. Tnere is a gap in the S side of the slab-built inner setting, possibly marking the position of an entrance passage, but this would have to be tested by excavation.

3. Meams Hill, Kinnordy
NO 373 573

Lying in the saddle to the NE of the summit of Meams Hill, approximately 150m beyond the end of the farm track which runs E from the unclassified Kinnordy-Glen Prosen road 500m N of Meams farm, is a well-preserved ring-cairn which is unmarked on the 1:50000 OS map. The cairn measures approximately 10m in diameter, with a central space some 5m across. Parts of the inner and outer kerbs can be traced.

4. Raedykes, Stonehaven
NO 832 096

This group of four cairns occupies the crest and eastern slope of a broad spur known as Campstone Hill which projects S from the higher ground around Curlethney Hill, approximately 300m NW of West Raedykes.

The south-easternmost of the group is a ring-cairn, its features clear despite heavy robbing for building-stone. The outer kerb is 9.4m in diameter and encloses an inner setting 3.9m in diameter within a ring of cairn material which rises 0.4m high. The outer kerb is most clearly visible on the SW, while the inner kerb has been almost entirely robbed out. A stone-circle some 17m in diameter formerly enclosed the cairn. Nine stones out of a possible original twenty survive.

Some 20m to the WNW and slightly higher up the spur are the remains of an oval cairn, measuring 8.5m by 7.7m and rising to 0.5m in height. It is bounded by a kerb of small boulders, but there is no clear sign of an inner setting in the robbed-out hollow at its centre, which might indicate that this is a plundered round cairn of Bronze Age date rather than a ring-cairn. There is no enclosing stone-circle. A further 15m to the WNW is a similar cairn. Measuring 7.9m in diameter and rising to 0.6m, there are only traces of a kerb on its western side. The central part of the cairn has been heavily robbed, leaving no trace of an inner setting or cist. Again, there is no enclosing circle.

The fourth, and most complete, cairn lies at the highest point of the group 80m NW of the first described. It is a fine ring-cairn 10.2m in diameter and 0.6m high. It stands within a circle 13.9m in diameter, of which five stones remain standing from a possible total of thirteen. The outer kerb shows signs of considerable elaboration, with possible grading of heights towards the SW. Here stand two tall stones, 1.1m and 1.7m high, with the broken stump of a third lying between them. At intervals around the curve of the kerb are other pillar stones, up to 0.9m high, which are clearly a designed feature rather than the product of random selection.

5. Strone Hill, Lintrathen
NO 292 567

On the SW flank of Strone Hill overlooking Lintrathen Loch, roughly 0.5 miles NNE of Foldend on the B951 Kirriemuir-Glenisla road. This ring-cairn stands within the later unenclosed settlement, and is most notable for its exceptionally small size. Measuring only 6m in diameter, with a central space 2m in diameter, it has an outer kerb containing at least two large slabs.

THE BRONZE AGE

*c.*2500 BC to *c.*700 BC

Around the middle of the 3rd millennium BC there occurred a technological revolution which transformed the nature of prehistoric culture in Britain. New migrants began to cross the North Sea from the lands around the mouth of the Rhine and began to settle in the British Isles. There is great debate at present as to whether this migration constituted an invasion, or that the new people arrived in small numbers and integrated quickly with existing Neolithic communities, but the weight of the evidence favours the former. The incomers formed a distinctive group among the earlier Neolithic folk, physically, culturally and, above all, technologically. With them they brought new styles of pottery, most notably the type of vessel from which early archaeologists gave them their name: the Beaker People. But the one skill which set them apart from the Neolithic farmers was the knowledge of how to work in metal.

The discovery of metal-working technology was one of the greatest revolutions in human development and occasioned a profound change in the structure of society. This was a revolution that went far beyond mere substitution of stone and flint by a superior material, for metallurgy required additional skills, such as the ability to identify the ores and how to smelt them, how to improve the metal through alloys and how to cast it successfully. These new skills are likely to have been jealously guarded since they gave power and prestige to those who knew them over those who did not. And yet, there is no evidence that the incomers used their superior technology to establish what could be termed social or political domination over the indigenous Neolithic population, archaeology instead pointing towards an intermingling of the peoples which was to produce the new cultural blend that was Bronze Age society. Nevertheless, this was no utopia and archaeology also points towards increased evidence for warfare, much of it perhaps stimulated by conflict over scarce resources. Possession of the materials for making bronze as much as the technology for its manufacture gave a different form of power: economic. Copper ore is found in only a few parts of Britain, and tin has an even more restricted distribution, so demand for the new metal in areas which lacked natural ore deposits stimulated trade, giving power to those who controlled the supply. Although copper is found in various parts of Scotland, much was still imported, but all tin had to be obtained in Cornwall.

Long distance trading contacts may first have been established in the Neolithic period, but these were developed and maintained throughout the Bronze Age, especially the trade in Cornish tin. Sea-borne trade seems also to have developed with the European mainland across the North Sea, perhaps representing the preservation of contact with the continental homelands of the earlier Bronze Age migrants. Evidence seems to point to a thriving trade in the period *c.*700 BC between parts of the NE coastal districts of Scotland and NW Germany, or the arrival of settlers about that time from the Continent. The strongest evidence is in the form of fine cast bronze brooches of a distinctive form from sites in Moray, and other pieces of high quality ornamental bronzework from sites in Aberdeenshire and Angus.

Throughout the wider NE of Scotland, it appears that the Beaker People at first settled predominantly in areas peripheral to the major centres of Neolithic culture, such as in the Garioch. Beaker pottery is found extensively throughout eastern coastal districts from the Tay northwards, indicating a considerable movement of people into this zone. Of course, they were not moving into empty territory, and the nature of their relationship with the indigenous population can only be conjectured. At several late Neolithic ritual sites in northern Scotland, however, there are indications of what has been interpreted as the takeover, desecration and deliberate 'slighting' of the stone circles and communal tombs of the older culture by the new. It is possible that the Neolithic people attempted to keep the incomers at arm's length if they could not be otherwise controlled, for their strange metal-working 'magic' may have been seen as a dangerous mystical challenge to the old order of things. This would certainly explain the development of early bronze-working traditions focused on areas peripheral to the Neolithic centres. We should not doubt the power of the incomers, however, and acts such as the burial of beakers in the heart of the henges and circles of the Neolithic peoples should perhaps be seen as a statement of the superior 'magic' of the metal-workers, a magic which was ultimately to win the day.

The prestige and power which the knowledge of metal-working brought, and the additional power which possession of metal tools and weapons gave to their owners, undoubtedly brought a significant change to the very structure of society. It is possible that the possessors of the new technology established themselves in an elite role in society, using control of supply to accomplish a grip over their bronze-hungry customers. Certainly, early Bronze Age society, as it can be reconstructed from the archaeology, was radically different to that which preceded it. The communal focus of the Neolithic cultures was shifted towards a clearly hierarchical structure, with a stratigraphy of ruling classes, warrior castes, farming peasantry and, most probably, slaves.

These changes are to be seen most clearly in new forms of burial practice. The communal tombs of the Neolithic, large-scale and long-lived, were already a waning tradition in the later 3rd millennium BC, but in the Bronze Age they rapidly disappear altogether. A new tradition of individual burials in stone-lined box graves – cists – became the norm. Some were inserted into the sides of earlier Neolithic cairns, as was the case in the excavated barrow at *Dalladies*. Often, however, the cists were dug directly into the soil and, probably dependent on the social status of the burial, a round cairn of stones raised over it. Most of the round cairns which are scattered extensively throughout Angus and Mearns should probably be dated to this period, as excavations at, for example, *Cairn Greg* and *Gilchorn* demonstrated. Many occupy prominent hill-top or skyline locations, as at *Hatton Cairn* and *West Mains*, Auchterhouse, often forming elements in extensive cemeteries, such as that which crowns *Brankam Hill* overlooking the Loch of Lintrathen.

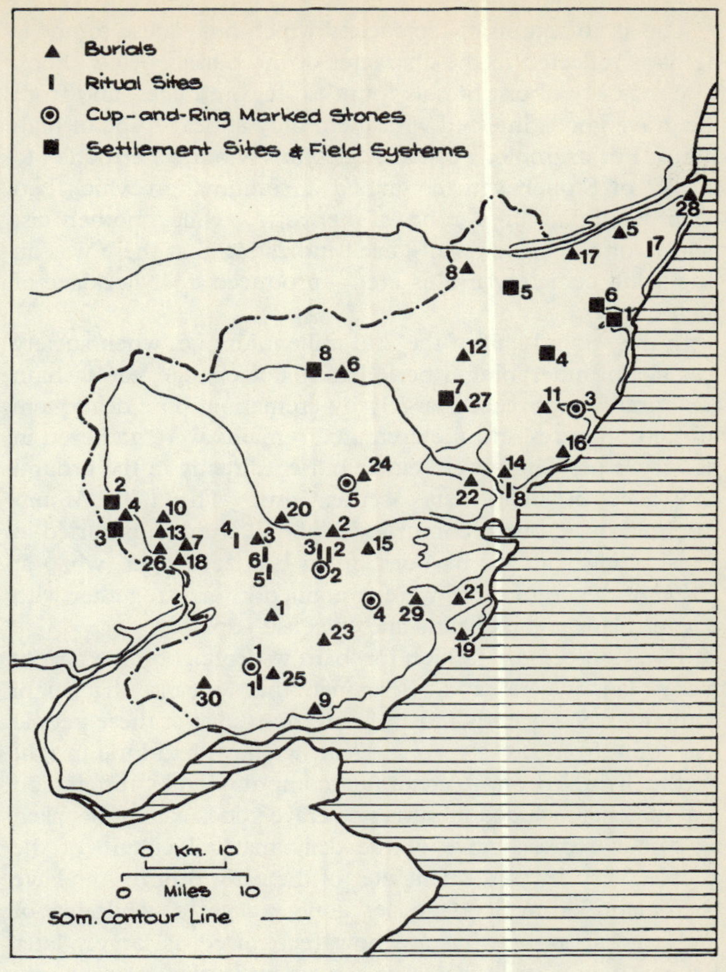

2. Bronze Age – settlement, burial and ritual sites.

The stratification of the society which built these tombs is perhaps reflected in the character of the burials below them. The majority of cist burials found so far are males, and from the grave goods interred with them they appear to be of high status. For example, a cist at Malcolm's Mount, Farrochie, to the W of Stonehaven, contained an inhumation which had been 'wrapped in a robe of network', while another cist nearby on the same farm – itself indicating that there was an important cemetery in this area – produced a jet necklace of high quality.

In the second half of the 2nd millennium BC, when society was again undergoing a period of major change, the fashion for burial was replaced largely by cremation. The dead were burned on pyres and the cremated remains were gathered in pottery urns. These were either buried directly in the ground or placed in small cists of their own. The *West Mains*, Auchterhouse, burial comprised a partial cremation buried in a cist along with his ox-horn hilted bronze dagger, while at *Gilchorn* the cremations were contained in urns together with dagger blades, glass beads and 'incense cups'.

The 19th-century fashion for 'barrow-digging' on the part of many landowners and clergymen has meant that until comparatively recently most of our knowledge of these people has come from burials. As a result, we have had little insight on the 'living' Bronze Age, a fact compounded by recognition that material included in burials as grave goods cannot be taken as strictly representative of the daily material culture of the people. Very few settlement sites of the early Bronze Age have been identified in Scotland, let alone excavated, while few of the large areas of what are now recognised as largely later Bronze Age or early Iron Age settlement in the upland zones have been examined in any detail. Stray finds of high-quality bronze and gold metalwork, especially jewellery, point towards a sophisticated, technically versatile and materially wealthy society, but no major 'power-centre' of this period has been examined archaeologically in detail.

Excavations outwith this region, at sites such as Tulloch Hill near Forres in Moray, or Dalrulzion near Blairgowrie in Perthshire, have shown that the extensive areas of settlement and field systems which have been identified, usually in the upland zones, have a life span that lasts several centuries. Tulloch Hill, certainly, had phases of settlement of both Bronze Age and Iron Age date in the areas examined, and it is likely that sites such as *Brewlands Bridge* in Glenisla and *Hill of Rowan* in Glen Esk, included below as Bronze Age, have a similar longevity. Most of these sites lie at comparatively high altitudes in areas which we would nowadays regard as highly marginal hill-farming territory. It is becoming apparent from the findings of excavation at such sites that occupation was not unbroken, and that the Iron Age settlement often represented a later recolonisation after perhaps several centuries of abandonment. Many, it is clear, were abandoned in the later 2nd millennium BC as the result of a drastic deterioration in the climate after 1200 BC. This saw colder summers, higher rainfall, and the rapid development of blanket peat in upland districts. As a result, large tracts of formerly cultivated land would have slipped beyond the productive margin, and it can only be guessed at the competition for good land which would have resulted. Famine is likely to have been an ever-present danger as society shifted towards the margins of survival, and it is likely that population levels were at the very least checked, if they did not in fact begin to decline.

It is perhaps no coincidence that in the later Bronze Age weapons become more common, both as grave goods and as components in hoards of scrap bronze. Competition over land, or over the population centres required to work it, may have sparked a struggle for survival which tipped society finally into its hierarchical mould dominated by a warrior-aristocracy. Much more research is needed, but it is possible that the increasingly-violent society which developed at this time led to the first moves towards the large-scale fortifications which began to appear in the early 1st millennium BC.

In contrast to the great number of probable Bronze Age burial sites which are liberally scattered throughout this region, there are few ritual monuments which can be dated to this period with certainty. The stone circle building tradition had been in decline in the late Neolithic; circles became smaller in diameter and contained fewer stones. Circle-building did not entirely disappear, but by the 2nd millennium BC small 'circles' with diameters of little more than 2m had replaced the great Neolithic rings. Angus and the Mearns, however, lies to the E of the centre of greatest density of this type of monument. Just as it was peripheral to the recumbent circle tradition of the NE Neolithic, it was peripheral, too, to the so-called 'four-poster' tradition of the 2nd millennium centred on upper Strathtay. The four-poster at *Balkemback*, to the N of Dundee, is a good example of this class. Instead, there seems in the Bronze Age in this area to have been a move towards single standing stones as the focus for ritual activity. The massive pillar stone at *Morphie*, on its terrace overlooking the River North Esk from the N, is a striking example of this class of monument. It appears to have formed the focal point for burials as well as ritual practice, and it is perhaps from this ancient role as an assembly point that later traditions of local courts meeting at stone circles or standing stones derives.

Bronze Age Sites

Settlement and Field Systems

1. Balnagight Wood, Findlayston, Stonehaven NO 845 892 to NO 849 892

On the SW facing slopes and ridge 500m ENE of Findlayston farm, N of the A957 Stonehaven-Banchory road, 2.25 miles NW of Stonehaven. The lower slopes of the hillside have been subject to modern agriculture, removing a large portion of what remains nevertheless an extensive area of field-system and clearance cairns. Some 120 cairns and a series of linear clearance heaps can be seen on the low ridge proper, while on the SW slopes is the field-system. This comprised at least three large rectilinear enclosures, up to 65m broad, dropping down from a 200m-long stony bank. The central field is subdivided into eighteen narrow strips. An oval enclosure at NO 847 892, which measures 19m by 17m within a low stony bank, possibly marks the location of the settlement with which the fields were associated.

2. Brewlands Bridge, Glen Isla
NO 183 617 to NO 188 617

This extensive area of settlement and field-systems lies on the lower slopes of the long SE ridge of Mount Blair on the W side of Glen Isla. The settlement is strung out along the tributary valley of the Alrick Burn, to the N of the unclassified road from Brewlands Bridge W to Blacklunans and the A93. The huts represent a mix of forms and it is probable that the visible remains form part of a long-lived settlement with occupation in extending from the Bronze Age down into the last centuries BC.

3. Burn of Kilry, Glen Isla
NO 212 574

This group of hut-circles lies adjacent to the road in the rough grazing to the W of the unclassified road from Bridge of Craigisla to Brewlands Bridge 1.5 miles NW of Little Kilry farm. The well-preserved footings of four houses lie close together on either side of the 350m contour, while a fifth lies 100m to the NW. The remains of a field system can be traced around the huts.

4. Cotbank, Glenbervie
NO 769 829

The S slopes of the broad ridge which extends eastwards from Cotbank farm, 1.25 miles N of Glenbervie, carry an extensive field-system with numerous clearance cairns. The fields are roughly rectilinear and are bounded by stony banks 2m thick and up to 0.4m high, measuring some 60m by 30m. One field is completely enclosed by banks measuring 32m by 27m. There are at least 25 cairns of up to 5m in diameter by 0.4m in height. There are no signs of the position of the settlement to which these fields pertained.

5. Garrol Hill, Mulloch
NO 716 903 to NO 720 902

This large field-system extends for up to 10 hectares across the S face of Garrol Hill, 700m SE of Midtown farm, S of the unclassified road from the B974 250m S of the Feugh Bridge at Strachan, to the A957 at Blairydryne. The system contains three hut-circles, the largest (NO 716 903) measuring 12.9m by 11.2m within a low stony bank. It has its interior levelled into the hillside on the E and its entrance is on the WSW. The remaining huts lie 6m apart 200m to the SE at NO 718 902. The western of the two is better preserved and measures 8.5m by 7.5m within a wall 2.2m thick by 0.5m high, with its entrance on the SSE. There is an enclosure on a knoll 130m SE of the first hut-circle. It measures 6m in diameter within a wall 1.1m thick and 0.30m high. Around the hut-circles are several stony banks up to 3m thick and irregular clearance mounds. There are some 30 small cairns on the heather moorland to the E.

6. Glenton Hill, Rickarton
NO 823 887 to NO 826 883

A complex of settlement and field-system extends over an area of some 11 hectares on the E flank of the hill, 0.5 miles SE of Rickarton off the A957 Stonehaven-Banchory road. The system contains at least five hut-circles and a possible enclosure. The circles lie in groups of two and three respectively, and vary in size between 3.5m and 8m in internal diameter. The enclosure lies at NO 825 884 and measures 7.8m in diameter by 0.4m in height, with entrances in the NNE and SSW. The field-system comprises a series of substantial embankments, 3m thick at the widest and rising to 0.6m in height, and lynchets up to 0.9m high at the E. There are at least 125 cairns and short stretches of bank on the higher W slopes. There is one complete field measuring 57m by 48m, which pre-dates one of the hut-circles – which is built against the negative lynchet on its SW side.

7. Herd Hill, Fettercairn
NO 617 763 to NO 616 761

On the S flank of Herd Hill, to the W of the track from Upper Thaneston farm which traverses the SW slopes of the hill, are the remains of an extensive area of settlement and field clearance. These consist of two hut-circles lying some 180m apart, and an oval-shaped platform which may mark the site of a third. The N hut-circle measures 8m in diameter within a wall which has spread to a stony bank 1.6m wide. The interior is dug back into the hillside on the N, and there is a clear entrance on the SSE. The second hut-circle is 7.5m in diameter and its interior floor has also been levelled back into the hill. Its entrance is on the S. The platform lies 50m NE of the first hut-circle, measuring 13m by 10m within a low wall with an entrance to the SE. There is an area of field clearance, scattered with cairns, in excess of 9 hectares lying around the huts. On the slopes below the N hut-circle are two prominent field-banks.

8. Hill of Rowan, Glen Esk
NO 465 792 and NO 484 794

Two extensive areas of field clearance cairns lie on the SW and SE flanks respectively of the prominent Hill of Rowan which rises at the junction of Glen Tarf with Glen Esk. The eastern of the two groups is clearly visible in the low-lying heathery ground on the N side of the unclassified road from Tarfside to Lochlee as a series of irregularly-shaped clearance cairns and long rickles of stones which appear to define the formerly cultivated ground. The second group lies adjacent to the footpath which swings round the W end of the hill from the same road between Dykeneuk and Blackness. There are several other areas of probably Bronze Age cultivation on the slopes above Glen Esk, one of the most readily-accessible occupying the level ridge of a broad headland projecting S into the main valley on the W side of the Burn of Turret at NO 541 810.

Burials

1. Arniefoul, Glamis
NO 408 449

On the NW ridge of Hayston Hill, 0.5 miles NE of Arniefoul farm. This unusual earthwork has been interpreted variously as a 'defensive earthwork' or the remains of a 'bowl barrow'. It consists of a circular, flat-topped mound, 15.2m in diameter and 1.8m in height, which is enclosed by an unbroken ditch with an upcast bank round its outer edge.

2. Battledykes, Oathlaw
NO 460 551

In farmland 0.3 miles SE of Battledykes farm. This round cairn was investigated in the 19th century, when two cinerary urns were recovered.

3. Bell Hillock, Redhall Cottage, Kirriemuir
NO 389 582

In the field to the NE of the cottage, S of the backroad from Prosen Bridge to Glen Prosen, 0.4 miles W of Prosen Bridge. This small cairn has been the target of excavation in the 19th century. Two small urns, a spearhead, and portions of a jet necklace were recovered from the mound.

4. Birkhill, Glenisla
NO 212 596

This grass-grown round cairn stands on the northern shoulder of Druim Dearg, approximately 0.4 miles SE of Birkhill farm, E of the backroad from Bridge of Craigisla to Brewlands Bridge. The superstructure may have been robbed for stone, but it survives to 7.9m in diameter and 0.9m in height. Part of the kerb, constructed of massive boulders, can be seen on the SW side.

5. Blakiewell, Maryculter
NO 864 986

At the edge of a forestry plantation in low lying ground to the W of the Crynoch Burn, 430m NW of Blakiewell farm, some 0.75 miles SSE of Kirkton of Maryculter. This kerbed cairn measures 14m in diameter within its boulder kerb. The NW half lies within the forestry plantation and, although planted, survives up to 0.6m high. The SE half, however, has been obliterated by agricultural action.

6. Blue Cairn, Tarfside
NO 494 797

Lying immediately to the E of the primary school in Tarfside. The cairn appears to have been heavily robbed for stone in the past, and survives now as a rubbly hummock on the lip of the old river terrace along which the village is built. Its E side has been cut away by the cottage building on that side, while its N side has been so severely robbed as to be impossible to trace without excavation, but on the S a fine section of its massively-constructed boulder kerb can be seen.

7. Brankam Hill, Bridgend of Lintrathen
NO 301 557

This well-preserved kerbed cairn stands on a slight platform on the SE slopes of Brankam Hill, on the N side of the B951 Kirriemuir-Glenisla road. The cairn measures 2.1m in diameter over a kerb of graded boulders, the largest of which is on the SE. On the summit of the hill, at NO 299 558, are at least twenty earthen mounds measuring up to 6m in diameter and no more than 0.3m in height, which have been identified as Bronze Age barrows.

8. Bucharn, Strachan
NO 659 929

Occupying a commanding position on the edge of a terrace projecting from the S slopes of the Hill of Goauch, 200m E of Bucharn farm, N off the B976, 0.6 miles W of Strachan. This massive bare mound of stones measures 27m in diameter by 4.5m in height. It stands on a bold platform which probably resulted from ploughing and field clearance in comparatively modern times, rather than representing a ritual pavement around the burial site. A similarly-proportioned cairn lies 1 mile to the E at Upper Shampher.

9. Cairn Greg, Pitkerro
NO 466 337

In farmland S of the B961 Dundee-Drumsturdy road, 1m E of Pitkerro House. This cairn was excavated in 1834, when it was found to contain a large central cist built on the old ground surface. The slab-built cist was cemented at its joints with clay, and was capped with two massive slabs, one above the other but separated by 0.3m of soil. The cist contained a Beaker and a riveted bronze dagger, but the skeletal remains had entirely decayed.

10. Cairn Motherie, Lintrathen
NO 271 594

On the northern summit of the elongated ridge of Creigh Hill, overlooking the Backwater Reservoir from the E. A substantial round cairn, 12.5m in diameter and 1.2m in height.

11. Cairn of Arthurhouse, Thornylea, Fordoun
NO 761 747

This cairn lies 600m N of Arthurhouse Cottage at the S end of a shelter-belt of trees on the crest of the long ridge which extends to the NE from the main spine of Hill of Garvock. It is oval, measuring 21m by 18.7m and rises to 3.3m in height. A second cairn lay nearby, but this had been largely quarried away by the early 19th century to reveal a cist within a kerb of boulders. In the Middle Ages a hoard of coins and a silver brooch had been buried just outside the kerb.

12. Cairn o' Mount, Fettercairn
NO 649 806

On the W side of the B974 Fettercairn-Banchory road, immediately S of the summit of the road. Occupying a prominent skyline position, this cairn, which measures 15.5m in diameter by 3.5m high, has been altered over the centuries to form a way-marker for travellers across this important hill-route.

13. Cairn Plew, Lintrathen
NO 264 584

On the southern summit of Creigh Hill, overlooking Backwater Dam. This round cairn has been badly disturbed by the construction of grouse butts. It survives up to 13.1m in diameter by 1.2m in height.

14. Canterland, Marykirk
NO 706 653

On the S summit of the long ridge of the Hill of Canterland, 1.25 miles E of Marykirk, accessible by farm track and footpath from Canterland. This fine cairn, which measures

9m in diameter by 0.7m in height, is surrounded by a ditch with external bank, from which it is separated by a 3m-wide berm. The evidence for disturbance of both the mound and bank probably date from the 19th-century excavation of the cairn. This revealed an empty central cist which apparently cut through an earlier inhumation burial, while to the E was a second cist containing an inhumation and several flints. Parts of a Beaker were recovered at the same date.

15. Carsegownie, Aberlemno NO 506 545

In agricultural land 0.25 miles SE of Caresegownie farm, 1.25 miles SW of Aberlemno on the B9134 Forfar-Brechin road. This round cairn is overgrown with whins and survives as a circular, stony mound up to 1m in height and 30m in diameter within a boulder kerb. Its irregular profile is the result of examination in the 1850s, when a short cist containing cremations in urns was found. The depression in the centre of the cairn marks the site of the cist. There were no secondary interments or cremations, but three or four long cists were revealed at its outer edge, suggesting that the cairn's life may have extended into the Iron Age.

16. The Cloch, Boghead, Johnshaven NO 781 679

On the summit of Cloch Hill 380m WNW of Boghead farm. Marked on the 1:50000 OS map as 'stone circle', this is the denuded remains of a substantially-built kerbed cairn. It measures 18m in diameter spread over the remains of a boulder kerb, but robbing has reduced the mound to a maximum of 0.5m. The cairn's name is derived from a prominent conglomerate slab (2.3m by 1.7m by 0.6m) set on edge to form one of the kerbstones on the SSE. This is flanked by two uprights which resemble the flankers of a recumbent stone circle, hence the attribution on the map, but the cairn is now recognised as part of a local style which features well-built kerbs incorporating such massive slabs.

17. Clune Wood, Durris
NO 793 950

This large cairn lies amongst forestry on the gentle NW slopes of Clune Hill, 150m WNW of the stone circle and ring-cairn (see above p.12 & p.20), 1.25 miles SE of Kirkton of Durris. It has been disturbed by unrecorded excavations at some stage in the past, and is further blurred through the construction of small enclosures from its stones, but still forms a substantial oval structure measuring some 20m by 16.5m and rises to a maximum height of 1.8m at the NW.

18. Cothelhill, Lintrathen
NO 291 549

In farmland on the E side of the backroad to Bridgend of Lintrathen, *c*.0.1 miles due E of Cothelhill. Known as 'Gallows Knowe', the cairn stands up to 3m in height by 30m in diameter. The summit was disturbed badly during World War II by the construction of an Air Ministry installation. The cairn has been investigated at various times in the later 18th and 19th centuries, with reports of at least three cists with burials.

19. Dickmountlaw, Arbroath
NO 655 436

On Dickmount Law, 0.5 miles N of Arbroath to the E of the A92 Arbroath-Montrose road. This large cairn, capped by a conspicuous stand of trees and contained within a modern enclosure wall, is a prominent sky-line feature visible from as far away as the coast of NE Fife. The depression in its summit possibly marks the site of an unrecorded excavation in the past.

20. Gallow Hill, Cortachy
NO 411 601

On the southern edge of Gallow Hill, 2 miles E of Cortachy on the backroad from Cortachy to Newmill of Inshewan. The much disturbed remains of two skyline cairns, approximately 125m apart.

21. Gilchorn, Inverkeilor NO 651 483

On the long ridge extending north-eastward from Kinblethmont Hill, 0.2 miles NE of Gilchorn farm, S of the B965 Inverkeilor-Friockheim road. Little remains of the cairn structure, most having been removed in the course of the second excavation in 1891. Before excavation, it stood 0.9m in height by 9.1m in diameter.

The first excavation, undertaken *c.*1808, revealed three cremations in urns and an 'incense cup', these apparently representing secondary interments, while at the centre of the mound was an apparently empty cist. Re-excavation in 1891 produced further secondary interments in the form of two collared urns. These contained the remains of two cremations, two incense cups, a glass bead, and a bronze blade. A pit cut into the old ground surface below the centre of the cairn was interpreted as the site of the cist discovered in 1808. Fragments of a bronze blade were recovered from its infill.

22. Glen Wood, Craigo, Logie Pert NO 678 622

In Glen Wood plantation, 0.3 miles SE of Glen of Craigo farm, W of the backroad from Hillside to North Water Bridge. The only surviving element of what appears to have been a barrow cemetery, the site being known locally as the 'Three Laws', the two others having been removed in the late 18th century, when a cist, skeleton, urn and 'ring' were recovered. The remaining mound appears to be a barrow, or earth mound, as opposed to a stone cairn. It consists of a low circular mound within a broad berm, enclosed by a ditch with upcast bank on its outer lip, the whole having a diameter of 36m.

23. Hatton Cairn, Labothie Hill NO 472 416

On the summit of Labothie Hill, 0.5 miles E of Carrot farm, to the E of the backroad from Mill of Inverarity to Gagie. Hatton Cairn is the only surviving member of a once extensive cemetery which spread along this prominent ridge site. The cairn was 'excavated' abysmally between 1876 and 1878, and the excavation report is so badly presented that little clear information concerning what was found can be extracted.

The excavation uncovered a large cist below the centre of the mound, which contained only an 'agate' knife blade. An unspecified number of other cists were also located, most lying on the old ground surface below the cairn, but one, clearly a secondary interment, overlying the primary central cist. Two of the secondary cists contained Food Vessels. All the cists apparently lay within a circle of large boulders set on edge, possibly the kerb of the cairn.

The eight other recorded cairns in the Labothie Hill cemetery lay within a few hundred yards of Hatton Cairn. These were removed for building-stone in the 19th century, and apparently contained cist burials with skeletal remains and urns. A cairn 0.5 miles to the NE on the summit of the hill, and a second mound, known as the Hare Cairn, on the lower ground 0.75 miles to the east, may represent outliers of the main cemetery complex.

24. Hill of Menmuir, Kirkton of Menmuir NO 516 650 to NO 524 657

The SE flank of the long ridge of Hill of Menmuir is speckled with some 500 small cairns spread over an area of 30 hectares. The cairns range from 1.2m to 9m in diameter, and dispersed through them are a series of stony banks, which would suggest that the majority are probably field clearance cairns. In the late 18th century, however, it appears that an inhumation was found beneath one of the mounds, indicating that some have a sepulchral function.

25. Huntingfaulds, Balgray NO 408 398

At the edge of the farm track, approximately 0.2 miles due N of Huntingfaulds farm. This much denuded cairn has been investigated on a number of occasions in the past. Excavation revealed a central cist and secondary cremation burials in urns.

26. Melgam Water, Lintrathen NO 262 565

Positioned on a low ridge of moorland on the S side of the Melgam Water, 0.3 miles SE of Pitewan farm on the B951 Kirriemuir-Glenisla road. This heather-clad round cairn, 13m in diameter by 1.2m in height, has been disturbed in the past. The remains of a short cist can be seen protruding through the cairn material at the centre.

27. The Ring, Hunter's Hill, Fettercairn NO 659 765

This cairn, of unusual type, lies immediately E of the farmtrack which runs between the B974 at Craigmoston and the same road at Gateside, skirting the NW slopes of Hunter's Hill, 1.5 miles NNE of Fettercairn. It comprises a stony mound 7.5m in diameter by 0.3m in height, within a bank 2m wide by 0.3m wide which encloses an area 19m in diameter.

28. Tullos Hill, Loirston, Aberdeen NJ 957 036

On the rising ground to the S of the Dee estuary between Torry and the Altens Industrial Estate. This is the remains of an important cairn cemetery, with four cairns surviving in varying degrees of preservation. The first three described form an intervisible group on the upper reaches of the hillside, while the fourth occupies a low-lying position on the NW slopes.

The SE cairn, known as Crab's Cairn (NJ 963 037), has been damaged and formed part of a field boundary. It measures some 14m in diameter and stands up to 1.7m high. Roughly 500m to the W is Baron's Cairn (NJ 957 036), forming a bold skyline feature crowning a low knoll. It measures 18m in diameter by 1.7m high, and has been used as the base for a trig point. Lying 800m to the SW is Cat Cairn (NJ 951 031), which once measured 22m by 19m and 2.5m in height. Tullos Cairn (NJ 959 040) lies apart from the main group lower down the hillside to the N. It is a bald mound of stones 20m in diameter by 2.5m high.

29. West Border, Friockheim
NO 593 490

Approximately 0.25 miles SW of West Border farm, adjacent to the line of the former railway. This round cairn, known locally as Cairn Knap, has been subject to quarrying at its NW side, but its outline can be traced in full. It stands 3m in height by 22.5m in diameter. There are reports of stone 'coffins' being unearthed in the side of the cairn.

30. West Mains, Auchterhouse
NO 315 377

On the summit of West Mains Hill, approximately 1.2 miles W of Mains of Auchterhouse. This substantial hill-top cairn is surmounted by a modern stone pillar and a trig-point. Measuring 21m in diameter by 2.5m in height, it has always been a prominent skyline feature. It was excavated in 1897, when a double cist was revealed at its core. This contained a partial cremation, with a riveted bronze dagger with the remains of an ox-horn hilt and a horn sheath mount. The cist was enclosed within a circular wall, roughly built from stones, and both it and the cist had then been covered by a small mound of earth or turf contained within a stone kerb. Over this mound had then been heaped a cairn of stones contained within a second kerb.

Ritual

1. Balkemback, Tealing
NO 382 384

In farmland N of the backroad from Tealing to Auchterhouse, 0.8 miles NW of Balkemback. This four-poster 'circle' consists of two upright and two recumbent boulders. The south-eastern stone has been marked with a number of cup-and-ring carvings on its eastern face, all connected to a vertical groove.

2. Blackgate, Lunanhead
NO 484 528

In the field immediately S of Blackgate farm, off the B9134 Forfar-Brechin road 1 mile NW of Lunanhead. Two stones survive from what appears to have been a setting of four (or possibly more). When one of the stones was blown over in the 1850s, an urn containing the remains of a cremation was revealed at its base. A thin fragment of stone recovered from the site in the 19th century, bearing cup-and-ring markings, is believed to have scaled off the larger of the two remaining stones.

3. Carse Grey, Forfar
NO 462 538

Not marked on the 1:50000 OS map, the remains of this small stone setting lie in woodland on the crest of the NE ridge of Carse Hill, 250m W of Carse Grey House. Three stones – one of which has fallen – remain of what was probably a four-poster setting.

4. Corogle Burn, Muir of Pearsie, Kingoldrum
NO 348 603

On the N side of the Corogle Burn, 1 mile SW of Muir of Pearsie farm, off the backroad from Kirriemuir to Easter Lednathie. Two of the stones of this four-poster setting appear to be aligned on two stones, both now fallen, situated approximately 19.8m to the south.

5. Fletcherfield, Kirriemuir
NO 401 525

In farmland adjacent to the track of the former Forfar-Kirriemuir railway line, 0.16 mile NW of Fletcherfield farm, off the A926 Forfar-Kirriemuir road. Both stones of this paired setting are now recumbent. A boulder incorporated in the old railway embankment 12.8m N of the stones may form part of an alignment.

6. Hill of Kirriemuir, Kirriemuir
NO 392 546

On the southern slopes of the hill, E of Kirriemuir cemetery. This massive standing stone stands 2.7m in height and is 1.9m broad at its base. It may have formed part of a paired setting, 19th century accounts mentioning the removal of a recumbent stone from nearby.

7. Hilton of Cairngrassie, Downies
NO 905 953

On a low rise 150m N of Hilton of Cairngrassie farm, 400m W of the A92(T) at Downies. This fine stone measures 1.3m by 0.6m at the base and rise to 2.1m in height.

8. Stone of Morphie, Morphie
NO 716 627

This magnificent stone stands in the stackyard of Morphie farm, immediately to the S of the unclassified road from the A92 to Marykirk 3.5 miles N of Montrose. The stone measures 1m by 0.7m at the base and rises to 3.4m in height. The stone was toppled in the mid 19th century, and an excavation prior to re-erection revealed the remains of a burial at its base.

Cup-and-Ring Stones

1. Balkemback, Tealing **(see above p.42)**

2. Blackgate, Lunanhead **(see above p.42)**

3. Kirkton Farm, Arbuthnott
NO 805 746

This sandstone block, found during ploughing in fields to the E of the farmhouse in 1976, is now kept at the farm. Measuring 310mm by 230mm by 130mm, it bears cup-and-ring and other carvings on three of its faces. On the upper face are three small cups linked to a central cup-and-ring by three radial grooves. The lower face has a cup-and-ring and three cup marks, three parallel grooves running from the latter – crossed by a fourth groove – onto the narrower end of the block to terminate in cups.

4. Letham
N0 528 498

At the junction of the unclassified roads from Dunnichen and Letham to Guthrie, 1.75 miles N of Letham. This boulder, referred to as the 'Girdle Stane of Dunnichen', is marked with several cup-and-ring carvings. It was re-used in the

Middle Ages as a boundary stone between the parishes of Kirkden and Rescobie.

5. Tullo Hill, Menmuir
NO 504 642

On the crest of the spur which projects SE from the main mass of Tullo Hill is a flat sandstone boulder measuring 1m by 0.8m by 0.1m, the surface of which carries about thirty-three shallow cup-marks.

THE IRON AGE

*c.*700 BC to *c.*500 AD

The early centuries of the 1st millennium BC saw the arrival of the newer technology for the smelting and working in iron in western Europe. From about 700 BC new waves of settlers, the Celts, were moving into Britain and bringing with them both this new iron-making technology and new styles in art, in bronze-casting, and new forms of fortification or settlement. This movement may have had much in common with earlier Bronze Age migrations, and there is still debate about the scale of the Celtic colonisation, especially over the issue of whether or not this amounted to an invasion. While there is evidence for apparently sudden and large-scale population movement in the 1st century BC from the Continent into SE England, which itself caused dislocation of existing population groups within these islands, the earliest phases of Celtic migration may have been small-scale and represented continuity of folk-movement patterns which had become established in the Bronze Age. Indeed, new colonists may have been trickling into Britain steadily for centuries, gradually intermingling with the older cultural groups. It is clear, however, that the incomers represented a significant element in the population, and before the first Roman expeditions into Britain in the mid 1st century BC their language and culture was dominant throughout the British Isles.

Our knowledge of Iron Age society is more detailed than our shadowy understanding of the Bronze Age. This is largely a result of contacts – commercial and confrontational – between the Celts and the Mediterranean world of the Greeks and Romans. Roman writers described the Celts as a tribal people with a highly structured society divided into a hierarchy of classes headed by a warrior-aristocracy and priestly elite, but founded on castes of peasant farmers and slaves. Warfare between both tribes and families within tribes played an important part in the life of the Celts: raiding and skirmishing appear as highly ritualised aspects of their social behaviour. Perhaps the best image is that presented in the much later tales of Cuchulainn and the Irish epic poems, where drunken, boastful warriors lived a ritualistic round of carousing, fighting and feasting. The warriors were also patrons of the smiths and craftsmen, loving to flaunt their wealth in outward show, and in the quality of the weapons which they bore. Fine metalwork, such as the hoard of armlets and the cast bronze bowl found at Balmashanner to the S of Forfar, give a vivid image of the skill and techniques of these Celtic craftsmen.

Our evidence for the tribal structure of Celtic Scotland is drawn mainly from two Roman sources. The *Life of Agricola*, written by his son-in-law, the historian Cornelius Tacitus, records the campaigns in Britain of the imperial governor in the late 70s and early 80s AD, while a famous map recording names and giving locations to the tribes was produced at Alexandria in the second quarter of the 2nd century by the geographer Claudius Ptolomaeus (Ptolemy). The evidence from both is highly contentious, and Ptolemy's map in particular is the subject of debate. Both, however, record an image of a land divided into the territories of a series of major tribes, one of whom in the N, the *Caledones*, led the last major resistance to the Romans' northwards advance. The war-riven society of the Celts was easy prey for the superior Roman military machine. Even when they combined as a confederacy against the invaders they proved incapable of offering serious resistance (see below p.69). By the 3rd century AD, however, Roman sources point to the existence of more substantial and stable confederacies amongst the Celtic peoples in N Scotland. It is currently the view that the ever-present threat from Rome in the S stimulated the formation of more enduring alliances which ultimately laid the foundation of the early kingdoms in Scotland. Tayside and Fife appears to have formed the heartland of one of these major confederations referred to variously as the Verturiones or Maeatae. Out of this fusion of tribes developed the later kingdoms of the Picts.

In NE Scotland, Celtic migration probably moved along the trade routes from N Germany which had developed in the early 1st millennium BC. Ideas, too, seem to have flowed along the same routes, and it is likely that it was via this conduit that the style of fortification most closely associated with the Celtic tribes of N Scotland, the timber-laced forts, were introduced. Forts of this class are distinguished by massive stone defences reinforced by timbers which ran horizontally through the ramparts. At some such forts the timbers caught fire, either by accident or hostile design, and their burning produced such intense heat in the core of the wall that the stones melted and fused, slumping into a slaggy mass. Sites which have suffered this fate are referred to as *vitrified* forts. This is not a class of monuments as such, despite claims made in some quarters that the firing was a deliberate action designed to produce a solid wall of impenetrable, fused stone. All that maps plotting the sites of vitrified forts do is chart the distribution of timber-laced defences. Some of the finest timber-laced forts – and vitrified forts – lie within Angus. The massive defences of the *White Caterthun* are amongst the most impressive of this class in Britain, while the ramparts of *Finavon Hill* and *Denoon Law* are striking testimony of both the skill of the builders and the scale of their work, even in their ruined states. Evidence for timber lacing has been noted at several smaller sites throughout the region, such as *Green Cairn* near Balbegno, and *Dundee Law*. The technique, moreover, appears to have remained popular into the early historic period, and it is possible that the first phase of work at sites such as *Turin Hill* may represent a late manifestation of timber-laced building.

The fortification of important settlements was presumably a response to the destabilisation of society which resulted from the climatic deterioration after 1200 BC. Some archaeologists have suggested that early forts were occupied only occasionally, serving as defended assembly points to which the local populations fled in times of war or raids, abandoned in more settled times in favour of undefended homesteads in the adjacent farmlands. Excavation at sites such as Eildon Hill North in Roxburghshire, however, has demonstrated clearly that these were indeed permanently occupied centres. Our present state of knowledge precludes

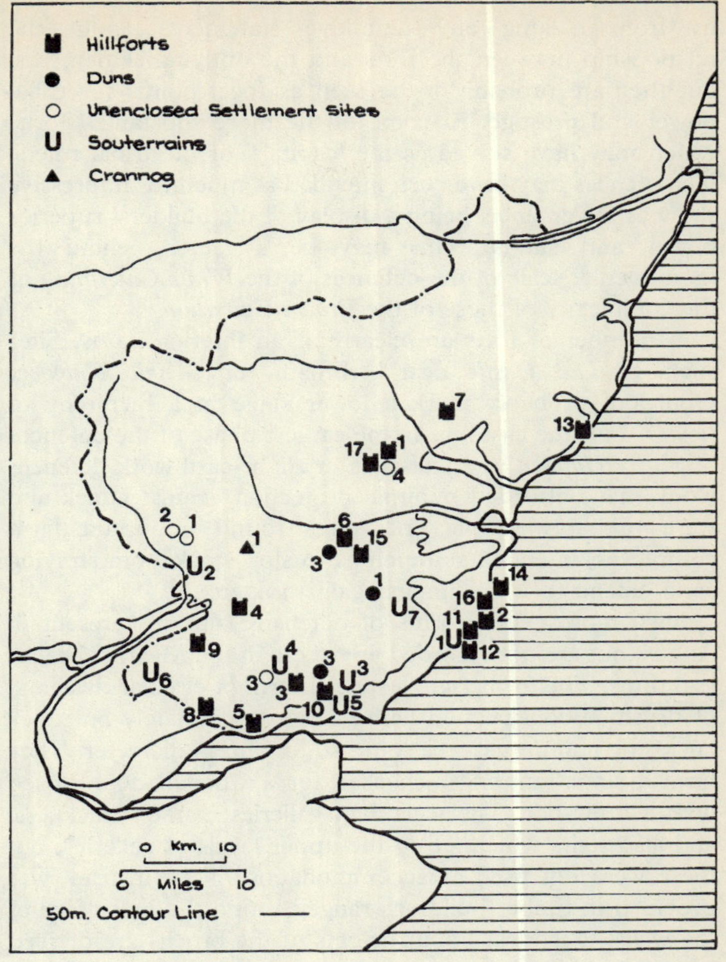

3. Iron Age monuments.

us from making any definitive statements about the relationship between the forts and the outlying settlements, but they are probably to be seen as focal points for tribal power and prestige. At some of the more substantial forts, which may have served as the 'capitals' of the tribal rulers, the defences may have been intended as much for impressive show as for defence, being a display of the builders' superior power and status. This may be a factor behind the monumental scale of the defences of the *White Caterthun*, or the complexity of those of the *Brown Caterthun*.

A number of forts are clearly of an inferior status. Sites such as *Lud Castle* near Arbroath, or *Meikle Knox* at Gourdon, probably mark a lower stage in a hierarchy of power. In some cases, as in the earliest phase of the defences of *Hurly Hawkin*, the palisades or slight earthwork defences would have afforded minimal protection against attack and were probably simply enclosures round important farm complexes, intended as much as to stop stock from straying as to defend their occupants against raiders.

Two more exotic forms of defensive site are present in Angus, but are not recorded anywhere in the Mearns: brochs and duns. The former are a special form of circular dwelling, of drystone construction with walls approximately 5m thick enclosing an internal area some 10 to 13m in diameter. They have a single entrance, checked for a wooden door closed with a draw-bar. The walls had galleries in their thickness, and also stairs which led to the upper levels of galleries, but these were not used as accommodation. This, instead, was provided in timber buildings ranged round the inner face of the walls. Our ideas about heights of the brochs are derived largely from the best-preserved site at Mousa in Shetland, and from major examples such as Dun Telve and Dun Troddan in Glenelg. These outstanding examples may have been originally up to about 15m high, but elsewhere, even allowing for extensive robbing of stone, it seems more likely that an average height of 5-6m was more common. Most were constructed largely in a tight period from the 2nd century BC to the 2nd century AD, and found most commonly in the Northern Isles, N and W mainland Scotland and the

Hebrides. Out of an estimated 600 or so brochs, only some 15 or so lie outwith these areas, mostly in a scattering between the Tay and the Tweed. Their origins as a building style are still subject to fierce debate, but the balance of opinion is that they evolved in the N and spread S. Why some were built so remote from their northern homeland, and separated from it by a wide region of broch-less country, is unknown, but it is possible that they represent either the product of bands of itinerant craftsmen building on commission, or were the homes of southward moving colonists who came into regions where the Romans had caused devastation and depopulation. Certainly, most of the Tay-Tweed group appear to date from the interval between the Flavian and Antonine incursions into Scotland. The broch at *Laws of Monifieth* appears to have been quite substantial, but those at *Craighill* and *Hurly Hawkin* are much smaller and should probably be seen simply as fortified homesteads occupied by farming communities – all lie in areas of good agricultural land.

The second class of 'exotics' are the duns, such as *Rob's Reed*, *St. Bride's Ring*, or the three strung out along the spine of *Turin Hill*. The term is actually quite a catch-all, being applied to a large and quite diverse range of monument. Most are found in the Hebrides and W coastal districts of the Highlands, and extending E along the major river-valley routes through the central Highlands. As a class, the duns are divided into a series of sub-classes, such as galleried duns, plain duns and ring-forts: the names are largely self-explanatory. The common feature to all is the massive dry-stone wall with which they are defended, ranging from 3m to 6m in thickness, either solid or, in the case of the galleried duns, containing a passage in the thickness of the walls. The circuit is usually pierced by a single entrance, checked for a draw-bar-secured timber door. Steps in the thickness of the wall, or against its inner face, provided access to the wall-head. The internal area could be as much as 16m in diameter, and contained timber, or less-substantially built structures. Plain duns usually have a smaller diameter, and in some cases it has been suggested that the whole of the inner space was roofed over. These structures, as with the brochs, appear to represent fortified farmsteads of some status, probably occupied by an extended family group. Dating of the duns is still imprecise as little archaeological examination has been undertaken, and what has been done tends to stress the great chronological range, spanning the period from the mid 1st millennium BC to the mid 1st millennium AD and beyond, over which they remained in vogue. Many, indeed, were built in the 1st or 2nd centuries AD, but had phases of occupation and redevelopment lasting into the post-medieval period. None of the duns of Angus have been excavated, but their rarity in the district suggests that they may represent a movement of colonists similar to that possibly represented by the brochs, or that they date to the migration of a Gaelic-speaking Scots colonists into Pictish territory in early historic times.

Many settlements of clearly 'Iron Age' date, other than these major fortifications, have been positively identified in Angus or Mearns. Most are unenclosed farming settlements located in the upland zones of the region, whose remains are still clearly visible on the ground, but large numbers of sites in the lower districts of E Angus have been identified through aerial photography. At the now destroyed excavated site at Douglasmuir near Friockheim, the crop-marks proved to mark the penannular ditches which defined the outer circuit of large, timber-built houses. Many of these sites probably represent continuity – or re-occupation – from Bronze into Iron Age, as is evident from the excavated site at Tulloch Hill in Moray, but several forms of house type appear to be purely Iron Age developments. One such is the so-called Dalrulzion type, named after an excavated site near Blairgowrie. This takes the form of an unenclosed circular house formed by two thin, practically concentric stone walls, the intervening space probably being filled with turf or peat for insulation. A ring of posts to support the roof members stood very close to the inner face of the wall, and in the centre of the floor was a hearth. Examples of this form have been recognised at *Brankam* and *Strone Hills* overlooking Lintrathen Loch, being especially common in the large areas of settlement to be seen in Glen Isla and across the border in Perthshire. Two other types, the ring-ditch – as seen at Douglasmuir – and the ring-groove, have also been shown through excavation to date from the last two or three centuries BC. The plan of the ring-groove house comprises one or two circular settings of post-holes together with one or two narrow penannular trenches in which wattle or split timber walls were seated. In the ring-ditch house, the roof members appear to have been seated in a very broad and shallow ditch. Examples of ring-ditch houses can be seen clearly to the E of the *White Caterthun*.

In the 1st and 2nd centuries AD there is the development of a further distinctive class of monument, the souterrain or earth-house. Older tradition calls these Picts' Houses, but they long pre-date the development of the historical Pictish people. They are, nevertheless, closely identified with the regions which came to form the heartland of the later Pictish kingdoms. Despite popular belief, these were not houses but were in fact elaborate storage 'cellars'. Excavations at sites such as *Ardestie* and *Carlungie* to the E of Dundee, show them to have been attached to large surface settlements, comprising possibly of groups of huts – as suggested by the original excavator at Ardestie – or as now seems more likely in view of the findings of the large-scale and modern excavation at Newmill near Perth, substantial timber-built roundhouses. Newmill, in fact, points towards souterrains as being elements of what were clearly sites of considerable status – the scale of the souterrain at *Pitcur*, for example, would seem to support this – connected to control of agricultural surpluses.

Only one enigmatic site in Angus and Mearns has been identified as a ritual complex of Iron Age date. This was at the now destroyed Neolithic barrow at *Dalladies*, where a complex of pits, post-holes and ditches stretching for some 400m by 30m over the gravel terrace above the North Esk – now quarried away – was excavated. There was an absence of normal domestic material from the site, although there appears to have been two possible huts, but the ditches seem to have filled rapidly with a dark soil containing an abundance of charcoal and calcined bone. Several horse and cattle skulls were also uncovered. The excavator described the site as religious but with a funerary function, since both cremation and disposal of the cremated remains occurred there.

Burials of Iron Age date are also quite elusive. Several long cists have been identified, such as those inserted into the Bronze Age cairn at *Carsegownie*, Aberlemno. At *Dalladies*, too, Iron Age burials had been inserted into the barrow. Aerial photography has identified a number of sites which may represent Iron Age – or Pictish – cemeteries, for example at Invergighty and Boysack Mills. The crop-marks for these show as small rectangular or circular enclosures surrounding low cairns which contain a central cist burial. At Boysack Mills, in the Lunan Valley W of Inverkeilor, the site was excavated in advance of gravel quarrying in 1976. One square-ditched enclosure and one circular were excavated in full, as were parts of two others. The square-ditch was some 5m square and surrounded a very deep central grave pit which contained an extended inhumation with the remains of an iron pin on his shoulder, lying in the remains of a wooden coffin. The pin was of a common, loosely-dated type, unfortunately allowing no firmer date than 1st-3rd century AD to be offered for the burial.

Iron Age Sites

Hillforts

1. **Brown Caterthun, Menmuir***
NO 555 668

Access from W by signposted footpath from the car-park at the crest of the unclassified road from Little Brechin to Bridgend, approximately 4.5 miles NW of Brechin. This complex earthwork is best appreciated from an aerial photograph, its form being blurred or obscured on the ground by the dense heather which cloaks the hill on which it stands. There is no other site comparable, although certain of its features find parallels in some simpler structures in southern Aberdeenshire. The complexity of its elements indicate at least three building phases, rather than a unitary design.

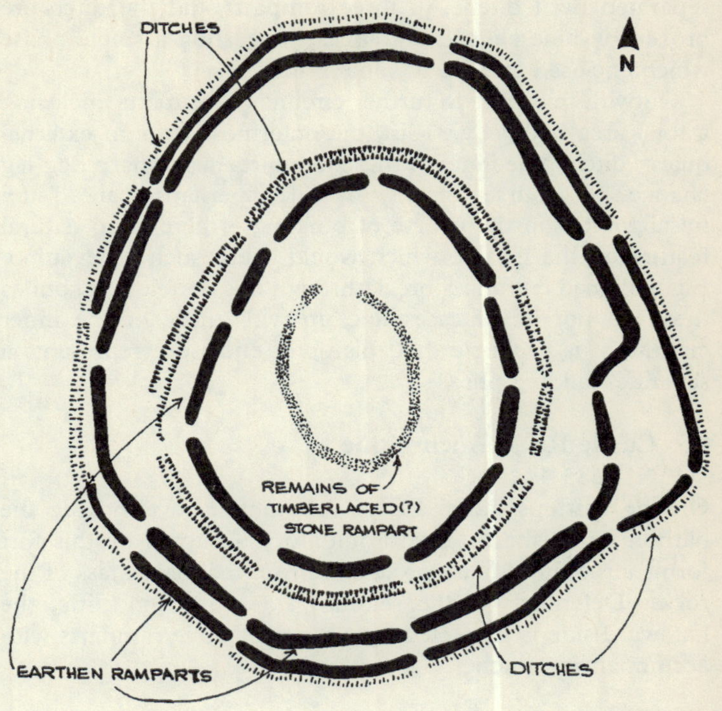

Figure 3. Brown Caterthun hillfort.

The central element is a small enclosure measuring 91.4m by 60.9m, defined by a ruinous stone wall, which lies slightly off the summit of the hill. This innermost circuit has a single entrance in the N side. At distances of between 18m and 54m outside the inner enclosure stands a substantial rampart, possibly marking the line of a stone wall. This has spread to as much as 7.5m in thickness, but stretches of boulders can be seen in various places along its outer edge. Immediately beyond this circuit are two further rings of rampart, separated by a ditch. All three ramparts and the ditch are broken by nine aligned entrances, suggesting a single phase which enclosed an area of some 2 hectares.

Outwith this are two further circuits of ramparts enclosing a total area 330m by 310m, the outermost with an external quarry ditch. The inner of these ramparts has a sharp dog-leg change of course in its E side, perhaps caused by misalignment in the course of building – there is no natural feature on the hillside which would cause such a deviation. Eight aligned entrances break through this double ring, but as these do not in all cases line up with those of the inner circuits, it is probable that this outer enclosure represents a separate building phase.

2. Castle Rock, Auchmithie
NO 683 442

On the clifftops 225m SE of Auchmithie, overlooking the harbour from the S. The promontory occupied by this fort forms a roughly square projection from the main mass of the rocks. Defended on the seaward sides by 30m cliffs, the landward side is protected by a series of three ramparts with accompanying ditches.

3. Craighill, Duntrune
NO 432 358

On the hilltop 360m NW of Craighill farm, S of the unclassified road from Tealing to Kellas. Of the multiple lines of defence which encircled the hilltop, only the innermost rampart survives to any great extent. The chief interest at this site, however, is the broch which was later built in the western end of the fort enclosure. Excavated in 1957, this measures 10.6m in diameter with walls 4.5m thick, of which only the lower courses remain. There is a cup-marked stone a short distance outside the entrance to the broch.

4. Denoon Law, Charleston
NO 355 444

Two miles SW of Charlestown on the unclassified road to Rochelhill and Denoon. This fort occupies the level summit of the isolated outcrop of the Law. The single rampart follows the outline of the hill, producing a trapezoid 113m by 67m internally. The rampart itself is of massive construction, still standing 4m high in places and spread up to 15m wide, implying that the remains of a timber-laced wall might stand at the core of this slumped ruin. On the NE and NW flanks of the hill, where the slope is gentler, are the denuded remains of three lines of rampart, probably contemporary with the inner circuit.

5. Dundee Law
NO 391313

The Law, a conical mass of basalt, dominates the skyline of the city and is a conspicuous landmark for a considerable distance around. The fort which occupies the summit has had an unfortunate history, its S end having been almost obliterated in 1923 by the building of the City's war memorial and summit access road, and its N end disturbed in the 1960s by the construction of a transmitter station. Excavation in advance of landscaping of the area around the war memorial in 1992, however, revealed that more survived than previously believed.

Late 19th century plans show a rectangle with an annexe at its N end, measuring overall 79.2m by 51.8m within a rampart spread up to 5.4m in thickness. Earlier plans, however, depict circular bastions at the angles and a spurwork covering an approach to the summit from the SE (up the line of the modern footpath and stairs), a layout which suggested a later date for building than was usually supposed. The 1992 excavations demonstrated at least three phases of occupation, with the surviving structural remains belonging largely to the final episode of occupation.

The earliest phase was represented by ephemeral traces of vitrified material from a demolished timber-laced rampart dating from the early Iron Age. Much of the vitrified material was found re-used as filling in a modern drain-slot. A soapstone cup-shaped lamp found in the 1923 building operations, now in Dundee Museum, probably belongs to this phase. A second phase is dated to the 2nd century AD on artefact evidence, mainly sherds of Samian pottery, a Roman product imported from manufacturing sites in Gaul. Structural evidence is less tangible, but a paved area uncovered represents either an open court or the floor of some large structure.

The third phase represented the defences of an earthen-walled citadel of the mid-16th century. This was a rectangle with pronounced bastions at the angles – the shape noted by the 1st edition OS map – with its entrance at the SE protected by an angled external spurwork. The N rampart of the main enclosure, plus stretches of the E and W walls, are relatively intact. The site is undocumented, but it is presumably contemporary with the English occupation of Broughty Castle from 1547-50 (see below p.152-3), and was possibly an outpost from which Dundee and the castle at Dudhope (see below p.163) could be overawed and monitored.

6. Finavon, Aberlemno
NO 507 557

Occupying an isolated hillock at the NE end of the Hill of Finavon, to the N of the unclassified road from Aberlemno to Finavon, 1 mile W of Aberlemno. This important hillfort is a conspicuous feature on the southern skyline to travellers on the A90(T). Roughly rectangular in form, it measures 153m E-W by between 30 and 38m N-S internally. The enclosing wall was found during the excavations by V.Gordon Childe in 1933-5 to be timber-laced, heavily vitrified in its upper levels (prominent masses of vitrified stone can be seen in various places round its circuit), 6m thick and still standing 3.6m high internally and 4.8m externally under the fallen rubble of its upper portions. The chief feature of the interior still visible is the rock-cut cistern towards the E end (the deep depression at the W end is a second well, possibly cut at a much later date), but a series of hearths found along the northern side of the enclosure during the excavations indicated the presence of lean-to buildings ranged against the inner face of the rampart. A radiocarbon date obtained from a plank found on the floor of one of these buildings in the course of a second excavation in 1966 has produced a date 665 ± 70 BC.

7. Green Cairn, Cairnton, Balbegno NO 633 723

In agricultural land on the S side of the B966, 1.25 miles SW of Fettercairn. Often confused with the medieval earthwork at Green Castle, also known as Finella's Castle, which lies some 4 miles to the NE (see below p.141). Despite having been subject to agricultural activity for many years, the defences of this vitrified fort still form a prominent feature on the skyline to travellers on the B966. It occupies a site with no obvious defensive merits on a broad terrace overlooking the former flood-plain of the River North Esk. Ploughing has reduced its rampart to a broad, stony mound which encloses an area roughly 45.7m by 15.2m internally. Lumps of vitrified stone visible amongst the plough-debris indicate that this was formerly a timber-laced wall. Excavations in 1973-4, the trenches of which were not back-filled and can still be traced, produced radiocarbon dates confirming a 6th century BC date for the earliest phase of occupation.

8. Hurly Hawkin, Liff NO 332 328

In the grounds of a private house at Liff. This important multi-period site occupies a position of great natural strength on a promontory between two deep water-courses at the Den of Liff on the S-facing slopes overlooking the E end of the Carse of Gowrie. The natural attractions of the site are obvious, the only easy line of approach being across the neck of the promontory from the N. Excavation between 1958 and 1967 revealed five phases of occupation at the site, each represented by a major change in the form of the structures represented.

The earliest phase of fortification was a palisaded enclosure without any major earth or stone rampart defences. This survived as a series of post holes revealed in the course of the excavations. It was replaced by a massively fortified promontory fort with twin lines of ditch and rampart thrown across the northern neck of the site. Subsequently, in the later 1st century AD, the inner rampart was deliberately levelled and a broch constructed over part of its site. This measured 12m in internal diameter within a wall 5.1m thick. The broch itself fell into disuse, probably in the 2nd century AD, and was plundered for stone to build a souterrain within the inner ditch of the fort. Finally, the souterrain's entrance was blocked up and the courtyard of the buildings associated with it partially destroyed.

9. Kinpurney Hill, Newtyle
NO 323 417

The prominent mass of Kinpurney Hill, crowned by the rectangular block of an 18th-century observation tower, is a conspicuous feature of the N side of the Sidlaw Hills above Newtyle. The summit of the hill is enclosed by a single rampart and ditch to form a large fort (6.6 hectares in extent), entered through a single break in the bank on the W.

10. Laws Hill, Drumsturdy
NO 492 349

In grazing land on the hilltop immediately to the SW of Laws farm to the S of Drumsturdy on the B961 Dundee-Monikie road. This once substantial hillfort was systematically plundered for stone in the early 19th century. It was excavated in 1859 by the owner of the farm, who published a detailed account of his work. The fort is defined by an oval enclosure 122m by 61m internally, within the remains of a timber-laced rampart some 9m thick, its outer face constructed of coursed blocks. The easier slopes at the E, W and SW flanks of the hill are protected by outer defences, also of timber-laced construction. Large quantities of vitrified stone were found in the inner wall in the course of the 19th-century excavations.

Within these defences, but apparently after the fort had

been abandoned for some time, a broch was constructed in the 1st or 2nd century AD. Only the lowest courses of this remain, its superstructure having been removed during the stone-robbing operations. The internal area measures 10.6m in diameter, within walls 4.8m thick.

11. Lud Castle, Castlesea Bay, Auchmithie NO 681 434

On the promontory at the southern end of Castlesea Bay, 0.5 miles S of Auchmithie. The headland occupied by the fort appears to have been subject to severe erosion in the past, leaving only a small portion of the structure intact. Rising to 30m from the sea, it is joined to the mainland by a narrow, concave isthmus, its eastern end cut by a single rampart running across the promontory. A stone spindle whorl was found on the site in the 19th century.

12. Maiden Castle, Carlingheugh Bay, Arbroath NO 670 422

On the promontory at the S end of Carlingheugh Bay, 1 mile E of Arbroath on the coastal path along the clifftops. The flat-topped promontory occupied by this fort is defended by 24m cliffs on its seaward sides and slopes steeply downwards from the E to W on the landward side. Here, a deep ditch and massive earth rampart cuts across the neck of the promontory to form a single, highly effective, line of defence.

13. Middle Knox, Gourdon NO 817 702

This small fort occupies the summit of steep-sided spur overlooking the sea 600m E of Middle Knox farm and roughly 0.5 miles SW of Gourdon. Measuring 79m by 36m within a denuded rampart which survives mainly at the N end as a rubble mound 3.1m thick, it appears to have had a single entrance midway along its NW side. There are traces of an outer rampart at the N end, where the spur joins the main body of the hill.

14. Red Head, Ethie
NO 701 474

On the coast 0.5 miles SE of Mains of Ethie farm, 3 miles E of Inverkeilor by unclassified road. This promontory site has been severely mutilated by the construction in the 1940s of a series of slit trenches and observation posts for coastal defence. From what remains, however, it would appear that the headland had been defended by a single ditch and rampart.

15. Turin Hill, Aberlemno
NO 514 535

Turin Hill lies between the lines of the B9113 Forfar-Montrose road and B9134 Forfar-Aberlemno road. The fort occupies the highest point of its ridge, 0.25 miles NW of West Mains of Turin farm on the B9113, from which the shortest but steepest climb to the summit from the S can be made.

Defended by rocky scarps along its S edge, Turin Hill is a site of great natural strength. The fortifications strung out along the ridge are complex and clearly represent several phases of construction. The earliest is represented by a double-ramparted oval enclosure 270m by 120m, covering an area of 3 hectares. It has been suggested that this phase was never completed. Within this, a smaller stone-walled fort was subsequently constructed. Measuring 152m by 39m, this bears close comparison with the fort on Finavon Hill 1.5 miles to the N. The wall appears to be timber-laced, but this has never been tested by excavation. This second fort was apparently abandoned and a stone walled dun, measuring 27.4m in diameter within walls 3.6m thick, was later constructed partly overlying the northern sector of its defences. The amorphous remains of two other duns lie 45m to E and W of this better-preserved example, indicating that this was a site of considerable importance in the Early Historic period.

16. West Mains of Ethie
NO 693 460

On the coast 90m SE of West Mains of Ethie farm, 3 miles SE of Inverkeilor by unclassified road and farm track. Excavated in the 1960s, this coastal promontory fort has revealed evidence of a complex settlement history in the form of a succession of timber-built round-houses in its interior. The promontory itself is defended by a broad band of triple ditch and rampart fortifications, possibly representing more than one phase of building.

17. White Caterthun, Menmuir*
NO 548 661

Access from the SE by the footpath from the Historic Scotland car-park at the crest of the unclassified road from Brechin to Bridgend, 5 miles NW of Brechin. This splendid hillfort, one of the finest Prehistoric ruins in Britain, is a complex of defences of at least two, if not three, phases of construction. The fort is roughly oval in plan, measuring internally 152m by 67m within the tumbled remains of a monumental timber-laced rampart. This inner wall was between 9m and 12m thick, broken by a single entrance at the SE. A short distance outside this wall was a second timber-laced rampart, 6m thick and of less substantial construction. The combined rubble spill from the collapse of these walls spreads over 30m down the hillside. The grass-grown interior has a rock-cut well at its W end, but no traces of original structures (the rectangular enclosure on the N side is of recent date).

Immediately outwith the timber-laced defences is a third circuit, comprising a low rampart with an external quarry-ditch. Between 30m and 69m below this are the remains of two further lines, possibly never completed. On the slopes to the E, outwith this lowest line of defences, are the footings of a number of circular houses (see below p.63). Lying on the slope between the timber-laced walls and the rampart and ditch, at the western end of the fort, is a large boulder measuring roughly 2m by 1m. The upper face of the stone is covered with seventy or more cup-marks.

Duns

1. Dumbarrow Hill, Letham
NO 551 479

This dun occupies a rocky height at the E end of Dumbarrow Hill, 150 NE of Hallkirk farm, N off the unclassified road from Letham to Arbroath, 1.5 miles SE of Letham. It is an oval structure, measuring 38m by 30m, including a 5m thick rampart. Some external facing stones are visible on the NW.

2. Kingennie, Wellbank
NO 575 354

This fragmentary ruin, known as St. Bride's Ring, lies in woodland just to the W of the unclassified road from Wellbank to Monifieth, about 1 mile S of Wellbank. It occupies the summit of a spur which projects N from the flank of Kingennie Hill, and is protected by steep slopes on all sides except the W. The ruins are overgrown and have been severely robbed in antiquity, but the remains of a wall 2.1m wide enclosing an area 16.7m in diameter can be traced.

3. Pitscandly Hill, Blackgate
NO 491 524

Standing on the SW edge of the long, gently-sloping terrace which extends SW from the summit of Pitscandly Hill, above steeper slopes on its S side, some 0.5 miles SE of Blackgate farm. Known as Rob's Reed, this heavily ruined dun has an internal diameter of 19.8m within a broad stony mound, 5.4m thick, which represents the spread and tumbled remains of its rampart.

Unenclosed Settlement Sites

1. Brankam Hill, Bridgend of Lintrathen
NO 299 556 to NO 302 557

On the SE flank of the hill, approximately 400m N of the B951 Kirriemuir-Glenisla road, are the remains of four house sites of varying forms. A circular house platform 9.5m in diameter may be accompanied by a similar platform occupied by the small cairn (see above p.33). There is also a hut-circle,

9m in diameter within an earthen bank, and two so-called Dalrulzion-type hut-circles, the larger of which is 18m in diameter.

2. Strone Hill, Bridgend of Lintrathen
NO 292 567 to NO 287 567

The W spur of Strone Hill above the B951 Kirriemuir-Glenisla road at the N end of the Loch of Lintrathen bears traces of settlement spread over an area of some 16 hectares, apparently largely of early Iron Age date. There are three main groups of hut-circles. The first is a compact group of four small huts and three larger structures positioned at the E end of the ridge below the steep summit slopes of the hill. The large hut-circles have an internal diameter of some 15m. Two are overlain by the smaller huts. A second group, comprising three Dalrulzion-type hut-circles, lies midway along the spur. The largest measures 17m in diameter, and one is partly overlain by its neighbour. The third group lies among an area of field clearance cairns on the crest of the ridge, positioned on a narrow terrace towards its W end. Here there are three hut-circles, each with a diameter of 7m within a low stony bank. Dispersed across the hillside are numerous clearance cairns – the largest with a diameter of some 8m – plus extensive field banks.

3. Tealing
NO 407 378

In rough ground, 360m SE of Tealing Manse. Excavated in the 19th century, this hut circle survives as an earth and stone bank with an entrance at the NW. The interior is grass-grown, with no indication visible of the paved floor mentioned in the excavation report.

4a. White Caterthun, Menmuir
NO 540 659 to NO 537 655

To the E of the highest point on the backroad from Menmuir to Bridgend, 1 mile N of Menmuir, there is an extensive area of settlement and field systems on the NW slopes of the White Caterthun. Three ring-ditch houses lie amidst an extensive system of fields – covering some 20 hectares – which are divided into both small rectangular plots and narrow strips, interspersed with clearance cairns. Two of the houses, the larger of which has an internal diameter of 15m within a 2m-wide ditch, lie about 20m apart on a low ridge. The third ring-ditch, measuring 15m in diameter within a 3m-wide ditch) lies some 120m to the NE.

4b. NO 549 660 and NO 550 661.
At least three more ring-ditch houses lie on the NE slopes of the hill, two immediately outwith the outer rampart of the fort (see above), and a third 160m to the ENE.

Souterrains

1. Arbroath
NO 644 422
At the NW corner of the Eastern Cemetery in Arbroath. Discovered during grave-digging operations at the end of the last century, only 6.7m of the souterrain passage survives (the rest being occupied by graves). No trace of the surface buildings associated with it has been identified.

2. Barns of Airlie, Airlie
NO 305 515
On the crest of the ridge at the western end of the second field to the W of Barns of Airlie farm, 0.2 miles N of Kirkton of Airlie. The surviving souterrain at Barns is one of at least seven found in the vicinity, five on or close to the farm. It is the most complete of all the souterrains still open, consisting of a stone-lined passage 20.4m long, 2m wide and lintelled at a height of 1.8m, roofed with slabs, one of which has been removed to allow access. There is a series of eight cup-marks and serpentine grooves cut into the underside of one of the slabs, possibly a re-used Bronze Age stone. It is probable that the entrance passage survives infilled at the E end of the main structure, but this has never been excavated. There are no surface indications of the hut complex which was served by the souterrain.

3. Carlungie, Newbigging* NO 511 359

Signposted from the A92 Dundee-Arbroath road, 1 miles E of city boundary of Dundee. Set in the middle of an enclosure of clipped grass amidst the arable fields of this fertile district, it is easy to appreciate the relationship between such sites and areas of cereal production. It is less easy, however, to appreciate the former appearance of the site from the manner of its consolidation and public presentation after its excavation in 1950–51.

Carlungie souterrain has been a large and complex structure, consisting of a long, sharply curving passage, 42.6m in length, with a secondary chamber which served as a workshop entered from it. Entered at its E end from a paved courtyard, it had three subsidiary entrances, one of which served the side chamber, and one running in from the N approximately one-third of the way along its length via a long narrow passage. The entire passage is roofless and in parts the side walls have been reduced to their lowest course of stone, leaving only a shallow gully in places to mark the

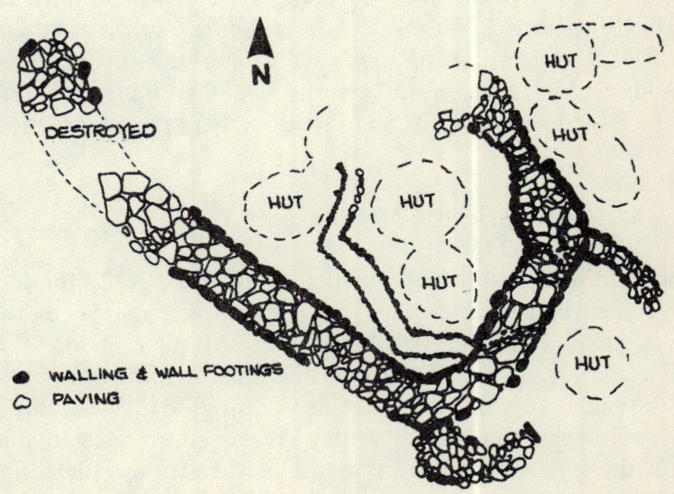

Figure 4. Carlungie souterrain.

course of the souterrain. During excavation, the remains of eight circular paved areas – interpreted as huts standing within the curve of the passage, but perhaps more probably zones of paving within a single larger timber roundhouse – were identified, but none has been marked out on the surface. A second, unexcavated souterrain is known to exist slightly to the SW.

4. Home Farm, Tealing*
NO 412 382

The souterrain and doocot (see below p.246) are signposted from the A90(T) Dundee-Forfar road along the unclassified road to Balgray and Auchterhouse. The souterrain lies in farmland and stands near the edge of a deep water-course immediately W of the farmsteading. The 24.3m-long souterrain consists only of its unroofed passage, which was cleared out following its chance discovery in 1871. It is 2.3m wide on average, with walls rising to 2m in height from a basal course of massive boulders, corbelled in near the top to narrow the space for roofing. During clearance several roofing-slabs were found on the floor of the passage. The entrance slopes down from the NE to a doorway defined by vertical flagstones. Just inside this, at the base of the northern wall of the curving passageway, a cup-and-ring marked boulder is built into the stonework. As at Carlungie, although surface structures are known to exist here, none are now visible.

5. Mains of Ardestie, Newbigging*
NO 412 382

Enclosed in arable fields immediately N of the A92 Dundee-Arbroath road, from which it is signposted, just W of the cross-roads with the B962 Monifieth-Monikie road. It is safest to park on the B962 N of the junction and walk round to the pathway leading to the site. Although damaged, this is one of the best-preserved of the Angus souterrains in that both the passage and the remains of the surface structures with which it was associated have been left open and consolidated after excavation in 1949-50.

The passage, which lost its northern end through modern agricultural action, and is roofless for its entire length, survives as a substantial stone-walled trench, 23m long. The lower courses of the walls are constructed from massive boulders, while the upper courses, which are corbelled in to narrow the gap to be covered by the roofing slabs, are of smaller coursed stones. The floor has been paved, but problems of water seepage during its lifetime led to the installation of a stone-lined drain under the middle of the paving. The main entrance, its opening defined by vertical slabs, is at the foot of a short, narrow passage which slopes down from the courtyard area formed on the surface in the inner arc of the curve, while a subsidiary entrance, which breaks the passage wall above floor level, comes in from the N and enters from a small structure of which only wall-footings survive. This itself opens into the first of a series of three linked circular structures, traditionally interpreted as huts, of which only the footings remain, running parallel to the curve of the passage. The 'huts' are graded in size from N to S, with the largest of the three at the N end. One of the boulders forming the ring of the largest hut is a re-used cup-and-ring marked stone. To the W of the huts a slab-lined pit is sunk into the ground. It has been suggested recently, in the light of the excavation of the large souterrain with substantial and sophisticated timber roundhouse adjacent to it at Newmill to the N of Perth, that rather than being the footings of huts, these four structures were merely defined paved areas associated with particular activities (butchery or metal-working) and that the principal surface structure stood slightly further to the W and was missed in the excavations.

6. Pitcur
NO 253 374

In the sloping field on the N side of the A923 Dundee-Coupar Angus road, directly opposite Pitcur farm, 2.5 miles SE of Coupar Angus. This is the largest by far of the surviving, open souterrains in Scotland, but it is deteriorating rapidly. The main passage, which has not been traced for its full course, is 57.9m in length, with an 18.2m-long subsidiary chamber opening from it. Only about 15m of the passage is still roofed, but in the open section several massive stones lie in the floor of the passage where they have fallen. A number of the stones in the passage carry cup-and-ring marks. There are no visible remains of the associated hut complex. A second souterrain was recorded on the farm in the 19th century.

7. Grange of Conon, Redford
NO 573 450

In agricultural land immediately to the SW of the unclassified road from the B961 1 mile N of Redford to Arbroath, 500m NW of Grange of Conon farm. Occupying an elevated position on the SE-facing slopes of Cairnconon Hill is the site of an Iron Age farmstead. Excavations in 1859 revealed a souterrain with an associated circular hut, of which only the corbelled circular chamber at the terminal end of the passage survives. The discovery of six long cist graves on the hillside to the NW of the souterrain indicates that this was an important area of settlement in the early 1st millennium AD.

Crannogs

Loch of Kinnordy, Kinnordy
NO 366 544

In the marshy ground at the NE end of the Loch of Kinnordy nature reserve, and not accessible to the general public, is a prominent mound of dry, stony ground. This, measuring some 80m in diameter and rising 2.5m above the surrounding bogland, is believed to represent the remains of an artificial platform, or crannog, on which a large hut-circle of late Bronze Age or Iron Age date would have been constructed.

ROMAN

*c.*83 AD to *c.*215 AD

In 78 AD the Roman governor and general, Gnaeus Julius Agricola, embarked on a series of campaigns aimed at completing the conquest of mainland Britain. By 80 his armies had reached the Tay in a reconnaissance campaign, an advance consolidated in the following season by a line of forts across the Forth-Clyde isthmus. In 82 he turned his attentions on SW Scotland, but in 83 he headed N and by the end of the summer had probably reached as far as Aberdeen. His new conquests were secured by forts strung along the southern edge of the Highland line, centred on Inchtuthil on the Tay SE of Dunkeld. This line extended NE through Strathmore, with forts at Cargill in Perthshire, and at Cardean, Inverquharity and Stracathro in Angus. The latter is the most northerly site in Scotland where a permanent Roman fort has been identified, but is unlikely to have been the northernmost garrisoned outpost of the Empire. Cardean has been excavated, but both there and at Inverquharity and Stracathro no clearly visible remains survive above ground.

With Strathmore held by garrisoned forts, Agricola pushed northwards into the last major area of good agricultural land and dense native settlement in Scotland outwith the Roman orbit. In 84 he marched against the tribal confederation of the Caledonians, and crushed their army at the unidentified site of *Mons Graupius*. Various locations have been proposed for this battle, the two most favoured being Bennachie in central Aberdeenshire and Knock Hill at the Pass of Grange in Banffshire, both lying along the line of temporary camps which stretches from *Raedykes* to Muiryfold. From there he pushed westwards along the Moray Firth, possibly establishing a line of briefly-held outposts as far as the district round Inverness. Final conquest, however, eluded Agricola, for he was recalled to Rome at the end of the year and pressures on the imperial frontier on the Danube forced withdrawal of troops from Britain. The reduced garrison could not hold the northern parts of the island, and by 86 all of Agricola's conquests N of the Forth-Clyde line had been abandoned.

In the 140s the emperor, Antoninus Pius, instructed his governor in Britain, Quintus Lollius Urbicus, to mount a fresh series of campaigns in Scotland. This, the Antonine occupation, led to re-building of forts in southern Scotland and the re-establishment of Agricola's old line from the Forth to the Tay, but no forts in Strathmore were re-commissioned. Indeed, the frontier was the Forth-Clyde isthmus, where Lollius Urbicus constructed the so-called Antonine Wall, and the few forts N of that were simply outposts controlling the road into the heart of native territory. Despite the shallowness of this re-occupation, which lasted less than two decades before its outpost forts were abandoned permanently, Roman might was recognised by the tribes of eastern Scotland who paid tribute in grain and other produce.

A final Roman re-advance into the region N of the Forth-Clyde line occurred in the early 3rd century AD. In the 190s Clodius Albinus, governor of Britannia, had stripped the province of soldiers in an attempt to win the imperial throne, with the result that control over the lands N of Hadrian's Wall was lost, and the frontier defences themselves were overrun. Chief amongst the enemies of Rome in the N were the Maeatae, a great confederacy of tribes based on the country between the Forth and the Mounth. They had slaughtered Roman officials and overseers, overrun the frontier defences, and raided deep into the Roman province. Thus, in 208, when Emperor Septimius Severus came in person to Britannia and based his court at York, it was against this people that his major campaign was directed.

The Severan campaigns aimed at the establishment of a secure northern frontier rather than at the conquest of the N part of mainland Britain. Accordingly, few forts N of Hadrian's Wall were re-occupied and the only major permanent garrisons established were a supply base at Cramond on the S bank of the Forth to the W of Edinburgh, and at Carpow on the S bank of the Tay near Abernethy in Perthshire. The emperor himself, commanding one of the largest armies to invade Scotland, marched far into the North

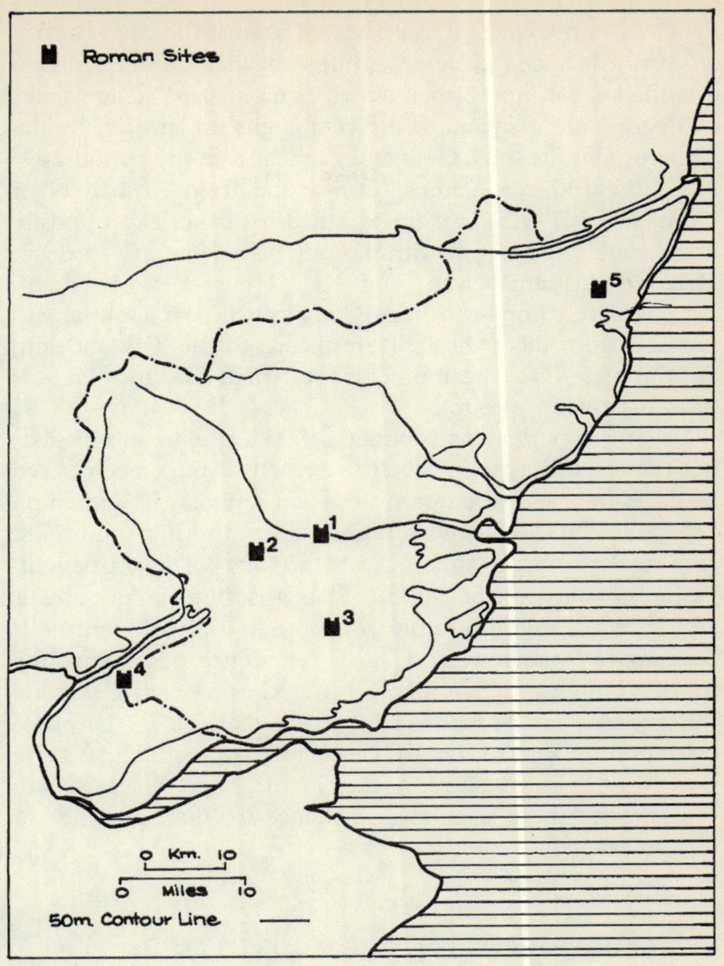

4. Roman sites.

East in a campaign of terror directed against the chief centres of the Maeatae. Several groups of temporary camps, classified according to their acreage (63 acres, 130 acres and 165 acres) are assigned to the campaigns undertaken by the emperor and his sons, Geta and Caracalla, in the period 209-211. The 130 acre camps form a line from Ardoch N of Dunblane in Perthshire, up Strathearn to the Tay opposite Perth, and on through Strathmore with sites at Cardean, *Battledykes*, Balmakewan, and Kair House near Fordoun. The 63 acre camps run from Craigarnhall near Doune, and run NE from there through Strathearn to the Tay and into Strathmore. The encampments at *Kirkbuddo* and *Lintrose* form part of this group.

Severus's campaigns brought the Maeatae to submission, but they swiftly rose in revolt in breach of the truce offered by the Romans. The emperor, by then seriously ill, settled on genocide, and the concentration of camps in Angus and eastern Perthshire points towards the focus of his onslaught. Perhaps luckily for the Maeatae, Severus died at York in 211 and his sons, eager to return to Rome to establish control of the Empire, patched up a hasty yet secure peace with the tribes. Although the Roman forts at Carpow and Cramond were quickly abandoned – by no later than 215 – the peace held until the end of the 3rd century. It is possible that there were further Roman campaigns in the N in the early 4th century, but there is no clear evidence for their presence or for their targets.

Roman Sites

1. Battledykes, Oathlaw NO 458 555

In farmland on Battledykes farm, 1.5 miles west-south-west of Oathlaw. This temporary camp, 52 hectares (130 acres) in extent, is ascribed to the campaigns of Septimius Severus against the Maeatae between 209 and 211. The site occupies a broad gravel terrace overlooking the Lemno Burn from the N. As with most of the so-called marching camps in Angus, little survives above ground. A short stretch of the western end of the S rampart can be traced where it skirts the northern edge of the shelter-belt woodland between Battledykes and Birkenbush farms.

2. Caldhame (Caddam) Wood, Kirriemuir
NO 378 555 to NO 386 563

Running through Caldhame Wood 1.25 miles N of Kirriemuir. This stretch of supposed Roman road is *c*.0.75 miles in length and runs diagonally through the wood from near its SW corner to a point on the B955 Kirriemuir-Cortachy road 60m S of its NE angle. Its identification as Roman is not accepted universally, but the recent discovery through aerial-photography of the crop-mark remains of a 1st-century Roman fort at Inverquharity on the River South Esk, 2 miles NE of the end of the presently identified stretch of road, strengthens arguments in its favour.

3. Kirkbuddo
NO 491 442

The SW corner of this temporary camp, the only part of its defences now clearly visible above ground level, are bisected by the B9127 Kirkbuddo-Whigstreet road, 0.5 miles E of Whigstreet. Covering an area of 25 hectares (63 acres) this site has been identified as part of one of the smaller series of temporary encampments built during the Severan campaigns in the period 209-211. Still relatively intact in the mid 18th century when it was surveyed by General Roy, it is now only clearly visible from the air, where its rampart can be seen to be broken by six entrances protected by *tutuli* – short stretches of detached rampart placed to cover the entrance gap some metres beyond the line of the main defences – apart from the upstanding portion of the circuit which runs through the forestry plantation known as Whigstreet Wood. On the N side of the road, the rampart can be seen as a substantial barrier fronted by a deep ditch of sharp V profile.

4. Lintrose, Campmuir
NO 220 376

Approximately 1 mile S of Coupar Angus, straddling the Angus-Perthshire boundary. Forming part of the same chain of temporary camps represented by Kirkbuddo (above No. 3), Lintrose dates from the Severan campaigns conducted between 209 and 211. In the 18th century the site was still sufficiently well-preserved to be surveyed in full by General Roy, but subsequent agricultural action has reduced it to only a few visible portions. The best-preserved stretch is formed by the southern end of the eastern rampart in the woods 90m SE of Campmuir.

5. Raedykes, Stonehaven
NO 841 902

This well-preserved temporary encampment, formerly believed to date from the campaigns of Septimius Severus in the early 3rd century AD but now assigned a 1st century date and attributed to Agricola, occupies a high moorland site some 3 miles NW of Stonehaven. The uneven topography of the land on which it lies has resulted in an irregular layout which seeks to make the best of unsuitable terrain. It is possible to trace most of the circuit of ditch and rampart, which encloses 37 hectares, and the six gates, represented by breaks in the main rampart protected by a short stretch of ditch and rampart (called a *titulum*) placed in advance of the gap. In the woods on the S side of the unclassified road between the A957 and the B979, 230m S of the main encampment, is a stretch of earth and stone bank 180m long by 1.2m high running parallel to the S side of the camp. This, it has been suggested, might represent an outer line of defence across the gentler slopes to the SE.

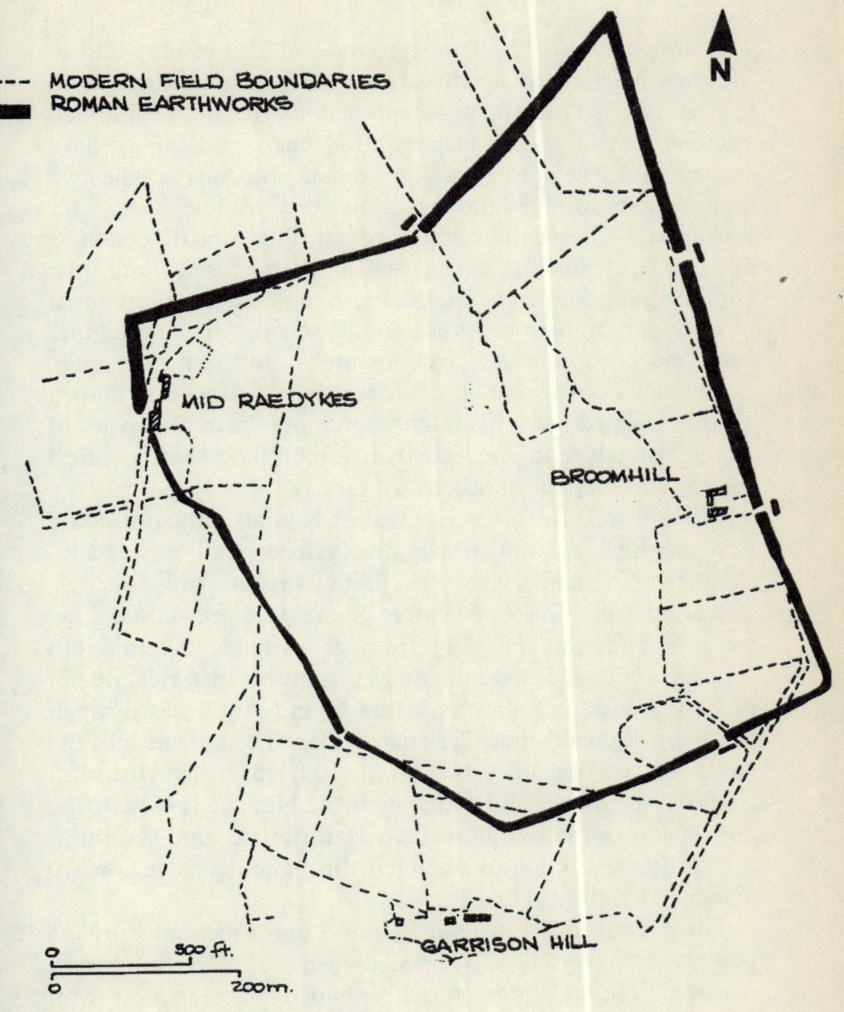

Figure 5. Raedykes Roman marching-camp.

PICTISH AND EARLY MEDIEVAL PERIODS

*c.*500 to *c.*1050

The devastation of the lands around the Tay estuary and in Strathmore wreaked by the armies of Septimius Severus in the early 3rd century, combined with the continued vulnerability of those districts to Roman raids, may have slowed the development of this region into one of the two main centres of native power in the early Middle Ages. This was to be the heartland of the southern Picts, the descendants of the Caledonian tribes which had fused into the confederation known as the Maeatae in reaction to the threat of Roman domination. Although this was by far the wealthier and more populous region, their northern kinsmen, descendants of the second confederation of tribes and known as the Dicalydones, being more remote from the risks of Roman attack, had succeeded in establishing their political supremacy over the southern tribes.

Proximity to the areas of greatest Roman influence could have positive as well as negative effects, and it was into Southern Pictland that the first Christian missionaries, operating from mission centres S of the Forth-Clyde line, were to penetrate possibly from as early as the mid 5th century. Indeed, despite the more prominent historical role of Columba and his followers in the N and W, it was through Southern Pictland that Christianity began to spread into the lands of the pagan tribes of the North East. Historical tradition associates this work with St. Ninian, to whom the conversion of the Southern Picts is attributed, and several of the earliest church sites scattered throughout this region are associated with his cult.

Early conversion to Christianity may account for the comparative scarcity of Class I Pictish stones in Angus and Mearns. These stones, roughly-shaped slabs incised with carvings on one face only, carry no Christian symbols or human figure sculptures, and are commonly ascribed to the pagan period of Pictish history. Their greatest concentration is in the country N of the Mounth, especially in the Garioch district of Aberdeenshire and extending across to Inverness and Easter Ross, a distribution which may reflect both the lateness of the conversion of the northern Picts to Christianity and the political dominance of their kingdom within Scotland. There are, nevertheless, several very fine Class I stones from Angus, such as those at *Aberlemno* and *Dunnichen*, which probably mark the chief centres of political and economic power in the area: only men of wealth and influence could afford to indulge in the patronage of the arts which is manifest in these stone monuments. It is perhaps an indication of the relative unimportance of the Mearns at this time in that it has produced little sculpture of any type from the Pictish period, the site at *Dunnicaer* near Stonehaven excepted.

While missionary activity in the land of the southern Picts may have been quite intensive by *c.*500, this does not mean that all the Picts in this region were converted to Christianity by that date. Indeed, if the example of the northern Picts is considered, conversion was a long drawn out process that took nearly two centuries to achieve anything like the spiritual domination of the bulk of the population. Greater exposure to outside influence, however, may have speeded up this process in the S. There are, nevertheless, few sites which can be identified with any certainty as centres of missionary work rather than having later medieval dedications to saints of the early Church. Nevertheless, some idea of the location of the more important centres can be obtained from the distribution of Class II Pictish stones and other sculpture carrying Christian symbolism. On this criterion, *St. Vigeans* near Arbroath would seem to have been a religious centre of outstanding importance. Later major churches can be postulated at *Restenneth* – which is probably the site of the church founded *c.*710 by the Pictish king, Nechtan mac Derile – and *Brechin*, where the round tower speaks of its importance as a centre of the Celtic Church into the 11th century.

Despite the historical importance of this region as the centre of Pictish power in the period from the later 7th through to the middle of the 9th centuries, and its subsequent

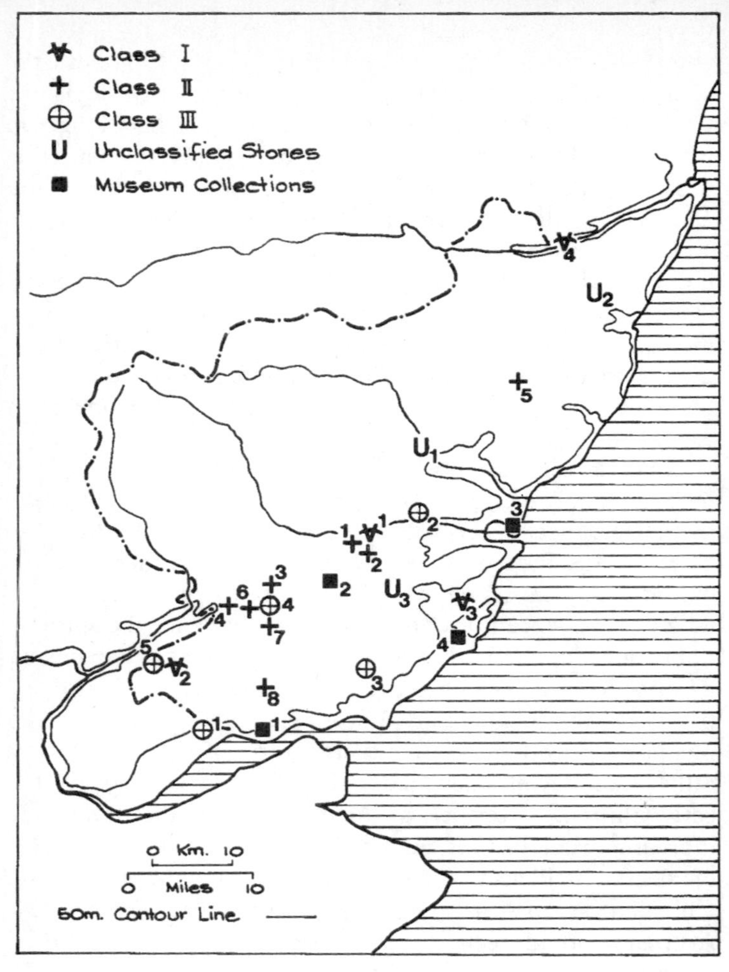

5. Pictish Stones.

importance as part of the new kingdom of the Picts and Scots from the 9th century onwards, there are few important fortified sites to which a definitively Pictish label can be applied. *Dunnottar*, or more probably the fortification on the headland now known as *Bowduns*, is one of the few major sites of early historic date which figures in contemporary written sources. The scale of both possible locations, and their outstanding strategic importance on the pivotal point of routes turning round the E end of the Mounth, implies that Pictish Dunnottar was a centre of at least regional power. There is no site of comparable scale in Angus, but here tradition at least points to the older hill-fort sites, such as *Turin Hill*, and the now vanished 'dun' at Dunnichen, as the seats of Pictish royal power. Excavations on sites in Banffshire – Cullykhan and Green Castle at Portknockie – both strongly-defended sites on rocky coastal promontories, suggests that more detailed examination of the supposedly Iron Age promontory forts of the Angus coast – such as *Castle Rock*, Auchmithie, or *Lud Castle* – might demonstrate a continuity at those sites from the late Prehistoric into the early Historic period. The limited amount of excavation on fortified sites in both Angus and Mearns, however, can only but distort our ideas of patterns of power and social hierarchy in historic Pictland.

A clear indication of the locus of wealth and power in Pictish society is given by the Class II sculptured stones. The greater density of these stones, which carry Christian symbolism and fine figure sculpture in relief alongside the older Pictish symbols of the Class I stones, in S Pictland in comparison to the land beyond the Mounth, may in large part be attributable to the late spread of Christianity amongst the northern Picts. Their greater concentration in the S, however, may also reflect the shift in the balance of political power within Pictland, with domination passing decisively from the N to the more populous and prosperous S in the late 7th century. Patronage of the arts, as represented by the magnificent Class II stones at *Aberlemno*, undoubtedly flowed from the court of a powerful and wealthy king, or from the household of a self-confident provincial lord.

The predominance of the lands of the southern Picts in the struggle for political mastery over all Scotland was reaffirmed after the middle of the 9th century by the takeover of the Pictish kingship by the Scots of Dalriada. Having consolidated their grip on the richest zone N of the Forth, the early Scottish kings were provided with a spring-board from which to launch their centuries-long drive for ultimate domination over all Scotland. The kings from Kenneth mac Alpin onwards were based mainly in Strathearn and Angus, as the later medieval concentration of royal estates in the Gowrie and Strathmore areas indicate, but it is clear that their power in this zone was not always unchallenged. Indeed, in the 10th century, there appears to have been a long-running and bloody feud raging between the royal dynasty and that of the rulers of Mearns, reaching a bloody climax in 995 with the murder of King Kenneth II near Fettercairn. The murder in 1094 of Kenneth's descendant Duncan II, eldest son of Malcolm III Canmore, at Mondynes in Fordoun parish in the Mearns, by one Maelpetair, described as 'earl of Mearns' in later sources, may represent a continuation of the feud.

Pictish and Early Medieval Sites

Fortified Sites

1. Bowduns, Stonehaven NO 884 845

Lying 500m to the N of the cliff-girt promontory crowned by the medieval castle of Dunnottar, forming the northern headland of the bay known as Castle Haven. The level-topped promontory known as Bowduns, extending to 6 hectares, is joined to the mainland by a narrow isthmus approximately 40m wide. Across this run the remains of a wide ditch with, on its inner lip, the indistinct traces of a rampart. The failure of trial excavations in 1984 at Dunnottar Castle to produce evidence of the Pictish fortress recorded there in the late 7th century (see below), and the proximity to Bowduns of the rock stack crowned by the supposed pagan Pictish cult centre at Dunnicaer (see below),

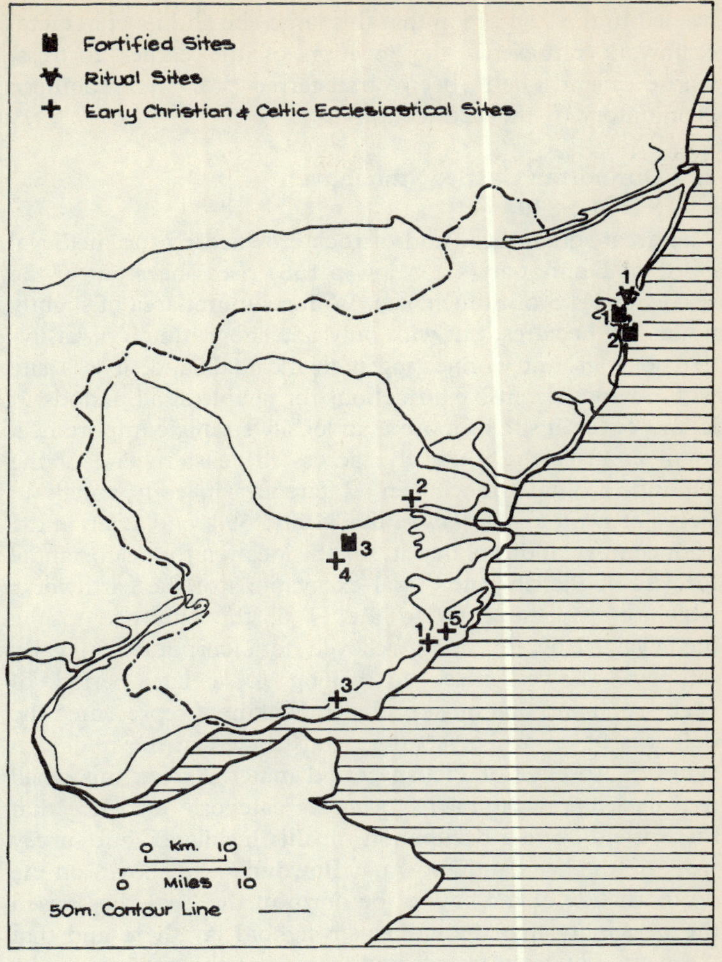

6. Pictish and Early Medieval forts and religious sites.

has led to the suggestion that this large site and its ephemeral earthwork represents the location of the earlier fortress, whose name had been transferred to the southern promontory by the 12th century.

2. Dunnottar Castle, Stonehaven NO 882 839

The great square headland of rock crowned by the medieval castle of Dunnottar (see below p.165) rises sheer out of the sea 1.5 miles S of Stonehaven. With a summit area of slightly under 3.5 hectares, but with only one short stretch of easily-defended ground connecting it to the mainland, it is a site with obvious defensive attractions for people at all periods. It is, moreover, a site of more than locally strategic importance, for it controls the routeways across the eastern end of the Mounth around Stonehaven. References in early annals to sieges of *Duin Foither/Fother* in 681 and 694, and again in the 10th century, indicate that it was the location for a substantial fortress of Pictish date. Trial excavations of the earthworks which crown the cliffs to the N of the entrance to the medieval castle, for long believed to incorporate an early rampart, showed these to belong to a late period of occupation and that most of the embankment represented the defences of an artillery battery constructed in the mid-17th century. Absence of Pictish-period material from this small trial excavation cannot be taken as categoric evidence that there is no Pictish occupation on this headland, but survey work on the headland known as Bowduns (see above) on the northern side of the bay to the north of the castle has raised the possibility that the earlier stronghold lay there and that the name has been transferred from it to the new castle site later in the Middle Ages.

3. Turin Hill NO 514 535 (see above p.60)

Ritual Sites

1. Dunnicaer, Stonehaven NO 883 846

The rock stack known as Dunnicaer stands at the southern edge of Strathlethan Bay, 50m N of the cliffs of the promontory known as Bowduns (see above), approximately 1 mile S of Stonehaven. The summit of the stack, accessible only to those possessed of technical rock-climbing abilities, was crowned until 1832 by the remains of a low wall. In that year three men, having succeeded in scaling the cliffs, amused themselves by throwing the stones into the sea. Amongst the stones were several bearing Class I Pictish symbols, of which five were recovered from the sea at the foot of the stack at intervals down to 1856. Four of these stones are now preserved in the private grounds of Banchory House in Aberdeen, while one is in the Marischal Museum in Aberdeen. These sculptures, it appears, were inset in the inner face of the wall which once crowned the summit, traces of which were still visible in 1982. It is suggested that the enclosure formed on the summit of the stack represented a pagan cult site, presumably associated with the large fort on the adjacent promontory.

Early Christian and Celtic Ecclesiastical Sites

1. Arbirlot NO 588 407

No remains of the early community at this site are currently visible. Its status is uncertain, but it had been laicised by the later 12th century. In *c.*1200 the Bishop of St. Andrews granted the church of Arbirlot to the monks of Arbroath, but the church lands there were retained by him as part of the bishopric estates.

2. Brechin* NO 596 601

The site now occupied by Brechin Cathedral (see below p.115) had been since at least the 10th century an important monastery containing a community of Céli dé and serving also as the seat of a bishopric. It is recorded first in the reign of Kenneth II (972-95), by which time it seems to have already been a large and influential establishment, whose wealth can be seen in both the fine sculptured stones now preserved within the medieval cathedral and in the round tower of Irish type attached to its nave. The Chanonry area around the cathedral is defined by a D-shaped enclosure with its straight edge to the S formed by the steep drop into the den, possibly representing the early line of the vallum which cut off the religious community from the secular world.

When written records of the church at Brechin first appear in the 12th century, the abbacy had become a lay office held by members of the same family. It appears, too, that the first named bishop, Samson (*c.*1130-69), belonged to the same kin. After him, however, the bishopric passed out of family control and was held from *c.*1178 to 1198 by Turpin, a man of Anglo-Norman descent and the first of the line of reformed bishops which continued down to the Reformation. The community of Céli dé survived until the early 13th century in one form or another, their prior, Bricius or Maelbrigte, being recorded down to 1220.

3. Monifieth
NO 494 325

Nothing remains of the monastery and community of Céli dé which stood on the site occupied by the old parish church of Monifieth. During work on the old church in the early 19th century, three Pictish slabs and a section of cross-shaft, dating from the 8th and 10th centuries respectively, were found embedded in the stonework. These are now in the National Museum in Edinburgh.

Although possession of the church, its dependent chapels, lands and rights were granted soon after 1200 by Gilchrist, earl of Angus, to the monks of Arbroath Abbey, the celi de appear to have survived until *c.*1220. In that year Earl Malcolm of Angus confirmed the possession of the lands which pertained to the abbacy (the *abthain*) in the hands of Nicholas, son of Bricius or Maelbrigte, priest of Kirriemuir, his descendents assuming the designation ‘of Monifieth’.

4. Restenneth*
NO 483 516

The site occupied by the 12th-century and later Augustinian priory (see below p.121) was, according to tradition, earlier that of a community of unknown type founded in the late 7th or early 8th century by St. Boniface, or Curitan, a Pictish bishop associated closely with Rosemarkie in Easter Ross, supposed founder, too, of early churches at Tealing and Invergowrie. Arguments that the lower portions of the tower which dominates the priory ruins date from *c.*710, when King Nechtan mac Derile of the Picts asked Abbot Ceolfrith of Jarrow to send him masons to build a church of stone, dedicated to St. Peter, have recently been challenged and a late 11th or early 12th-century date is now preferred.

5. St.Vigeans, Arbroath
NO 638 428

The red sandstone medieval parish church of St.Vigeans (see below p.138), signposted from the A92 immediately N of Arbroath, occupies the site of what was clearly an important ecclesiastical centre of the Pictish Church. The superb collection of sculptured stones housed in the adjacent museum (see below p.98) date from *c.*700 to 900 and underscore that importance. Nothing is known of its history, and it was already long defunct by 1178 when the church was granted to Arbroath Abbey.

Pictish Symbol Stones
Class I

1. Aberlemno*
NO 523 559

In a recess in the drystane field dyke on the S side of the B9134 Forfar-Brechin road opposite the village hall. Car-parking at the hall. An irregular leaning pillar of sandstone. The stone is incised on one face with, from top to bottom, a serpent, diagonally set double disc and Z-rod, and mirror and comb symbols. At the base on the rear of the stone is a series of small cup-marks, hinting at the reuse of an earlier standing stone. A few yards to the E is a rough pillar of red sandstone.

This stone is very worn, but in good light the traces of a curving incised design and a wavy line can be seen on its roadside face. Both stones have been moved to the roadside in this century, unlike the monumental Class II slab a few yards further to the W (see below), which stands in its original position.

2. Keillor, Newtyle
NO 273 398

On a mound on the N side of the unclassified Pitcur-Newtyle road, directly opposite the track to High Keillor farm. A rather weather-worn Class I slab. At the top is what appears to be a wolf-like animal, a double disc and Z-rod in the middle and a mirror symbol at the bottom. There are reports of cist burials from the mound on which its stands.

3. Kinblethmont House, Inverkeilor
NO 639 471

In the private grounds of Kinblethmont House. This fragment was found approximately 275m N of the house in 1952. At the top there is incised a crescent and V-rod, under which is an elephant symbol, and at the bottom the upper portions of a mirror and comb.

4. Park House, Park
NO 780 976

Set on a pedestal in the private grounds of Park House, 0.5 miles SW of Park, between the A93 Aberdeen-Crathes road and the River Dee. This fragment, which bears part of a flower symbol, a crescent and V-rod, and a mirror and comb, was brought here in 1821 from a site at Keith's Muir approximately 1 mile to the NE.

Class II

1. Aberlemno*
NO 523 559

In a recess in the drystane dyke on the S side of the B9134 Forfar-Brechin road, opposite the village hall in Aberlemno. Parking at the hall. This splendid, if weathered, cross-slab stands in its original position, a fact which is hastening its deterioration as traffic pollution and salt spray from passing vehicles in winter corrodes the soft sandstone. To minimise winter damage, the stone, like its neighbours, is encased in a wooden sheath over the winter months, during which time it cannot be seen.

The roadside face carries the cross in relief, its head superimposed upon a wheel decorated with interlace, with raised circular bosses in the centre and in the rounded angles of each arm, and raised rectangular bosses at each arm end. The cross-shaft is divided into panels of interlace. The background is also divided into panels: interlaced animal motifs at the top; angels with bowed heads in the next level down; a second interlace panel; at the bottom animal figures.

The reverse is better-preserved. At the top is a large crescent and V-rod over a double disc and Z-rod. Below these is a lively hunting scene moving from right to left and top to bottom. Two trumpeters blow a fanfare as two horsemen ride past. Below these are two more riders, a hound and a warrior on foot with a square shield on his left arm. Beneath these, hounds are bringing down two deer. At the bottom of the stone, in separate panels, on the left is a centaur figure trailing a foliated branch over his shoulder, and on the right a representation of David slaying a lion. Both of the narrow sides of the slab are decorated with an incised running spiral design.

2. Aberlemno Churchyard*
NO 523 556

In the churchyard, parking behind the church. This is one of the finest stones of southern Pictland. The slab has been neatly dressed and trimmed, tapering on either side towards its gabled head. The carving is still very crisp and sharp.

The cross head is decorated with low relief interlace in the arms, and a spiral-filled circular panel in the centre in place of a boss. The head is superimposed upon a narrow, halo-like wheel with blank circular depressions occupying the rounded angles between each arm (the hole is modern). The shaft is divided into panels of interlace. Above the cross, deer-like creatures crouch in the space between the border and the cross-head. The lower portions of the slab are filled with animal interlace. On the right, the upper section of interlace is formed by two intertwined dragonesque creatures, jaws biting each other's bodies. Below this, a pair of exquisite sea-horses face each other, snouts and raised fore-hooves touching. On the left is a running spiral interlace made up of three dragonesque beasts.

The rear of the slab is the subject of conjecture concerning the circumstances in which it may have been carved. At the top is a 'tuning-fork' or notched rectangle and Z-rod, and triple disc symbols. Below these, divided from them by a raised border, is a battle scene between two differently equipped groups of warriors. From the left come Pictish infantry and cavalry, distinguished by their sharp noses, pointed beards and back-combed hair. The foot soldiers wear knee-length tunics, carry shields with spiked central bosses, and long spears or short-bladed swords. The horsemen are similarly equipped, but wear shoes with long pointed toes and fight with spears held overarm. The enemy, most probably Northumbrians, ride in from the right. They wear hemispherical helmets with prominent nose-guards (the Picts are bare-headed), long tunics or mail byrnies, carry round shields, and fight with swords or slender-shafted spears or javelins. That they have been defeated by the Picts is shown in the upper row of figures, where one of the helmeted warriors is galloping to the right, his sword and shield discarded behind him, pursued by a mounted Pict. At the bottom, another Northumbrian is shown prostrate on the ground with ravens feeding on him. The favoured interpretation sees this as a representation of the battle of Nechtansmere or Dunnichen, fought in 685 between the Picts and Northumbrians near Letham, 6.25 miles to the S. There, Ecgfrith, king of Northumbria, and his army was destroyed by the Picts under Bridei mac Bili. The stone at Aberlemno, however, may date from as much as a century after the battle was fought.

3. Cossans Farm, Glamis*
NO 401 500

Signposted from the A928 Glamis-Kirriemuir road 2.25 miles N of Glamis, on the edge of an area of higher land 0.5 mile E of Cossans farm, approximately 1.25 miles E of the main road along farm tracks. The stone, which has been broken in the past and re-erected, is a guardianship site, but the field in which it stands may be under crop.

Known as St. Orland's Stone, this slab occupies an elevated position overlooking the now drained marshes around the River Dean. The cross face has been damaged when the stone was broken in the past, part of the shaft having been broken away below the head. What remains is enriched with rolls of spiral interlace. It is suggested that the empty circular depression in the centre of the head may have contained a decorative metal plaque. The panels on either side of the shaft are filled with assorted monsters.

The reverse is made up from one panel enclosed within a frame formed by the bodies of two serpentine monsters. At the top are crescent and V-rod and double disc and Z-rod symbols, below which the face has been deliberately damaged by the removal of some symbol from the stone. Under the damaged section are two pairs of riders with hounds, a boat containing six people, and at the bottom of the panel a bull is being attacked by a monster.

4. Eassie*
NO 353 574

Within a purpose-built shelter in the SE angle of the old church of Eassie (see below p.132), 2.25 miles W of Glamis on the A94. This stone lay in a nearby stream for many years before being brought into the church, hence the considerable wear. The cross is decorated with panels of interlace and fretwork. In the background, the panels above the head to right and left have the figures of angels - that on the right has largely scaled off - while below on the left is a rather gangly-looking warrior carrying a square shield and with his spear resting over his shoulder. On the right is a fine sculpture of a stag, an odd-looking beast with its tail between its legs, and a running hound.

The reverse, which is divided into two panels, is more worn. The upper panel contains a damaged 'swimming elephant' or Pictish beast symbol at its top left corner, below which is a cramped double disc and Z-rod. Under these, three figures in knee-length tunics and long cloaks carry staves and process from left to right. To their right is what looks like a tree growing out of a pot. It is often described as being 'in flower', but the flowers look like severed heads impaled on the branches. To its right is the figure of a man with a rod or sword resting on his shoulder. The lower panel has largely disappeared, but the remnants of what appear to be three cows can be traced.

5. Fordoun Church, Fordoun
NO 726 784

In the vestibule of the 19th-century church is a slab recovered from the base of the pulpit of its predecessor, built in 1788, which occupied the site of the medieval parish church. It bears a cross, part of a fish-monster, a double disc and Z-rod, and a hunting scene of three horsemen with dogs. There is an ogam inscription on the edge and an inscription in Hiberno-Saxon minsicule letters on the carved face.

6. Glamis Manse, Glamis
NO 386 468

In the garden of the manse opposite the parish church in the village. This slab is often referred to, on no good grounds, as King Malcolm's Stone. It has been roughly dressed on the cross face only and provided with tapering sides and a pedimented top. The cross itself is an accomplished piece of sculpture, its arms and head filled with panels of interlace of differing styles and complexity. In the space below the pediment, above the cross-head, are the very worn remains of what appear to be two beast heads with a human head between them. The four panels in the spaces above and below the cross arms are filled with incised or low-relief sculpture. At the top are a small beast and a centaur brandishing axes in each hand to left and right of the cross respectively. In the bottom left panel two bearded men wearing short tunics fight with axes, above whom is a cauldron suspended from a pole supported by two forked sticks. Two pairs of human legs protrude from the top of the cauldron. On the bottom right there is a doe's head over a triple disc symbol.

The reverse is undressed and it is probable that this was originally a Class I stone which later had a cross added to its other side. Roughly in the middle of the slab are a series of incised symbols: a serpent, a fish and a mirror. The stone, whose original position is uncertain, was moved to its present site in the 18th century.

7. Loanhead, Glamis
NO 394 465

In woods on the northern slopes of Hunters Hill, 0.5 miles ESE of Glamis village. The stone stands on the left hand side of a track through the woods, 140m W of Loanhead farm. Like the much larger Glamis Manse stone this appears to have been originally a Class I stone adapted by the dressing of one face and the addition of Christian sculpture. The cross is richly ornamented with interlace and fretwork and divides the background into four panels. At the top left is an angel, opposite which is a beast-headed man. The lower panels contain two deer, two beasts, and at the bottom right-hand corner a triple disc and a flower symbol. The reverse of the stone has been badly damaged, but there are traces of the incised carvings of a beast, a serpent and a mirror symbol.

8. South Balluderon
NO 373 375

In a small fenced enclosure on agricultural land at South Balluderon farm, 2 miles N of Kirkton of Strathmartine on the unclassified road to Auchterhouse and Tealing. Known as Martin's Stone, this slab lacks the upper section of its one sculptured face. What survives is the lower arm of a shaft-less cross, within which is carved a horseman riding from right to left. Under the cross there is a second horseman, a swimming elephant and a serpent and Z-rod symbol.

Class III

1. Benvie Kirkyard, Benvie
NO 329 314

In the old kirkyard, to the E of the unclassified Benvie to Fowlis Easter, 0.75 miles N of its junction with the A85 Dundee-Perth dual carriageway. This small cross-slab stands upright near the fragmentary ruins of the old parish church of Benvie, and is probably in its original position. The cross, which is on the W face, is ornamented with interlaced dragonesque animals, while the background is divided into panels with angels above the arms of the cross and intertwined beasts below. On the E face are two armed warriors on horseback, the upper rider being accompanied by a dog. Both edges of the slab are decorated: to the N a key pattern; to the S a pair of interlaced serpents.

2. Brechin Cathedral, Brechin
NO 596 601

At the W end of the cathedral's S aisle. It is believed that this cross-slab stood originally in the old churchyard at Aldbar, 2 miles SW of Brechin. The quality of the sculpture is overall quite poor, that on the reverse of the slab being crude in comparison to the work at, say, Aberlemno. The cross is decorated with interlace and key patterns, set on a background composed of panels which contain animal and human figures. Above the cross-arms are two beasts, while on either side of the shaft are figures in clerical robes. On the reverse, a pair of seated ecclesiastical figures are positioned over a large central panel containing a depiction of David rending the lion's jaw, with his symbols round about him (a harp, staff and a horned sheep, with a mounted warrior and two donkeys below).

3. Camus's Cross (the Camustane), Panmure
NO 520 379

On a grassy knoll near the head of an avenue leading to the Panmure Testimonial monument, 0.5 miles SE of Craigton. The Camustane is unusual in this region in that it is a free-standing cross. It is sculptured on both faces, each divided into three panels. On the E a Crucifixion scene occupies the top panel. Below is a centaur, and in the bottom panel are scrolls of foliage. On the west, the top panel contains a figure of Christ supported by bowing angels. The lower two panels contain pairs of ecclesiastical figures (sometimes interpreted as the Evangelists), holding books. Both sides of the cross are sculpted with scrolls of foliage.

The cross was moved to its present position in the middle of the nineteenth century from a site approximately 2m to the N, where it appears to have stood on a Bronze Age burial mound. The mound was excavated at the time of the cross's removal, and was found to cover a burial accompanied by a Food Vessel and a gold pommel mount or armlet.

4. Glamis Church, Glamis
NO 386 648

On a window ledge in the parish church. This fragment represents the bottom half of a cross-slab, the lower portion of the interlace-decorated shaft surviving at the front. To the right are the lower portions of a four-legged animal, possibly a wolf, while on the left are the legs and lower torso of a walking man. On the reverse, only the legs of two men standing close together survive.

5. Kettins Churchyard, Kettins
NO 238 391

Standing against the N wall of the churchyard in the village of Kettins. This large slab is now very worn and difficult to read. It appears to have been sculptured on one side only. What remains are traces of interlace and fretwork on the shaft of a cross, and in the panel to the right of the shaft various beasts and human figures with the heads of birds or animals.

Unclassified Stones

1. Edzell, Edzell Castle
NO 584 691

In the small museum in the Summer House of the Castle Garden. This fragment of sculpture was found during grave-digging in the old churchyard (see below p.133). It represents one arm and the central boss of an elaborate free-standing cross, carved on the front with a key pattern and with several small spiral-decorated bosses on the rear. At the centre of the front is a hemispherical boss covered with interlace.

2. Nether Auquhollie (the Lang Stane), Rickarton NO 823 907

This fine tall stone, measuring 0.43m by 0.66m by 0.7m at the base and rising to 2.35m in height, stands by the edge of a farm track 380m NW of Nether Auquhollie farm off the dead-end road from the A957 to Easter Auquhollie. There is an untranslated ogam inscription on its SE edge. It is possible that the stone is the last survival from an older (Neolithic or Bronze Age) stone circle which has been removed in the course of agricultural action.

3. Pitmuies, Guthrie NO 566 499

In the garden of a cottage on the S side of the A932 Forfar-Friockheim road, immediately W of the junction with the unclassified road to Gardyne. The lower portion of a cross slab with crosses on both faces. The stone is very worn and only some small sections of scrollwork can be made out at the base of one of the shafts.

Museum Collections

1. Dundee Museum, Albert Square, Dundee NO 403 305

An important collection of Class I-III stones from various sites in the vicinity of Dundee and elsewhere in Angus.

a. A Class I slab found in 1962 approximately 25m E of Aberlemno church. It carries incised decoration on one face only, consisting of a horseshoe above a swimming elephant.

b. A Class I slab which formerly stood in a field to the SE of Strathmartine Castle farm, 1.5 miles to the NW of the city. Incised on one face only, it has a crescent and V-rod symbol and a swimming elephant.

c. A Class I slab from Dunnichen. It is inscribed on one

face with a flower symbol, a double disc and Z-rod, and a mirror and comb. There are pecked vertical grooves down both sides, possibly indicating that the stone was perhaps being prepared for dressing and re-carving as a Class II. A replica cast of the stone has been erected at Dunnichen.

d. A portion of a Class II slab from Tealing Church. The cross side has remains of key-patterning in the lower section of the cross-shaft, and, in a panel to the right of the shaft, the intertwined figures of a serpent and a fish monster. On the reverse is the remnant of a panel containing an elephant symbol.

e. A recumbent gravestone of Class III style. This was discovered in the 19th-century in the old kirkyard at Kirkton of Strathmartine, now on the NW edge of the city suburbs. Decorated on its upper surface with a rather battered border composed of spiral work, it contains a recessed panel depicting two fighting serpents. At the 'head' is a damaged socket which would have held the tenon of an upright cross. The cross itself has not survived.

2. Forfar Museum

Amongst the collection at Forfar Museum are groups of stones moved there recently from the cemetery in Kirriemuir, where they had been on display since their discovery during the demolition of the old parish church, and from Menmuir Church. These comprise:

Kirriemuir:-

a. A Class II slab. The cross is carved with rich interlace and in the panels around it are, at the top, two bird-headed figures, and on either side of the shaft two clerics holding books. The rear is divided into two panels. The upper contains a pair of figures bowing to each other while holding a disc-shaped object between them, possibly St. Paul and St. Anthony meeting and breaking bread. To their right is a third figure, full face to the viewer. The lower panel has a seated figure at its centre, on whose left there is a mirror and comb symbol and to the right an object enclosed by a rectangular frame.

b. A second Class II slab, the cross has key-pattern decoration, with a panel at the foot of the shaft containing a pair of beasts. The background is divided into two panels. On either side of the cross-head are kneeling angels. To the left of the shaft is the figure of a striding man, his hair pulled into a bun at the nape of his neck, beard trimmed to a neat point. His right hand holds the folds of the plaid which is wrapped round his shoulders, while his left grasps a staff and what looks like a small square shield. On the left of the shaft a crow pecks at a dead stag, below which are two running hounds and an unidentified animal.

The rear has a rather cramped double disc and Z-rod at its top left corner. The remainder of the face is dominated by the figures of a mounted warrior, under whom is a mounted hunter and hound in pursuit of a stag.

c. This is the lower part of what appears to be a Class II slab, but no symbols survive on the remaining portion. The interlace-decorated cross divides the lower portion into panels to right and left of the shaft, both containing interlaced beasts. On the rear is the lower half of a mounted warrior, beneath which is another rider accompanied by his hound. The edges of the stone have been dressed, but interlace survives on the left side only.

d. A fragment of cross-slab comprising the lower portion of the stone, but lacking also its back and left side. The surviving panel contains an angel, while there is interlace down the right hand side.

e. A small Class III slab. This has plain, undecorated crosses on both faces, while the panels in the background of the crosses are filled with interlace.

Menmuir:-

f. A battered and weather-worn Class III slab. The cross has key-pattern and interlace work, and to the right of the shaft is the figure of a cleric. The reverse is busily carved with two riders one above the other, a spiral fish-like monster, an animal with its legs doubled up beneath it, and a man holding a club.

g. This is the fragment of a slab, the tenon in its base indicating that probably it was originally mounted on a recumbent gravestone. The front has a panel containing the figure of a rider, while the reverse has the lower portion of a man.

h. A fragment of sculpture showing part of a hunting-scene on one face and what has been interpreted as part of a cross-head on the other.

i. and j. Two sculptural fragments with crosses on one side only.

3. Montrose Museum, Panmure Place, Montrose

a. Described as Class II but with no symbols remaining on the undamaged portions, this stone was found at Farnell near Brechin. The cross-shaft is enriched with interlace, while the background contains fretwork and interlaced animal figuring. The reverse is damaged, but formed a single panel framed by two serpent-like monsters whose heads face each other at the top. On the undamaged section are: at the top the figure of an angel; in the middle a cross; below this two figures beneath a tree and flanked on either side by serpents.

b. Often described as Class II on account of a possible debased double disc symbol on the rear, this slab from Inchbraoch (Rossie Island) is in fact a Class III stone. The quality of the carving, figuring and layout is crude, representing the output of a sculptor who had not trained in one of the main centres of sculpture.

The cross is decorated with fretwork in the central square of its head, while the shaft and arms are filled with uneven-looking scrolls or spirals. To right and left of the cross-head are what are meant to be interlaced serpents, but looking more like a ball of wool attacked by a cat! On the left of the shaft is a grinning, four-legged creature either suckling a smaller animal or having its belly attacked by it. On the right a tall, beast-headed man is attacking a smaller human figure.

On the overcrowded rear is an array of human and animal figures. At the top left an elongated reptile curls around two decorated discs (the possible double disc symbol), its form being matched on the right by a small, fawn-like creature below which an elongated wolf-creature is waiting to pounce. Within this frame is an armed rider mounted on a donkey-like steed, possibly representing a hunter in pursuit of the passive doe below him to the left, which is also being attacked by a hound. To the right of this is another beast. Below this is a seated human figure, to the left of which is a depiction of Samson, a scabbarded sword at his waist, attacking a surprised-looking Philistine with the jawbone of an ass.

c. This is the upper part of a Class III slab which was also found in the old burial-ground of Inchbraoch. The front has an interlace-decorated cross with winged, beast-headed men in the panels above the cross-arms. On the reverse is a mounted warrior.

4. St.Vigeans Museum, Arbroath*
NO 638 429

Housed in a converted cottage immediately to the N of the churchyard from which most of the stones were recovered, this Historic Scotland maintained museum is signposted from the A92 on the northern outskirts of Arbroath. This is one of the largest and most important collections of Pictish stones, ranking alongside the large group at Meigle in Perthshire and in the National Museum in Edinburgh. There are thirty-two stones in the collection and space does not allow a full description here. The finest of the stones is the so-called Drosten Stone, named from the inscription which it bears in a small panel near the foot of one of its narrow sides. This reads DROSTEN IPEUORET (or IREUORET) [E]TTFOR CUS, arranged in four rows. It is suggested that the second row commemorates King Uurad, son of Bargoit (UORET), who reigned 839-42. The cross-face bears a handsome cross-shaft flanked by interlaced animals, while the reverse has some rather late-looking and crude Pictish symbols, beasts, and an interesting figure armed with what appears to be a crossbow. Perhaps more interesting is the prosaically-labelled No 7. This is a very mutilated stone, having been re-shaped and its rear planed flat. On the remaining side, however, are portions of an exquisitely carved interlace cross-shaft, flanked by a series of figure scenes. To the left of the shaft two priestly figures are up-ending a naked man into a small container, possibly representing burial, baptism, or perhaps ritual drowning. Below this, two clerics carrying T-headed croziers move from left to right. On the right of the shaft the seated figures of St.

Paul and St. Anthony break a disc of bread between them, the beak of the bird which miraculously provided this gift still remaining, but the rest has been cut away. Below this is a very peculiar representation of a small kneeling man, again apparently naked, in the act of what appears to be cutting the throat of a standing bull. Much of the symbolism behind these scenes is lost to us, but it seems that in this ostensibly Christian stone, both Christian and pagan traditions are intertwined.

THE MIDDLE AGES

*c.*1050 to *c.*1600

The death of Macbeth, slain in battle at Lumphanan in Aberdeenshire at the hands of Malcolm III in 1057, opened a new chapter in the history of this region. Although the struggle for domination of Scotland between the increasingly powerful kings of the Canmore dynasty and their rivals based in the N, descended from Macbeth's stepson, Lulach, was to last into the 12th century, and two more dynasties of pretenders to the Scottish throne were to mount their challenge with support from the northerners, destiny had come down irreversibly on the side of the southern kings. Nevertheless, until the early 12th century Scottish royal power was weak N of the Mounth, and both Angus and Mearns remained vulnerable to attacks from the N through the mountain passes. The last significant attack came in 1130 when Angus, grandson of Lulach, and ruler of Moray, led his army deep into Strathmore. His invasion ended in defeat and death at Stracathro, and failure meant that the Scottish king, the energetic and ambitious David I, would follow up his victory by ensuring that the heart of his realm was never again exposed to such a threat. The result was the beginning of what can only be described as the Scottish conquest of the North, a process that was to last for over a century, but one which moved the internal frontier of the kingdom decisively to the N and W within a few decades.

The mainstay of the royal advance into the N was a programme of aristocratic colonisation. From the beginning of the 12th century the Scottish crown had been encouraging the settlement within Scotland of men of Anglo-Norman background, men who imported with them new ideas in terms of government, military science, and the Church. These colonists, often land-hungry younger sons with no prospect of inheritance back home, became the spear-head of a movement which saw the establishment of new lordships, held by men unswervingly loyal to the Scottish kings, deep into formerly hostile territory. To encourage settlement by such men, whom David and his successors needed to assist them in their policy of modernising Scotland – of converting it from a comparatively backward and unsophisticated Celtic realm into a more strongly centralised and modern kingdom of the European 'feudal' model – royal estates were often given as the central component in a new lordship held by the incomer on terms which involved some degree of military service. Most held their lands for the service of one knight in the royal army, a 'valuation' which perhaps translated more usually into a rent in money. The progress of these incomers is most often marked by the spread of mottes – earthworks crowned originally by timber castles – which are seen as a distinctively Anglo-Norman and Continental phenomenon. The mottes at *Barry* and *Downie* in Angus are good examples of this type of monument. The advance into the N saw the provision of defence in depth and the securing of the major routes into the land beyond the Mounth. Royal castles at *Cowie* and *Kincardine* complemented those further N at Kildrummy in Mar – later given to the earl – and at Aberdeen, while the motte of the Giffards at *Strachan*, and that at *Durris*, represent intermediate stages in baronial hands controlling the routes across the Dee.

Native families participated fully in the process of colonisation in the N, the earls of Fife, Strathearn and Atholl, all of Celtic descent and reluctant to allow foreign colonisation within their own spheres of influence, were perfectly happy to function as Anglo-Norman knights and receive new lands on the same terms as the incomers in the newly-conquered territories. Native families of less status, moreover, continued to play a prominent role in local government, giving the lie to the widely-held popular belief that 'Normans' were introduced by the Scottish kings and quickly usurped the position of the native nobility throughout the kingdom. In Angus in particular, several native families continued to prosper throughout the Middle Ages, the most notable being the Ogilvies.

Hand-in-hand with the spread of the new forms of land tenure and lordship which the Scottish crown was encouraging in the 12th and 13th centuries came a radical shake-up in the structure of the Church. As we know so little about the organisation of the late Celtic native Scottish Church – what material we have was generally written by later medieval, generally hostile, Roman clerics – it is difficult to gauge truly the degree of corruption and decadence with which it was afflicted. It seems to be the case that many of the old monastic sites were at best in decline, at worst having been laicised and fallen into the hands of dynasties of laymen who still exercised the office and privileges of abbot. Nevertheless, there are indications that at some sites, possibly including *Brechin*, communities of monks known as *celi de* – Vassals of God – descendants of an evangelical, reforming movement in the native Church, continued to function. The laxness of the old system and the gradual slipping of Church property into lay hands, however, was anathema to the new tide of spirituality sweeping Europe in the 11th and 12th centuries. With kings such as David I and Malcolm IV convinced of the superiority of the reformed Church, and having witnessed its workings at first hand in England and France, the days of the old order were numbered.

The process of reform of the Scottish Church took several generations, but it should be seen as a part of the same movement which saw the Anglo-Norman colonisation and the spread of royal authority. To carry through the reforms, the kings introduced foreign clerics to fill the vacant bishoprics of Scotland. There was no widescale displacement of native clerics; whenever a vacancy arose the king would simply 'advise' the appointment of one of his preferred men. With reform-minded clerics established in the bishoprics, the overhaul of the rest of the system could progress. Probably working closely with the nobility, whom the Church needed for patronage and support, a system of parishes based largely on the pattern of secular lordships gradually came into being by the 13th century. These formed the bedrock of Church, and to a certain extent civil, government. At the same time as the structure of the Church was being overhauled, new elements in the form of monasteries of the reformed orders of monks and canons were being established. These were largely royal foundations, such as *Arbroath Abbey*, requiring great investment in capital terms. They were founded as pious acts, for the principal role of the monks or canons who inhabited them was to say masses and prayers for the soul of the founder, and to provide a superior spiritual leavening for society in general, but they brought, often indirectly, much more earthly benefits. The monasteries were very much centres of alien culture and education, which served to introduce innovative techniques in crafts and trades, and especially in agriculture, into Scotland. They tended to be substantial landowners who ran their estates for profit, surpluses being sold on for cash, or traded overseas for luxury goods which could not be produced at home. Their economic importance in the commercial development of Scotland cannot be understated.

A third strand in the modernising of Scotland lay in the foundation of the burghs. These were privileged trading centres which commanded local monopolies as exclusive markets for goods produced in their hinterlands. They served both to draw in the surpluses of the agricultural communities around them, to provide a conduit for the produce of the monastic estates, and to channel these ultimately into overseas trade. Their spread in many ways marked the expansion of royal power, for they were founded by the crown and often came to serve as seats of royal administration in the localities – the bases for sheriffs and law courts – and as outposts of royal government in frontier zones.

The great advances of the 12th and 13th centuries can be seen very clearly in Angus and the Mearns. This, until the wars of Independence, was to be one of the most settled and prosperous zones of the kingdom N of the Forth. For kings such as William the Lion and Alexander II, this was one of their more regular areas of residence at a time when the king moved around the country from castle to castle. Hunting at *Kincardine* was certainly a lure, and the location of many of the Angus and Kincardineshire residences on the northward routes made them obviously regular homes to kings who were campaigning in Moray and Ross. They lay, too, in the heart of an area of several royal estates, and it was probably to consume the food renders from his Angus lands that the 13th-century kings and their households came to the important royal castle at Forfar.

Settlement and stability is the hallmark of the region in the 13th century. Its prosperity is reflected not only in the magnificent architecture of *Arbroath Abbey* or *Brechin Cathedral*, but also in the buildings of some of the finer small parish churches, such as *Logie* and *Pert* in Angus, or *Cowie* in Kincardineshire. The aristocracy, too, were prospering as the produce of their estates and rising rents boosted incomes. Prosperity for them saw a shift from building in earth and timber to a flaunting of their new wealth in stone and mortar. The sadly ruined remains of the curtain wall at *Red Castle*, or the shattered fragments of *Old Panmure*, do not reflect the turbulence of the period, but rather underscore the wealth of their owners and the stability of the time. It was probably in the burghs, however, that the clearest evidence for this prosperity was manifest. There, wealth was lavished on the Church – usually reflected in the 13th-century by the development of smaller establishments, such as friaries, hospitals and almshouses – few of which survived the Reformation, and whose buildings have long since been swept away. The exquisite ruin of the chapel of the *Maison Dieu* at Brechin is poignant testimony to the vanished splendour which resulted from noble and burghal pride. Apart from their plans, little has survived in the burghs to reflect their 13th-century heydays, but the continued importance of early burghs such as Dundee, Forfar and Montrose offers clear evidence of their medieval commercial success.

Even without the traumas of the Wars of Independence, this Golden Age would have faded rapidly in the 14th century. A deterioration in the climate brought crop failure, cattle murrains and famine, soon to be followed by the first in a long series of devastating outbreaks of plague. War, however, proved to be the fatal catalyst, and Scottish trade entered a long slump that only gradually reversed in the late Middle Ages. The Wars also brought a dramatic reshaping of the power structure within Scotland, many of the old families being swept away in the bitter civil wars which accompanied the struggle to maintain Scottish independence. Old lords, such as the Comyns at *Durris*, or the Balliols at *Red Castle*, were forfeited and their lands granted to new families who had proven their loyalty to the Bruce family. Several centres of royal government, such as the royal castles at Dundee and Forfar, were demolished and never rebuilt. These upheavals continued throughout the 14th century, the Bruce settlement being largely reconstructed again after 1371 by their Stewart successors. Indeed, it was under the Stewarts that several of the families most closely identified with Angus, such as the Lyons, the Lindsays and the Ogilvies, established their local pre-eminence.

The great days of the 13th century had also seen a waning in the spiritual zeal which had characterised the Church and fuelled the process of reform. Through most of that century the target of noble and royal generosity had been the various orders of friars, whose original purity and simplicity had fired the imagination of the laity, and whose role in society – preaching to a population largely starved of an active part in religion – had won them great public support. Their role, as ministers to the people, saw the foundation of numerous friaries in the major towns, such as *Dundee* and *Montrose*, a process which continued until the eve of the Reformation. By 1300, however, even the friars were losing the reputation for spiritual purity which they had once enjoyed. Nevertheless, despite widespread recognition by society at large of the failings of the Church system, there was little agitation for change: non-conformity was heresy.

It was probably at parish level that the failure of the medieval Church was most evident. Here, at what should have been bedrock level, there was a steady deterioration in standards throughout the Middle Ages. The decline was largely due to the failure to attract a high calibre of recruits into the ranks of the parish priesthood. Few ambitious men were prepared to live with the obscurity of parish service when their university training could guarantee a passport to riches in the upper ranks of the clergy, usually in royal service or in diocesan administration. This problem was compounded by the fact that much of the wealth of the parishes, derived from the teinds (tithes) paid by the parishioners, had been diverted into the coffers of the major monasteries. This process, known as appropriation, began with the grant to the monastery of the right to appoint the parish priest. This developed into a right to appoint one of its own number to the position, in effect giving it the right to use the revenues for its own purposes. This brought great wealth to the monasteries – by the end of the Middle Ages roughly 80% of Scottish parishes had been appropriated in this way – but with no firm legislation to ensure that the monasteries fulfilled their obligation to provide a good level of pastoral care locally, religious standards had slipped to a dangerously low level. The level of appropriations was already a major problem in the later 12th century. At the time of its foundation, *Arbroath* received control of the churches of *St. Vigeans*, *Ethie*, Dunnichen, Kingoldrum, Maryton, Newtyle, Banchory-Ternan and *Glamis*. To these, before 1250, it had added *Inverkeilor*, Barry, Monikie, *Nigg*, Inverlunan, *Guthrie*, Mains, Kirriemuir, Ruthven, Monifieth and Murroes, all within the district covered by this volume, as well as several others scattered from Inverness to Northumberland.

One immediately obvious result of this diversion of revenue into the hands of the monasteries was that little was spent on the enlargement and elaboration of the parish churches. This is a major reason behind the simplicity of many pre-Reformation churches in Scotland. At *Pert*, for example, the rebuilding of the church in the 13th century was the last major structural work undertaken there until the 16th century, when the old church was fitted up for the new style Protestant services. Civic or local pride, however, could play a redeeming role, wealthy burgesses or lairds, or the craft and merchant guilds paying for rebuilding, restoration or embellishment. Thus at *Dundee*, which was appropriated to the Fife abbey of Lindores, the burgesses paid for the construction of the enormous 15th-century church as a statement of their wealth, confidence and as a symbol of superior status over their rivals in Perth.

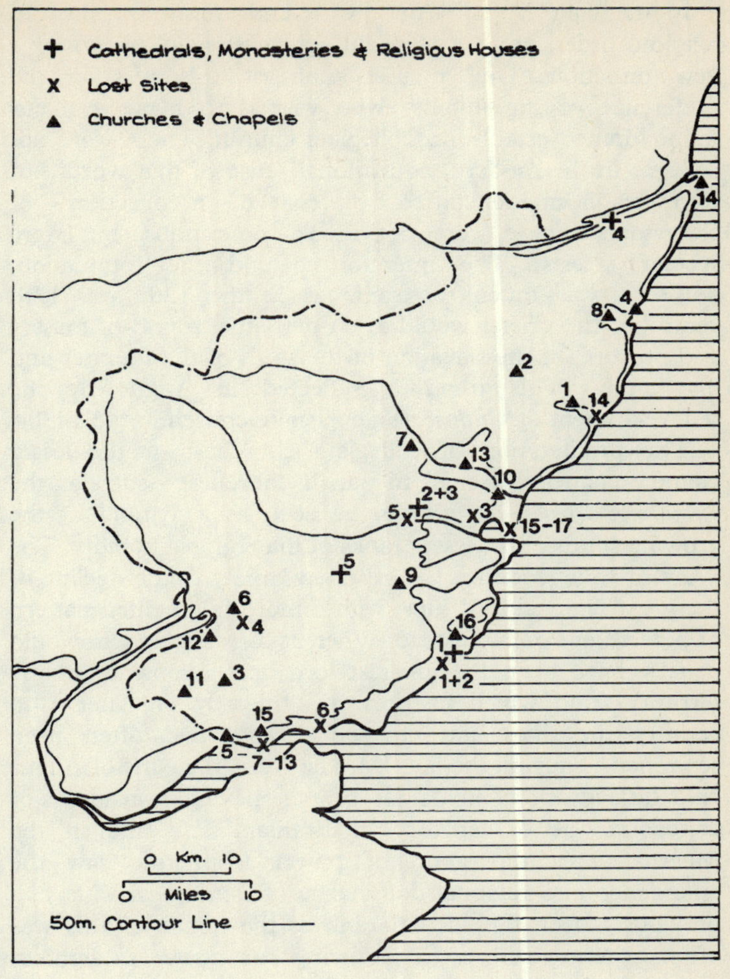

7. The Middle Ages – cathedrals, monasteries, religious houses and parish churches.

In the later Middle Ages, with enthusiasm for the old religious orders at a very low ebb, expressions of piety took a new direction. One manifestation of this was in the preference of the nobility who wished to make a major foundation to establish a collegiate church. These were not colleges in the modern, educational sense of that word, but were establishments staffed by a college – a collection – of clergymen. These were not monks or canons, but were secular priests. The intention behind the foundation, however, was much the same as in the 12th and 13th centuries: the priests would say a perpetual round of masses and prayers for the salvation of the souls of the founder and his family. This trend is reflected in Angus by the redevelopment of *Guthrie* as a collegiate church in the 1470s.

The proliferation of collegiate churches, or the lesser chantry chapels attached to parish churches – such as the *Arbuthnott Aisle* – is also to be seen as a symbol of the growing status of the lesser ranks of the regional nobility. The Wars of Independence had resulted largely in the decline of the great regional lordships, with a more fragmented pattern of power developing instead. Whereas formerly an earl would usually have been the greatest lord and landowner in the territory from which he drew his title, by the later 14th century the titles and control of land had often been separated. Thus, in the later Middle Ages, the earls of Angus held little property in Angus proper, having instead major concentrations of territory in Lothian, Fife and in the Mearns. This separation of power from title saw the emergence into regional dominance of families in what had previously been the second rank of the nobility. This was often accompanied by a jockeying for power as families sought to establish monopolies of control over offices, titles and jurisdictions. This in the later 14th century saw Ogilvy domination of the office of sheriff of Angus, and in the 15th and 16th centuries witnessed the grip of the Scrymgeour family over the burgh of Dundee. This jockeying for power, however, could lead to conflicts where personal interests collided, a situation worsened by the emergence of political factions in the later Middle Ages.

Despite a tendency for local rivalry to spill over into feud – as in the case of the Guthries and Gardynes – there is little evidence to support the widely-held belief in the general lawlessness of the later Middle Ages in Scotland. Indeed, the proliferation of castle-building in this period should perhaps be seen more as a sign of the stability of the times, for the wealth needed to build new stone castles could not have been generated in the midst of such supposedly unsettled conditions. Certainly, despite the obviously defensive attributes of many of the new castles and towerhouses of the later 15th and 16th centuries, the emphasis in the buildings is on comfort and domestic convenience. The architectural refinement of many of the buildings, as at *Edzell*, *Balbegno*, *Dunnottar* or *Melgund*, suggests that castle-building was more a statement of one's social status, pretensions and wealth than the result of a desire for security. The proliferation of castles, too, however, also marks the rising importance of the lairds in local politics as the power of the greater nobility gradually changed in its nature and declined as a territorial factor. Here, again, a new superior status was reflected by the building of a stone castle. Similarly, the freeing of Church property from ecclesiastical control and its diversion into lay hands released great wealth into the nobility and lower ranks of the gentry, the latter often gaining finally secure tenure of the estates which they had feued from the Church. It was such formerly ecclesiastical wealth which funded the building of *Crathes*.

Cathedrals, Monasteries and Religious Houses

1. Arbroath Abbey, Arbroath*
NO 643 413

Signposted, at the N end of the High Street. The massive red sandstone ruins of the Abbey of St. Thomas the Martyr dominate the skyline of the town centre. The abbey was founded in 1178 by King William the Lion and colonised by Tironensian monks from Kelso Abbey. Royal benevolence made it one of the wealthiest monasteries in Scotland, with estates spread through Angus, Kincardineshire, Aberdeenshire and Banffshire. Building started soon after 1178 and, although the E end was completed by 1214 when King William was buried before the high altar, the church was not consecrated until 1233.

Entry to the ruins is by the magnificent W processional doorway of the church. Its round-headed Romanesque archway indicates that this was one of the earliest portions of the structure to be built. The doorway is deeply recessed and richly decorated. Its prominence and depth stems from the thickening of the W front into a barrel-vaulted projection designed to support a gallery, called a tribune, which opened into both the church and to the exterior of the building. Its outer face was finished with three gableted archways standing proud of the main wall of the church. These have gone, but the openings in the main wall and the angled scars of their roofs remain. The gallery opens into the nave through six narrow, pointed-headed archways. Above it on the exterior wall was a band of blind arcading, the heads of which survive, while over that and filling the whole of the upper stage of the gable was a great wheel window, of which only the lower half remains.

Flanking the doorway were two massive western towers clasped at each corner by boldly projecting stepped buttresses. The lowest stages of the towers were decorated with elaborate wall-arcading composed of two staggered layers, one superimposed over the other to give a false sense of depth. The shafts of the arcades have vanished leaving the heads hanging in space. Above these were two tiers of massive lancet windows. The N tower was carried a stage higher than the S, but this uppermost level has been almost totally destroyed. The towers were unfloored voids which, it has been suggested, were intended as western transepts similar to those at Kelso, or at the other major Tironensian abbey of Kilwinning in Ayrshire. Unlike Kelso, however, they do not form an integral part of the interior space of the church, for the main arcade of the nave was carried across the inner walls of the towers as though they did not exist.

Behind this massive screen is a void where the nave once stood. The outer wall of the S aisle, pierced at ground level by two processional doorways into the cloister and in its upper stages by the aisle windows with their lower half infilled to accommodate the lean-to roof of the cloister walk on the exterior, survives to its full height. The aisles themselves are reduced to the bases of the piers which carried the main arcade, except at the NW tower. The tower's S wall preserves the full arrangement of pointed-arched main arcade, triforium (blind storey) with two pointed-arched openings divided by a slender central shaft all contained within a larger round-headed archway, above which were the clerestorey windows. As can be seen from the archway which links the last remaining pier to the S wall, and from the scarring on the wall of the S aisle, the aisles were roofed with stone groin vaults.

Moving east, the massive piers which supported the central tower, and the whole structure of the N transept, have been reduced to rubbly stumps of masonry and the stone plinths which supported the pillars. The S transept is better preserved, its gable being one of the landmarks of Arbroath. In its W wall, above a tier of blind arcading, are the remains of two huge lancets which rise the full height of the building, pointed heads externally, round-headed internally. The walling which separates the windows, and the jamb of the S lancet, are pierced by mural passages – used for maintenance of the upper levels of the building – carried across the window voids on wooden platforms. The inner face of the S gable is more complex. The lower half has three tiers of arcades, the bottom two pointed-arched and blind, the upper round-arched and opening in front of a gallery which carried one of the mural passages. Descending in the thickness of the wall to a doorway in the SE angle of the transept is the stair by which the monks reached the church from the dormitory for the night-time services. Above these arcades are two large lancets, the western partly blocked to accommodate the roofline of the dormitory which abutted the transept in the E range of the cloister. The apex of the gable is filled by a large round window – the Round "O" of Arbroath. This originally could not be seen from inside the church as the transept had a flat timber ceiling and the window lit the large space under the rafters above this.

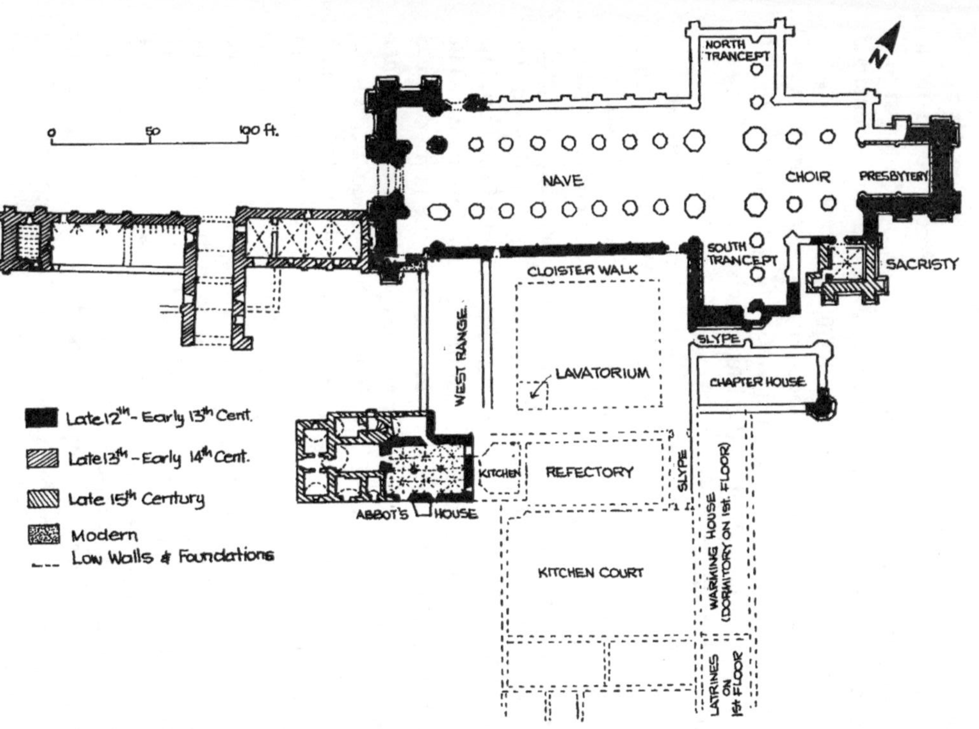

Figure 6. Arbroath Abbey.

To the E of the transept the church is again reduced largely to foundations and pier bases, except on the S. The principal survival here is the two-storeyed sacristy building erected in the 15th century. Entered by a doorway from the easternmost bay of the S aisle of the choir, this was where the altar vestments were stored and where the officiants at the mass robed and disrobed. The lower storey is a high, vaulted chamber with a small strongroom in the thickness of the SW angle opening from it. This served as a treasury where the precious altar vessels and other valuables were stored. The upper floor of the sacristy is not accessible.

The E end of the church, comprising the unaisled presbytery which extended beyond the monks' choir, has survived in part. Lit from the S probably by two tiers of large lancets, and two levels of lancets surviving from a probable three in the E gable, this area which housed the high altar of the church and the tomb of the founder, would have been a sea of light at the end of the long, gloomy tunnel of the nave and choir.

Of the cloister, which is strangely small in comparison to the monumental scale of the church, little remains beyond low walls and foundation lines, although the height of its buildings can be gauged from the roof-lines which scar the S wall of the nave and transepts. In the E range, the only substantial stonework is an isolated stack-like fragment which represents the NE angle of the chapterhouse. The W range has likewise disappeared, as has most of the S range – which housed the refectory and kitchens – and the kitchen court which stood to the S of this. At the W end of the S range, however, there is a superb late 12th-century vaulted undercroft which adjoined the abbey kitchens. This served as vaulted cellarage below the more important chambers in the upper floor, now fossilised within the later building known as the Abbot's House. The original abbot's chambers, completed *c.*1200, incorporated and projected westwards from the angle junction of the W and S ranges, and had as their principal component a large first-storey hall. This structure underwent several phases of elaboration and extension, reaching its present form by about 1500. It now houses the site museum.

In the later 13th century a massive gatehouse range containing the principal entrance to the abbey precincts was built westwards from the SW tower of the church. This comprises two long ranges of two-storeyed buildings separated by the gatehouse proper and culminating at its W end at the head of the High Street in a fortress-like tower. The eastern half of the structure possibly contained the guesthouse, while the upper floor of the western half served as the court-room of the regality court of the abbey. Through the centre of the building ran the vaulted entrance pend, originally defended by doors and a portcullis operated from the chamber above.

Arbroath Abbey's great wealth ensured that it occupied a prominent place in the affairs of the nation. In 1309 Robert I's chancellor, Bernard de Linton, was appointed abbot and it was here that the letter of the Scottish barons to Pope John XXII known as the Declaration of Arbroath, which he probably drafted, was sealed and issued in 1320. This same wealth, however, ensured that the abbey or influence over it came to be a sought after prize. Amongst the most lucrative positions in the gift of the abbot was that of bailie of the regality court, an office held by a layman who would preside over the courts held to settle disputes or try crimes committed in the territories under the jurisdiction of the abbey. By the middle of the 15th century the powerful Angus family of Ogilvy had come to regard this office as their preserve, but in 1446 this was challenged by the Lindsays. When the earl of Crawford, head of the Lindsay family, was killed during attempts to reach a negotiated settlement, open battle broke out in and around the abbey between the supporters of the two families. Although the Lindsays were victorious on the day, the office of bailie was confirmed in Ogilvy hands.

By the end of the 15th century, in common with many of the major monasteries of Scotland, the abbey had come to be held by a succession of royally-appointed commendators – lay-abbots or non-residents – including the younger brother of King James IV, who was Duke of Ross, Archbishop of St. Andrews and already commendator of the abbeys of

Holyrood and Dunfermline. In 1517 James Beaton, the first of three of that family to hold the commendatorship, gained control of the abbey. Following his appointment to the archbishopric of Glasgow in 1523, he secured the abbey for his nephew, the notorious Cardinal David Beaton. Beaton was a frequent resident at the abbey, which he continued to hold in commendam after his elevation to the archbishopric of St. Andrews in 1539, but is remembered most as a plunderer of its resources, much being granted to support his mistress, Marion Ogilvy, and her family. Shortly before his assassination in 1546, Cardinal Beaton transferred the abbey to the control of his nephew, another James Beaton, who in 1551 became archbishop of Glasgow. The abbey then passed to the control of the Hamilton family and, following the Reformation, was ultimately converted into a secular lordship for them. The buildings had begun to be stripped for materials by the 1580s and became a common quarry for the town, still being plundered for stone as late as 1800.

2. Brechin Cathedral, Brechin*
NO 596 601

In the Chanonry area to the SW of the city centre, entered from the E via Bishop's Close, the N via the lane opposite the car park in Church Street, or from the W via Chanonry Wynd. Brechin is one of the smaller Scottish cathedrals, its scale reflecting the comparative poverty of the medieval diocese in comparison with the wealthier sees of Aberdeen, Dunkeld and St. Andrews which surrounded it. It is, nevertheless, a building of quality and contains some important feature, most notably the fine round tower of probably late 11th or early 12th-century date.

The round tower, at the SW angle of the nave, was originally a detached tower of Irish type, serving as a belfry and as a refuge in troubled times. Rising to 26m, the walls of fine ashlar have a pronounced taper towards the top, which is crowned by a 14th-century octagonal spire with lucarnes in four faces. The windows are small and plain, and all are positioned in the upper levels of the tower. Access to the tower was through the doorway in its S side, 2m above

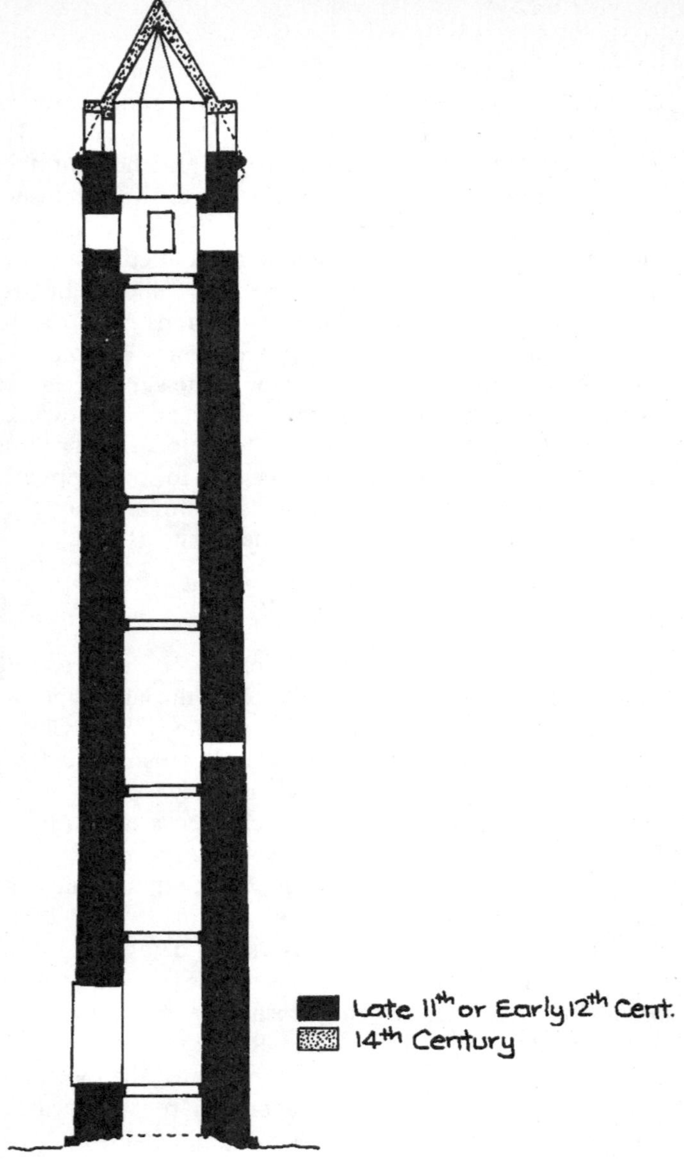

Figure 7. Brechin Round Tower, section.

modern ground level (the blocked door into the nave of the church was a modern alteration). The doorway is a narrow, round-headed archway with tapering sides set into a heavy frame with elaborate sculpted decoration. The outer edge of the frame and edge of the doorway proper are contained by continuous bands of flattened bead moulding. At the apex of the arch is a figure of the Crucifixion, Christ's feet resting on a platform, his arms extended along the outer frame of the surround, and his head rising above the frame. Outwith the frame, to right and left of the springing point of the arch, are two blank panels apparently intended for sculpture. Half-way down the frame of the door are two clerical figures in high relief, while the sill of the doorway extends to either side to terminals carved in the shape of mythical beasts. That to the left is a dragonesque figure from whose mouth hangs a human leg. The interior of the tower, which is not accessible to the public, was divided into seven storeys by timber decking, access from floor to floor being by removable ladder.

The original church associated with the tower occupied the site now filled by the nave. This church was rebuilt or enlarged in the later 12th century, architectural fragments from a fine Romanesque doorway or arch recovered in the restoration of the cathedral in 1900 showing it to have been a building of refinement. The oldest surviving portions of the present fabric, however, date to *c.*1230. Of this period is the lower part of the W front, containing a recessed processional doorway, and the nave arcades. The piers and responds are mainly plain octagons, but two in the N aisle are of clustered shaft form. Unusually, the rather small windows of the squat clerestorey (there is no triforium stage) are placed over the piers of the main arcade rather than over the centre of each bay. Along the wall-head at clerestorey level is a carved cornice decorated with nail-head quatrefoil design. This is to be seen most clearly on the S side. The side walls of the nave aisles are modern reconstructions which replace the walls demolished in 1806 when a single oversailing roof was provided over the nave and aisles, covering the clerestorey windows. There were no transepts, but a pair of small opposing chapels, added in the early 14th century at the NE and SE angles of the nave, gave a cruciform plan to the church. These chapels were also demolished in 1806, as was a porch in the N wall of the nave, but were reinstated as part of the modern restoration. Internally the church is rather dark, despite the splendid decorated window inserted in the W gable in the late 14th century.

The finest feature of the 13th-century work is the unaisled quire. This was abandoned at the Reformation and the E gable and NE half of the N wall represent a rebuilding in 1900–01. It is probable that the quire was originally much longer – possibly 25.6m long – and bore close comparison to those surviving at Dunblane and Dunkeld cathedrals, which share the same plan of aisled nave and aisle-less eastern limb. The side walls are pierced by tall lancets, undecorated externally, but internally with groups of three slender detached shafts with moulded caps and bases dividing the splays, while the moulded arches internally are decorated with an enriched dog-tooth design.

In the later 13th century work commenced on the square NW tower. The vaulted ground floor contains some beautifully-executed carving in the capitals of the angle shafts from which the vaulting springs. The tower rises from a stepped plinth, has massive buttresses at the S and NW angles and an octagonal stair tower at the NE angle. It is divided into four stages by plain stringcourses, and it would appear that the upper levels belong to later 14th century, building work probably having been interrupted by the disturbances of the Wars of Independence. References to work on a belfry during the episcopate of Bishop Patrick Leuchars (1351–83) must refer to the completion of the tower.

Around the cathedral it is possible to trace the layout of the medieval chanonry, and some of the buildings at the W end incorporate medieval remains or stand on medieval sites. The cathedral was non monastic, but was run from the 13th century by a college of secular canons, each possessing a separate manse in its own grounds within the chanonry, or walled precinct of the cathedral. The entrance was through a gateway from the High Street at the E end of Bishop's Close. The springers of the gate arch can still be seen in the walls on either side of the opening, but the arch and the tower which surmounted the gate have gone. To the N of the gate was the Bishop's Palace, no trace of which survives, then working W were the manses of the Treasurer, Sub-Dean, Archdeacon, Chancellor and Precentor. At the W end was the College or Song School, flanked to the N by the manse of the Canon Vicar and to the S by that of the Canon of Kilmoir, to the E of which on the S side were those of the Dean and the Canon Pensionar. Brechin had been the seat of a Celtic bishopric and a monastic community including a body of Céli dé (see above p.83). The round tower and collection of fine early carved stones – including an excellent dragon-headed hog-back gravestone, and a magnificent panel depicting the Virgin and Child – are the chief survivals from this period. The Celtic organisation appears to have been left intact until the later 12th century when a non-Celtic bishop, Turpin, was introduced. By 1200 the officials of a regular medieval diocese had begun to appear and, despite signs of a revival in the influence of the Céli dé and their prior in the period down to 1214, by 1220 the Celtic elements had been subsumed into the new organisation. A synodal chapter of the see – that is made up of all the clergy of the diocese – had appeared by 1214, but by around 1230 this was superseded by a chapter of cathedral canons headed by the dean after English fashion. Despite the poverty of the diocese, which contained only twenty-three parishes, there were fourteen prebends. Few of the bishops of this impoverished see played any great role in Scottish affairs, and it is perhaps significant that the only major addition to the cathedral – the NW tower – was completed in the episcopate of Patrick Leuchars, chancellor of Scotland under David II.

3. Brechin, Maison Dieu Chapel* NO 596 604

Signposted, in Maison Dieu Lane off Market Street to the N of the town centre. Although now reduced to only a long portion of the S wall and a section of the E gable, the ruins of the chapel which served the Hospital of St. Mary the Virgin are the most substantial remains of such an establishment to survive in Scotland. The remaining section of the S wall is 12.2m long, probably representing a little over half of the original length of the building. The wall rises from a broad plinth, broken half-way along its surviving length by a fine recessed doorway with richly moulded hood. To the E and W of the doorway, their sills resting on a stringcourse, are fine lancets, two to the E and one and the eastern jamb of a second to the E. The short section of the E gable ends at the jamb of the first of what was probably a trinity of windows. Internally, the windows have plain but striking moulded details. Between the two eastern windows, which formerly lit the altar from the S side, is an arched recess with the mutilated remains of a piscina for washing the chalice after mass.

From the style of the windows and doorway, it is clear that the chapel formed an original component of the hospital, or almshouse, founded between 1261 and 1267 by William, lord of Brechin. The hospital buildings, which lay to the N of the chapel, have been obliterated completely. Governed by a master and two chaplains, who, together with the bedesmen maintained there, were to say masses and pray for the soul of the founder, the Maison Dieu was a well-endowed small establishment. From the Reformation, its revenues were controlled by the burgh for the support of the poors' hospital, while the title of preceptor was held by the masters of the grammar school.

4. Maryculter NO 844 999

In the private grounds of Maryculter House, overlooking the River Dee, 8 miles WSW of Aberdeen on the B9077 Aberdeen-Durris road. Originally joined with Peterculter on the N side of the Dee in Aberdeenshire, the church of which was controlled by Kelso Abbey. In 1239 Walter Bisset of Aboyne granted his lands of Maryculter to the Knights Templar for the foundation of a house of that Order. Despite a promise made to Kelso that their parochial rights would be

Capo long barrow.

Colmeallie stone circle.

Stone of Morphie, standing stone.

The White Caterthun, hillfort and field system.

Red Castle, Lunan Bay.

Tealing souterrain.

Aberlemno, Class I Pictish stone.

Aberlemno Kirkyard, Class II Pictish stone.

Restenneth Priory.

Brechin, chapel of the Maison Dieu.

Dundee, St. Mary's Tower (the Old Steeple).

Mains Castle.

Dudhope Castle.

Finavon Doocot.

The Morgan Tower, Dundee.

Kinneff Kirk.

Boddin, lime kilns.

safeguarded, in 1287 Maryculter was separated from Peterculter. On the suppression of the Templars in the early 14th century their properties passed to the Hospitallers, who retained possession until the Reformation. Of this once important church, only the lower courses of stone work remain, despite it having continued to serve as the parish church until 1787.

5. Restenneth Priory, Forfar*
NO 482 516

Signposted from the B9113 Forfar-Aberlemno road 1.5 miles E of Forfar, on a promontory of land projecting into the marshy hollow formerly occupied by the Loch of Restenneth. The priory is the successor to an earlier Celtic establishment on the same site, dedicated to St. Peter, possibly that which the Pictish king Nechtan mac Derile built *c.*710 with the assistance of masons from Northumbria (see above p.85). It was for long supposed that the lower portions of the tower which still dominates the site belonged to this early community, but current thinking places its construction well into the 11th century.

In *c.*1161–2, Malcolm IV granted St. Peter's church, its lands and dependent chapels, to the canons of Jedburgh on the understanding that they establish a prior and convent of canons there. The priory which resulted from this grant remained a dependency of Jedburgh throughout the Middle Ages. Work on replacing the older buildings on the site may have commenced soon after the foundation of the priory, but it was not until 1243 that its new church was dedicated by David de Bernham, bishop of St. Andrews, in whose diocese it stood. Restenneth suffered damage during the Wars of Independence, Edward I of England granting a request by the abbot of Jedburgh for a gift of timber from the Forest of Platar in Angus for the rebuilding of the church and conventual buildings. In 1322, Robert I confirmed all its privileges and possessions possibly in connection with the burial there of his son, John. David II confirmed this and all earlier royal grants in 1344, out of regard for the memory of his brother. Despite these royal connections Restenneth remained a small house and from the later 15th century onwards various attempts were made to unite it with Jedburgh, the Chapel Royal, and, ultimately, the archbishopric of St. Andrews. Despite this, however, it maintained a separate existence until 1560, when it passed along with the rest of Jedburgh's property into the hands of the Hume family.

The chief remains of the priory are the tower, which is the most conspicuous landmark of the site, and the quire of the church to its E. The tower is the work of several periods, this being apparent from the changes in the masonry at different levels. The lowest portion is pierced in its E and W faces by high round-headed archways, and has a tall and narrow doorway, its round-headed arch cut from a single block of stone, on the S side. This formed a western porch or tower attached to the early church on whose site the quire was built. The tower was later heightened and shortly after 1400 was crowned with the stone-built broach spire which is the most distinctive feature of the ruins.

The tower is off-centre towards the S of the quire and nave of the 13th-century church, into which it has been wholly incorporated to form a partition between the canons' quire and the nave (which served as the parish church for Forfar until 1591). This suggests that the earlier church was narrower than that built for the canons, whose S wall followed the line of the older building, but whose N wall lies roughly 2m further to the N. The quire as it stands is largely 13th-century. It was a simple structure lit by a range of fine lancets in all three walls. The trinity of windows in the E gable have lost their heads, but those in the side walls (originally five on each side) reflect their original form. In the S wall are the remains of the sedilia where the officiants at the mass sat, a piscina for washing the chalices after mass, an aumbry or cupboard in which the consecrated waifers for the mass would have been stored, and a later tomb-recess. At the W end of the S wall is the blocked door through which the canons entered the church from the dormitory for the night services.

The nave and the majority of the cloisters have been

reduced to the lowest courses of stonework, but the general plan of both can be determined. The nave was aisle-less, its roofline marked by the scar which slants across the W face of the tower. Shorter than the quire, the W front of the nave lay on a line with the inner wall of the western range of the cloister. The dimensions of the cloister are clearly defined by the high, featureless walls which formed the inner faces of the S and W ranges. Of the E range, which contained the chapterhouse, only foundations remain.

Lost Sites

1. Arbroath, The Almonry and Chapel of St. Michael NO 643 413

The 12th-century almonry (where there was daily distribution to the poor and the infirm of the left-overs from the monastic refectory) stood at the head of the High Street opposite the W doorway of the abbey church.

2. Arbroath, Hospital of St. John the Baptist NO 404 626

Fragments of stonework from the hospice are incorporated in the late 19th-century Hospitalfield House which occupies the site. Possibly founded in the 13th century, it is on record by 1325 but appears to have been on the verge of ruin by 1490 when it receives its last mention in the records of Arbroath Abbey.

3. Arrat, Hospital of St.Mary Magdalene NO 646 590

The old churchyard at Arrat, 2.5 miles E of Brechin on the A935, marks the site of the 'Maidlin Chapel' or Hospital of St. Mary Magdalene. Never a well-endowed establishment, it was in decay by the middle of the 15th century and in 1456 its revenues were annexed to the altar of the Holy Cross in Brechin Cathedral.

4. Balgownie, Hospital of St. Mary the Virgin NO 362 464

A chapel here is first recorded in 1418, and in 1476 it was

described as the chapel or poor's hospital of St. Mary the Virgin. In the hands of the Lyon family by the later 15th century, it had probably ceased to function long before the Reformation. The ruins of what appears to be a 19th-century cottage occupy the site.

5. Brechin, The College or Sang Schule NO 595 601

Founded in 1429 by Walter Stewart, earl of Atholl, Strathearn and Caithness and lord of Brechin, last surviving uncle of King James I, as a college of chaplains or choristers. Earl Walter provided a building to house the clergy at the western end of the Chanonry of the cathedral, part of which was given in 1579 to the burgh by the last chaplain. The burgh authorities were paying the master of the grammar school of Brechin by 1580 and the old college building continued in use as the burgh school until 1814. It is possible that part of the old buildings at the W end of Chanonry Wynd incorporate portions of the College.

6. Broughty Ferry, Hospital NO 465 304

It is believed that the site of the hospital lay near to, or under, that occupied by the later 15th-century castle (see below p.152). Land here was given to Arbroath Abbey by Gillebrigte, earl of Angus, in *c.*1188 with the intention that the abbey establish a hospital for the use of pilgrims and travellers crossing the Firth of Tay. If the association with the castle site is correct, the hospital must have ceased to function before 1490 when Andrew, lord Gray, began construction of the tower-house.

7. Dundee, The Leper House NO 408 307

The Leper Hospital, probably founded in the later 12th or 13th century, lay outside the E port of the medieval burgh. It had fallen into decay by the mid-16th century, its revenues being given in 1554 to the Maison Dieu of Dundee. An attempt to restore the house in 1556 failed and by 1564 the site of the buildings was being leased for cultivation.

8. Dundee, Maison Dieu or the Almshouse NO 400 299

On the sloping ground to the S of what is now Perth Road, part of the western portion of the site is occupied by St. Andrew's RC Cathedral. The Maison Dieu, a hospital or almshouse controlled by the order of Trinitarian Canons, was established soon after 1390 on ground immediately to the W of the Nethergait Port of the burgh. After the Reformation the buildings passed into the control of the burgh and continued to be used for the support of sick or 'decayed' burgesses. The hospital was rebuilt in 1645 and continued in use until 1746. No trace of the building remains.

9. Dundee, Hospital of St. John the Baptist NO 429 307

It is possible that the chapel, which is first recorded in the 15th century, is of greater antiquity. Occupying a headland on the old shoreline 1.25 miles E of the burgh port, its exposed position probably resulted in its burning by the English garrison of Broughty Castle in 1548. Still ruinous in 1560, it and its lands were leased for cultivation by the burgh in 1562. The churchyard continued in use throughout the 17th century. The site is now overlain by the modern dockyards.

10. Dundee, Hospital of St. Anthony NO 405 307

The exact position of this foundation cannot be established with certainty, but may have stood on the N side of the Seagait near the site of Butchart's Court. Land for the support of a hospital of six beds was given in 1443 to the Augustinian canons of Vienne, and a chaplain of the hospital was still in office in 1565.

11. Dundee, The Greyfriars NO 401 304

The wealthiest Franciscan house in Scotland, the friary is believed to have been founded between 1234 and 1289 by

Dervorgilla Balliol, grand-daughter of David, earl of Huntingdon. The Scottish clergy met here in February 1310 to declare their support for Robert Bruce. The friary was burned by the English in 1335 and 1385, being rebuilt on a grand scale after the last event. In 1543 it was plundered by a Protestant mob, recovering only to be sacked by the English in 1548, and by 1559 the friars had abandoned their ruined convent. The buildings were demolished in 1560 for building-stone for the new burgh tolbooth, and in 1564 Queen Mary granted the site and the gardens of the friary to the burgh for use as a burial ground – the Howff. The friary buildings proper lay immediately outside the town walls on a site in the angle bounded by Bank Street on the S and Barrack Street on the W.

12. Dundee, The Grey Sisters (Poor Clares) NO 394 303

One of the last pre-Reformation foundations of this type, the nunnery of the Grey Sisters was founded in March 1502 on a site outside the West Port of the burgh. The buildings, which included a chapel of St. James, appear to have occupied a rectangular block of land bounded by what became Brook Street, Guthrie Street, North Tay Street and Brown Street. The property was sold in August 1560 and demolished soon after.

13. Dundee, The Blackfriars NO 399 299

The Dominican friary of Dundee was established between 1517 and 1521 on land outside the burgh to the N of the Nethergate. The new house was sacked by a mob in 1543 and burned by the English in 1548, never recovering from this latter blow. In 1560 the ruins of the building were demolished and the stone used for strengthening the harbour wall.

14. Inverbervie, Carmelite Friary NO 831 727

Little is known of the history of this obscure house of

Carmelite friars, established shortly before 1443. Its site is said to have lain towards the N end of the burgh, but no trace of its buildings remains.

15. Montrose, Hospital of St. Mary the Virgin NO 713 585

The original hospital appears to have occupied a site in the Clayhalf of the burgh between Murray Street and the old shoreline of the tidal basin on the W. It was apparently founded in the reign of Alexander II (1214-49) as a leper house, but functioned as a poor's hospital in the later Middle Ages. In 1510-12, the then Master of the Hospital, James IV's secretary, Patrick Paniter, built a new hospital on a fresh site further to the NE, which in 1516 was placed in the care of the Dominican friars. Nothing of the medieval buildings survives.

16. Montrose, The Blackfriars NO 713 586

This was one of the poorer houses of the Order in Scotland. It was founded in 1261 and built on a site to the N of the hospital. Damage sustained during the Wars of Independence required the building of a new church in 1359. No trace of the friary building survives.

17. Montrose, The New Hospital.

Shortly after 1510 Patrick Paniter, secretary to James IV and master of the Hospital, moved that establishment from its old site in the burgh to a new location on the E side of what is now Northesk Road N of the burgh. In 1516 he gave the running of the hospital over to the Dominican friary in the burgh, an act which considerably augmented the wealth of that establishment. Despite an act of 1560 authorising the expulsion of the Dominicans, a prior, sub-prior and two friars were still in residence in 1564, but by 1571 the property had been given over to the burgesses. Portions of the buildings still survived in the early 18th century, but the site was built over later that century.

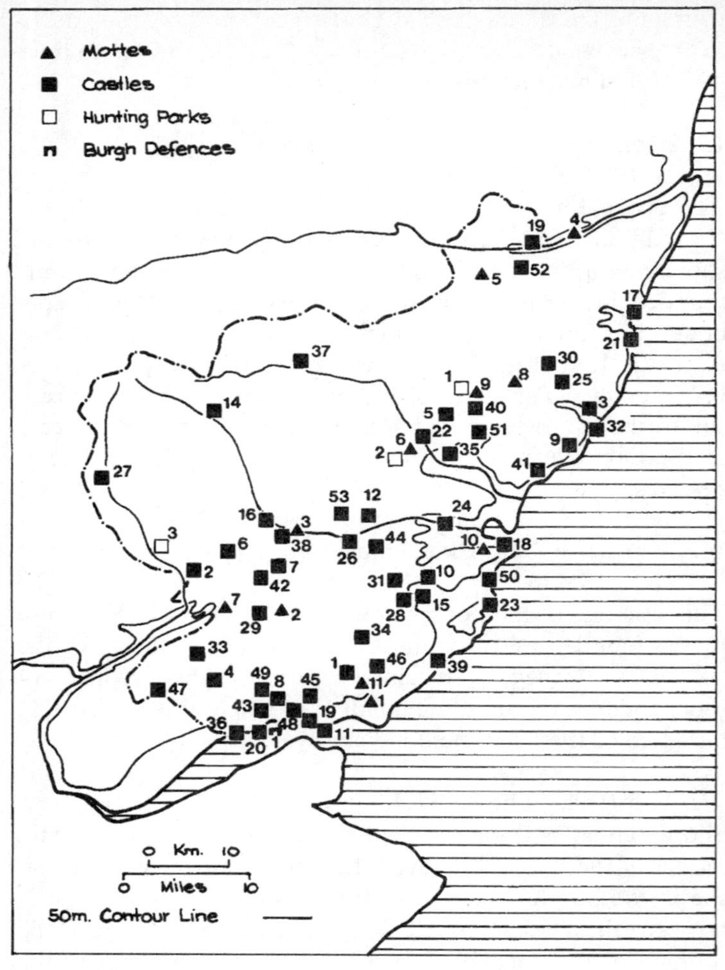

8. The Middle Ages – mottes and castles.

Churches and Chapels

1. Arthbuthnott
NO 801 746

Signposted off the B967 Inverbervie-Fordoun road two miles NNW of Inverbervie. St. Ternan's Church is one of the finest small medieval parish churches of Scotland. The site is an ancient one, having been occupied by a Celtic community over which the bishop of St. Andrews had come to exercise authority by the 12th century. Disputes over control of the church and its lands were settled in the bishop's favour by 1206, soon after which construction of the present structure was begun. The chancel was consecrated in August 1242 by David de Bernham, bishop of St. Andrews. The bishops, however, did not monopolise control of the church, the Allardyces and Arbuthnotts, the two principal local families, playing a prominent role. At the end of the 15th century Sir Robert Arbuthnott commissioned a major building programme, commissioning also the then vicar, James Sybbald, to produce a Psalter, Missal and Office of the Blessed Virgin for presentation at the altar of St. Ternan. All three books survive to the present.

In plan, the church is an elongated rectangle divided into nave and slightly narrower chancel, with an octagonal bell-turret in the W gable and a large two-storeyed apsidal chapel projecting S from the chancel. The chancel predates 1242 and much of the nave fabric is probably also of 13th-century date. The chancel is 8m long by 4.7m wide and opens from the nave through an acutely-pointed archway. Original windows survive in the N and S walls – plain, narrow slits externally, widely splayed with pointed heads internally – but the three in the E gable are modern. The door in the N wall led to a sacristy.

Much of the nave was rebuilt after a fire in 1889, but its 16th-century character was successfully preserved. The plain N wall is pierced by a round-arched doorway, while in the S there is a similar door and three large, flat-topped, mullioned windows of 16th-century style. On the right of the S doorway is a holy water stoup. The W gable and its conical-capped turret are part of Robert Arbuthnott's work of *c.*1500.

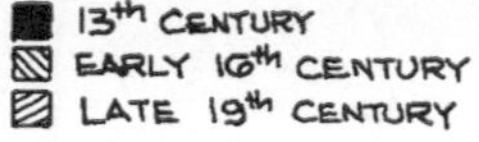

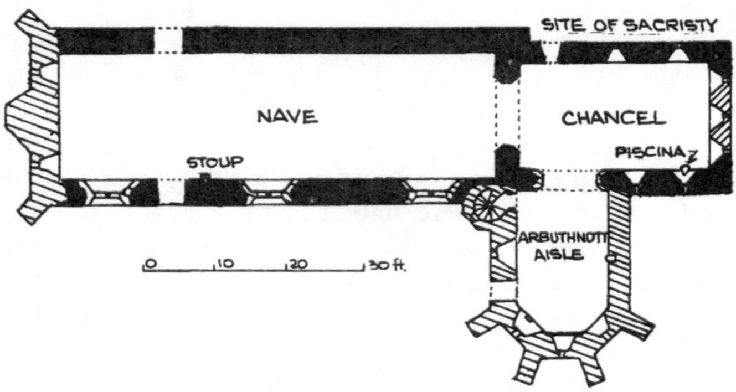

Firgure 8. Arbuthnott Church.

Sir Robert's greatest contribution is the Arbuthnott Aisle. This was completed by 1505, when its builder presented the service books commissioned from the vicar to the altar of the church. It is a magnificent example of the effort of a local laird to embellish his parish church and a reflection of the strength of popular devotion in some quarters on the eve of the Reformation. Designed primarily as a burial vault and chantry, it is entered from the chancel through a wide round-headed archway cut through the 13th-century S wall. The only surviving monument is the tomb of Sir Robert's son, James, now topped by a 13th-century effigy. The aisle is 6.2m long by 3.9m wide, with a barrel vault in its lower storey rising to 5.48m. The apse is roofed by a semi-octagonal vault. The windows are tall and narrow externally, containing single lights with delicate trefoil heads, but are splayed widely on the inside so adding to the air of spaciousness. At its NW angle a doorway opens onto a spiral stair in an octagonal turret in the re-entrant between the nave and the aisle. This leads to the priest's chamber on the upper floor. Of the same dimensions as the room below, it is lit by three plain, square-headed windows provided with window-seats, two in the apse and the third and largest, protected externally by a massive iron grille, in the W. There is a holy water stoup by the doorway and a small aumbry with trefoliated head. The external decoration of the aisle is restricted to four buttresses projecting from the apse. These rise above the roofline to finish in canopied and pinnacled finials and are provided at the level of the chapel windows with richly-carved corbels and canopies for saints' statutes.

2. Auchenblae
NO 727 784

At the S end of the village. This small church, dedicated to St. Palladius and consecrated in 1244 by David de Bernham, bishop of St. Andrews, was formerly the parish church of Fordoun. The only evidence for the 13th-century building is the piscina, possibly reset, on the S side of the altar. The three windows in the S wall and the N doorway all date from a major rebuilding in the early 16th century.

3. Auchterhouse
NO 343 382

At Kirkton of Auchterhouse, off the A927 Dundee-Newtyle road. The main part of the present church appears to date from a major rebuilding in 1775, but inspection shows it to contain portions of its medieval and 17th-century predecessors. The nave was largely reconstructed in 1630 and its S doorway which combines Classical and late medieval forms dates from that time. The chancel likewise underwent refurbishment at that time, the date being recorded in a panel in the E gable, but the acutely-pointed chancel arch and deeply-recessed square-lintelled S door are both of the late 15th century.

4. Cowie, Stonehaven
NO 884 873

On the clifftops adjacent to Stonehaven golf course, 1 mile N of Stonehaven. The original dedication of this site was to St. Nathalan, who carried out early missionary work in the area of the Mounth and Strathdee, but this was later superseded by a dedication to St. Mary when the church was given parochial status and separated from the parish of Fetteresso. The E gable, pierced by a trinity of fine lancets, and eastern two thirds of the building belong to a late 13th-century church consecrated in May 1276 by William Wishart, bishop of St. Andrews. The western third represents the remains of a 15th-century extension, while a doorway in the S wall of the chancel points to a refurbishment in the 16th-century.

5. Dargie, Invergowrie
NO 351 301

At the E end of the village, 0.25 miles NE of Invergowrie railway station. Sadly vandalised in recent years, the ruins of St. Peter's Church were for many years in a dangerous condition and fenced off for the safety of the public. Although this is an ancient site, identified as one of the churches founded by St. Boniface in the early 8th century, no part of the present building appears older than the 15th century. Evidence of early origins, however, survives in the form of a fine Pictish sculptured stone which was preserved at the site until the 1960s.

The old church, overshadowed by two late 18th- and 19th-century burial aisles appended to its northern side, measures 14m by 4.8m. There are two doorways in its S wall, the E having a flat lintel, the W with a round-headed arch cut from two stones, and two windows. The cusped head of the round-arched W window is carved from a single stone, while the E window has a flat lintel and was formerly mullioned. Internally, the church has been stripped of most of its medieval features, but a holy water stoup survives to the right of the W doorway, while in the W gable there is a simple aumbry to the N of the altar site.

6. Eassie*
NO 353 474

Signposted from the A94, 2.25 miles W of Glamis. The Class II Pictish stone preserved in a glass-panelled shelter in the SE corner of the church is evidence for the early origins of this site (see above p89), but no architectural features of the present building date from earlier than the 17th century. There is, however, little reason to doubt that the bulk of the fabric of the simple rectangular building belongs to the church dedicated in 1246 by David de Bernham, bishop of St. Andrews.

7. Edzell Church, Old Kirkyard, Edzell
NO 705 480

In the old graveyard, 1.25 miles W of Edzell on the unclassified road from Edzell to Glen Lethnot and Menmuir. Lying to the S of the roadway, which separates it from the plough-blurred remains of the motte (see below p141), are the vestiges of the parish church of St. Laurence. The remains formed a chantry chapel and burial aisle of the Lindsays of Glenesk, apparently a late Medieval addition to the S side of the church, entered from the nave by a wide archway. The only original feature is a piscina in the long E wall, against which stood an altar. In 1952 a fragment of a free-standing Celtic cross was found in the churchyard (see above p.93), indicating that St. Lawrences occupied a site of considerable antiquity.

8. Fetteresso
NO 854 857

At Kirktown of Fetteresso, *c.*0.5 miles W of Stonehaven. The church of St. Caran of Fetteresso, consecrated in May 1246 by David de Bernham, bishop of St.Andrews, was formerly the 'mother-church' of an extensive parish which, until 1276, included the chapels of Cowie to the NE and Dunnottar to the SE. The only features of medieval date are the doorways opposed to each other in the N and S walls, both of which are of the early 16th century. The N aisle is post-Reformation, built in 1602 for the Fullartons whose arms appear on a panel in its walls. There was an extensive reconstruction of the building in the 18th century.

9. Guthrie
NO 567 505

In Guthrie, 1.5 miles NNW of Friockheim. Most of the

medieval church was swept away in 1826 and replaced with the present characterless structure which overlies part of the site of the original choir. Until the 1470s, this was simply the parish church of Guthrie, but in 1479 it was erected into a collegiate church by Sir Alexander Guthrie. Guthrie's father, Sir David, had planned this earlier in the 1470s and had extended the choir to accommodate extra clergy. Drawings of this building made in 1818 show a low, undistinguished structure 23.5m long by 3.8m wide, with two square mullioned windows and a round-arched doorway in the S wall of the choir.

In 1479 Sir Alexander Guthrie added the southern aisle which is the only remaining portion of the old church. This stood to the S of the nave, its E wall level with the rood-screen which separated the nave from the choir. It was entered from the nave through a wide, round-arched opening – the blocking wall is modern – and has a large square mullioned window in its S gable. Internally it is relatively featureless, with only a piscina and aumbry in the blank E wall to mark the position of the altar. Formerly, however, it was roofed internally with a timber barrel-vault, painted with scenes of the Crucifixion and the last Judgement. These were removed for conservation in 1955 and are now in nearby Guthrie Castle, where sections of the timber rood-screen are also preserved.

10. Logie, Mains of Logie, Hillside NO 706 635

Overlooking the River North Esk at Mains of Logie, off the A937 5 miles NNW of Montrose. The chancel of the church dedicated in August 1243 by David de Bernham, bishop of St. Andrews, is the only portion of the parish church of Logie Cuthel to survive. At the Reformation it was united with Pert (see below) to the NW, to form the new parish of Logie-Pert, and a new church was built 2.25 miles to the WNW. The chancel, which stands in a circular enclosure on the S bank of the River North Esk, is structurally complete, but lacks its roof. Three slender 13th-century lancets grace the E gable and there is a later window in the S wall, probably introduced at the same time as the sacrament house built into the N wall adjacent to the position of the medieval altar. The nave had been demolished by the mid 19th-century and the former chancel arch replaced with a blank wall.

11. Lundie
NO 291 366

In Lundie, 8 miles WNW of Dundee off the A923 Dundee to Coupar-Angus road. A glance at this building suggests that most of its structure dates from the 18th century. The bulk of the fabric of the ashlar-built main body, however, is the 12th-century nave of the parish church of St. Lawrence the Martyr, built by the powerful Durward family who controlled the lands of Lundie. All of the original window and door arrangements in the S wall have been replaced, but a single slit window survives near the E end of the N wall. Alterations in 1786 saw the demolition of the apsidal chancel – a large Classical mausoleum now occupies its site – and the fine late 12th-century chancel arch was built up. Although this cannot now be seen, it is fossilised in the thickness of the wall.

12. Nevay, Kirkinch, Eassie and Nevay
NO 312 441

At Kirkinch, 3 miles ENE of Newtyle off the unclassified Newtyle to Eassie and Nevay road. Although this is a site with strong Celtic associations, the ruins of the present church appear to be largely of late medieval and post-Reformation date. The W doorway, with its round arch carved from a single stone, may be late medieval and there is a grave slab bearing the date 1597 built into the wall of the church.

13. Old Pert, North Water Bridge
NO 644 660

On the S side of the A90(T), 1.75 miles ENE of Stracathro Hospital. The ruined church overlooks the River North Esk. The E gable, supported by a prominent central buttress, is pierced by two slender late 13th-century lancets, while there is a single lancet in the W gable. The doorways at the NW and SE have flat lintels with rounded shoulders, that at the

SE clearly being an insertion. There is a blocked lancet towards the E end of the S wall, but the remaining (now blocked) S windows are post-Reformation.

14. St. Fitticks, Girdle Ness, Aberdeen NJ 963 049

Overlooking Nigg Bay to the E of Torry in Aberdeen. Despite its proximity to the seat of the medieval bishops of Aberdeen in St. Machar's Cathedral, a mere 3 miles to the NW, this, the former parish church of Nigg, lay in the diocese of St. Andrews. The medieval church, of which only the mutilated and much-altered opposed doorways in the N and S walls survive, was consecrated by Bishop David de Bernham in July 1242. The windows are all of 17th-century form, and the building appears to have undergone considerable reconstruction in the post-Reformation period.

15. St. Mary's, Dundee NO 402 302

In Dundee city centre. Of the medieval church of St. Mary which replaced the earlier burgh kirk of St.Clement, only the massive W tower which dominates the city-centre skyline remains. Known to Dundonians as the Old Steeple, this massive bell tower dates from a comprehensive reconstruction of the church in the mid-15th century. The tower is 12.2m square and rises some 50m to the saddle-backed roof of its cap-house. Although heavily restored in the 19th century and suffering a heavy-handed sand-blasting in the 1960s, most of what remains represents the original scheme. It is a striking statement of the probable quality of the other medieval churches of the burgh, now lost, and of the wealth and pride of the merchant burgesses of Dundee.

Most embellishment has been lavished on the W front. At the lowest level is the processional doorway, consisting of two richly-decorated round-arched openings contained within a larger elliptical archway. In the spandrel over the centre arch was originally a carving bearing the arms of the diocese of Brechin and a depiction of the Virgin Mary, to whom the church was dedicated. The crude representation of a pot of lilies was carved in the 1960s by a workman on the sand-blasting operation. Above the doorway is a magnificent traceried window which rises the full height of the lowest internal stage of the tower. Above it is a smaller, round-headed window filled with tracery, over which there is a narrower pointed-arched window divided into two lights. The tower is divided into two stages above this last window, 29m above ground level, by a broad parapet walk, its screen wall pierced by quatrefoil-shaped openings and capped by richly-carved pinnacles. The N and S walls of this lower stage are plainer, the N being unbroken to the level of the parapet, the S having only a pointed-headed two-light window at the same level as the similar window in the W wall. Below the S window is a carved panel with a figure of the Virgin. The E wall presents a similarly cliff-like appearance. Just above the roof-ridge of the nave is a worn armorial panel, while at the level of the pointed windows of the W and S walls is a square-headed opening framed by four carved corbels which possibly supported a clock-face.

Above this parapet are two belfry stages separated by a bold stringcourse. The lower has three lofty pointed windows in each of the E, S and W faces, but only two in the N as part of the wall here is occupied by the boldly-projecting octagonal stair-turret which rises the whole height of the tower at its NE angle. The upper stage is slightly wider than the level below and is pierced by two windows in each face over the solid sections between the windows below, except in the N where there is only one window. The tower is crowned by a second open-work parapet, now lacking its pinnacles, within which is a saddle-back-roofed cap-house. The tower was designed to be finished with an imperial crown spire similar to those of St. Giles in Edinburgh or King's College Chapel, Aberdeen, but although provision was made for this it does not seem to have been carried out.

Internally, only the lowest stage is of any note. This is a lofty chamber, the centre of its vault pierced by an opening through which the bells could be hoisted into the upper storeys. In the E wall is the blocked-up archway which opened into the nave.

The massive strength of the tower admirably suited it for defensive purposes, and in 1651 it was used by the burgesses as a safe store for their valuables during the assault on the burgh by Cromwell's army under the command of General Monck. When the town fell in September 1651, Robert Lumsden the governor and some of his garrison continued to hold out in the tower until smoked out and massacred. Despite this, the church and tower remained relatively intact though dilapidated – the nave had to be rebuilt in the 18th century – until a spectacular fire in 1841 destroyed the transepts and E end and forced a total reconstruction of those portions.

16. St. Vigeans
NO 638 429

On the northern outskirts of Arbroath, signposted from the A92 Arbroath-Montrose road. The church of St. Vigeans, which occupies a prominent flat-topped conical mound on the W bank of the Brothock Burn, was formerly the parish church of Arbroath. The dedication to the Irish St. Fechan and the rich array of Pictish sculpture from the vicinity housed in the adjacent museum (see above p.98) indicate that this was a Celtic church of some importance. Nothing of the present structure, however, is of earlier than late 12th-century date.

The E and W gables of the 12th-century church form the end walls of what is now the N aisle. This was enlarged in the 13th century by the addition of a S aisle with projecting square tower at its W end, the completion of this work probably being marked by the consecration of the church in August 1242 by David de Bernham, bishop of St. Andrews. In the 15th century the arcade between the 12th-century nave and 13th-century S aisle was removed and new four-bay arcades constructed to the N and S, with a wholly new S aisle built. This extended church was reconsecrated in 1485. In 1871 the old square-ended chancel was demolished and replaced with a buttressed apse, a further aisle of three bays added to the N side, and the W tower raised in height and finished with a parapet enclosing a saddle-back roof.

Mottes

1. Barry
NO 533 347

The prominent mound of Barry motte stands adjacent to Grange of Barry farm, to the W of the unclassified road from Barry to the A92. The church of Barry was granted to Arbroath Abbey by William the Lion in 1189, at which time there is no mention of a secular lordship there, the land probably being a royal estate. Construction of the motte would therefore appear to postdate *c.*1200.

2. Brigton, Douglastown
NO 417 466

In agricultural land 200m SW of Brigton House, 0.25 miles S of Douglastown on the B9127. This large ditched enclosure, an oval measuring 60m by 35m, is probably of medieval date. The ditch, which is heavily silted, is 13m wide and 1m deep.

3. Castle Hill, Inshewan
NO 445 572

The overgrown and eroded earthwork remains of this stronghold lie on the edge of the steep N bank of the River South Esk, 500m WNW of Inshewan House, to the S of the unclassified road from Tannadice to Memus, 2 miles W of Tannadice. The history of the early ownership of the site is unknown.

4. Castle Hill, Durris
NO 780 968

On the S bank of the Dee 0.5 miles NE of Kirkton of Durris off the B9077. The tree-covered motte lies adjacent to a track in agricultural land overlooking the river. On the summit, whose irregular outline measures roughly 39m by 32m, are traces of masonry of uncertain date. This was the caput of the royal thanage of Durris, the castle of which is on record by 1264 when the cost of repairs there were accounted for in the sheriff of Kincardine's exchequer returns. The keepership of the Forest of Durris was in the hands of John Comyn, earl of Buchan, in 1292. Following the forfeiture of the Comyns by Robert I, the lands of Durris were granted to the Frasers, builders of the earliest portions of the nearby mansionhouse.

5. Castle Hill, Strachan
NO 657 921

In agricultural land immediately S of the B976, 1 mile W of the village of Strachan. The motte is a flat-topped natural gravel mound which rises 6m above the surrounding flood-plain of the River Feugh. In the Middle Ages it occupied an island between separate channels of the river, in the centre of what was an area of marsh. Excavation in 1980–81 revealed several phases of development in the 13th century. The centre of the summit platform was occupied by a large timber hall with bowed ends, around which were grouped ancillary structures with a variety of domestic and industrial functions. The summit was contained within a timber palisade. Dating evidence pointed towards construction in the middle of the 13th century, which is at variance with the documentary records.

Strachan was granted between 1189 and 1195 to William Giffard of Yester in East Lothian. The lands were granted in forest, and it seems likely that the hill country to the S of Strachan was preserved as a baronial hunting-ground. Although its primary function was undoubtedly as a hunting-lodge, the position of Strachan at the N end of the strategic Mounth routes from Strathmore into Mar rendered it attractive to the crown to have a dependable vassal in possession of them. The Giffards retained possession until early in the reign of Robert I, when they were forfeited for supporting Edward I. The excavation revealed dramatic evidence of destruction in the early 14th century, probably in the course of Robert's 1308 campaign against the Comyns in the NE. Robert I subsequently granted the land to Alexander Fraser, but there is no evidence that the Frasers rebuilt the old castle.

6. Castle Hillock, Edzell
NO 584 688

In agricultural land directly opposite old Edzell churchyard, approximately 1 mile W of Edzell village on the unclassified road to Glen Lethnot, and within sight of the later castle. The original centre of the lordship of Glenesk, this once substantial motte has been seriously reduced by ploughing and its defences are now quite blurred. This stronghold was the seat of the Stirlings of Glenesk into the 14th century. On the death of Sir John Stirling, his heiress, Katherine, resigned her rights into the hands of Alexander Lindsay, son of Sir David Lindsay of Crawford, who received royal confirmation of this in 1358. The old castle remained the centre of the lordship until replaced in the early 16th century by the new stone towerhouse 300m to the NNW.

7. Castleton of Eassie, Eassie
NO 333 466

The farmhouse of Castleton of Eassie, lying immediately N of the A94 2.5 miles NE of Meigle, is enclosed within the impressive earthwork remains of a probably 12th- or 13th-century castle. A rectangular mound, its summit measuring 88m by 67m, is flanked on the NE and SE by a 15m-wide and 5m-deep ditch, with an internal bank on the NE. On the NW and SW the sides of the mound have been scarped. The causeway across the ditch at the SE may mark the position of the original entrance.

8. Fordoun House, Fordoun
NO 735 770

In agricultural land S of the B966, 250m E of Fordoun House, 1.25 miles NW of Fordoun. This roughly rectangular moated enclosure measures 75m by 42m internally, within a ditch 7m wide. It probably represents the site of a lightly-defended timber 'manor' of medieval date.

9. Green Castle, Kincardine
NO 668 765

The earthwork enclosure occupies a prominent knoll on the E bank of the Devilly Burn at the point where it exits from its narrow glen into the Howe of the Mearns, 650m NW of Mill of Kincardine farm, and clearly it is sited to control the important Cairn o' Mounth road (the B974) which runs along the opposite side of the glen. It is a trapezoidal enclosure measuring 65m by 35m within massive ramparts 14m thick and up to 3.3m high above the interior, 10m high above the 11m wide ditch. There are outer ramparts to the NW and SE and the entrance is in the NE. While it is impossible to date this site without excavation, and there is no surviving documentation to reveal its history, the form of the defences point to an early medieval rather than prehistoric date. It is possible that its legendary associations with Finella, daughter of the mormaor of Angus, and her murder there in 995 of King Kenneth II, point to origins as the principal seat of the early rulers of Angus and Mearns. It is more likely, however, that it is a 12th-century predecessor of the royal castle at Kincardine (see below p.192).

10. Maryton Law, Maryton
NO 682 556

This small motte, which now stands in a plantation of trees, occupies a strongly defensive site on a headland projecting NE towards Montrose Basin from Maryton Law, 300m S of the A934 at Maryton. It survives as a steep-sided truncated cone with a level summit, measuring 7.5m in diameter.

11. Old Downie, Monifieth
NO 519 365

The prominent earthwork of the motte is clearly visible from the unclassified road from Drumsturdy to Panmure, 0.5 miles E of the souterrain at Carlungie, standing in the field immediately S of the farm. The earliest reference to the lands occurs in 1254, when the royal thanage of Downie was in the hands of one Duncan de Dunny, but whether or not he built the motte is unknown.

Castles

1. Affleck Castle, Monikie
NO 494 388

To the S of the unclassified road between the B962 and B978 0.3 miles WNW of Monikie. Affleck stands below the S-facing slopes of the Downie Hills, ideally sited for exploitation of its estate's resources of upland pasture and lowland arable. Although overshadowed by the house which superseded it, it remains one of the finest late 15th-century towers in Scotland, lacking only the barmkin wall and the out-buildings which clustered in the courtyard.

The lands belonged in the Middle Ages to the family of Auchinleck, or Affleck of that Ilk. The estate is first recorded in 1296 when its lord, Matthew le Napier, swore fealty to Edward I of England. It is not known if this Matthew was ancestor of the Affleck family. The family had fallen on hard times in the early 15th century, but their fortunes were restored under the patronage of the Lindsay earls of Crawford. A deed drawn up for Earl David in 1466 and confirmed by King James III in 1471 set out the boundaries and rights of the lordship in detail and secured them against encroachment. Building of the tower probably commenced soon after, and the present structure was certainly in existence by 1501.

The tower, built of sandstone rubble, rises to four storeys and an attic. Usually described as L-plan, it consists of a rectangular main block with a small projecting jam at the S end of the E side, which contains the stair for most of its height. The doorway is in the ground floor at the re-entrant between the main block and jam. It has a round head beneath the empty surround for an armorial panel and a niche for a saint's effigy. Several of the upper windows retain original external grilles. The corbelled parapet, angle turrets, cap-houses, attic gables and chimney stacks are all 16th-century. The parapet has a projection directly above the doorway, allowing the defenders to drop unpleasant objects on unwelcome visitors.

Within the door is a short passage which opens to the left on the main stair of the tower, while directly ahead a door gives access to two cellars. This level is unvaulted, the ceiling being formed by the timber floor of the storey above. The first floor chamber, entered along a short passage from the stair, formed the common hall of the castle. It is an uncongenial room for, although provided with three large recessed windows with seats, there is neither a fireplace nor latrine. It is roofed with a stone vault.

The lord's hall on the second floor was a fine chamber, roofed with timber, provided with three deep recessed windows with seats, a latrine in the thickness of the SE angle and a deep wall press. At the N end the floor was originally raised in a dais for the lord's table, behind which is a handsome fireplace. The main stair stops at this level and anyone wishing to reach the third floor or battlements had to cross the hall to continue via a stair built in the SW angle of the tower. This freed the upper level of the jam for small rooms, the first of which is reached by a narrow stair in the thickness of the E wall. It is hardly a comfortable apartment, provided with only two tiny loopholes and a nook for a lamp. Opening from it is a latrine chamber provided with a peep-hole through which an occupant could watch the hall below.

The third storey was the solar, a room of exceptional quality provided with three recessed windows with seats, a splendid fireplace in the E wall, a latrine in the thickness of the S wall, and a large wall-press at the NW. Two small mural chambers in the N wall may have contained bunk beds. The gem of the tower, however, is the vaulted chapel in the jam entered through a miniature 'chancel arch' in the SE angle. The carving of the archway is exquisite, as is the overall finish of the chamber. Immediately inside on the right is a holy water stoup decorated on its base with carved shields. In the S wall is a beautiful piscina and a fine trefoil-headed window which side-lit the altar which stood between the two corbels on the E wall. Candles perhaps stood on these corbels, but it is more likely that they carried a wooden panel behind the altar painted with religious motifs. The stair continues from this floor to the parapet where it finishes in a cap-house crowned with a parapeted platform. A small cap-house over the jam formed a watch-chamber, again with a parapeted platform reached by an external stair.

2. Airlie Castle, Airlie
NO 292 521

In wooded private grounds 4.5 miles NE of Alyth. The castle occupies a site of great natural strength on a promontory overlooking the confluence of the Melgam Water and the

River Isla, protected on two sides by precipitous drops of over 30m to the river. The present building is of three distinct phases, the earliest portions dating from the second quarter of the 15th century, with alterations in the late 16th or early 17th century and the addition of a new block in 1792–3.

The oldest work is the massive curtain wall which cuts off the promontory, originally further protected by a rock-cut ditch. The wall is 36.6m long, 3m thick and rises to 9m in height, forming a cliff-like screen pierced by only two slit windows with widely splayed apertures towards the courtyard, and by the original entrance. Off-centre in this wall is the gate-tower, pierced at its foot by the high arched gateway leading into the entrance pend. The original defensive scheme probably had a drawbridge over the ditch, but this has gone. Behind this are the grooves for a portcullis, worked from the chamber over the pend, and beyond that stout double doors. Over the arch on the inner face of the tower are corbels for supporting a timber walkway. The upper levels of the tower appear to be 16th-century.

Licence was granted to Walter Ogilvy of Lintrathen by James I in 1432 for the construction of Airlie, which was complete by 1458 when his son, John, received confirmation from James II of possession of the castle and lands. Airlie remained the seat of the Ogilvies until 1640 when, following its capture and partial demolition by a Covenanting army commanded by the earl of Argyll, the family moved to Cortachy (see below p.159), which they had purchased from the Ogilvies of Clova in 1625. Airlie remained an Ogilvy property and is still in their hands.

3. Allardyce Castle, Inverbervie NO 818 739

In private grounds at the bottom of the valley of the Bervie Water, off the B967 1.5 miles NW of Inverbervie. Although there has been a castle of the Allardyces of that Ilk on this site since at least the 14th century, the present structure is largely of late 16th-century date. The building forms two sides of a courtyard, but all trace of the barmkin has been removed, leaving the castle standing in isolation as an elongated L. Its core is formed by the angle of the L, both wings having been extended in the late 17th century. The pended entrance to the courtyard runs through the basement of the eastern extension. This extension is narrower than the original house, and in the re-entrant angle formed between them on the courtyard side there is a superb stair-tower corbelled out from first floor level. This is decorated by extensive use of label corbelling, an architectural device much-favoured in NE Scottish castles of this date. The upper stages of the tower are corbelled out further to form a cap-house, access to which is by a stair in a smaller turret corbelled in the angle between the main stair and cap-house, while the top floor of the tower has a second turret corbelled out on its SE angle.

Although there were men calling themselves 'of Allardyce' in the 13th century, it was not until the reign of Robert I that the family of Allardyce of that Ilk acquired the lordship. In the early 15th century David Allardyce was shield-bearer to Robert, duke of Albany, governor of Scotland during the minority and captivity in England of James I. The property descended through the male line of the family until the end of the 17th century, when they passed through an heiress to the Barclays of Urie. The Barclay-Allardyce family remained in possession until 1854 when the line died out. After serving for many years as a farmhouse, and suffering badly in a fire, the castle has now been restored and is occupied as a private residence.

4. Auchterhouse
NO 331 373

In wooded grounds to the W of the A927 Dundee-Newtyle road, 2.5 miles NNW of Muirhead. The core of the present building is a towerhouse of the early 16th century, while a ruined second and much earlier tower (called the Wallace Tower) lies just to the SE. This pairing of free-standing towers as part of a single residential complex is not uncommon in Scotland, e.g. at Huntingtower outside Perth. The S wall and southern end of the E gable of the tower are reduced to foundations, but the springing of a barrel vault on the N wall shows that this was the vaulted basement of a small towerhouse. In the NW angle are traces of a spiral stair which led to the first floor, entered through a doorway with shouldered lintels, which suggest a date of construction in the early 14th century. The original entrance appears to have been at first floor level.

The main building underwent considerable alteration and extension in the 17th and 18th centuries and is now an hotel. It contains some of the finest examples of Jacobean plasterwork ceilings and fireplaces to be seen anywhere in Scotland. The exterior, which is harled and whitewashed, has been simplified in the 18th century with the removal of turrets etc. A stair-tower, corbelled out in two stages as it rises, projects from the S front.

Auchterhouse was an Ogilvy possession in the 15th century, passing in *c.*1478 through the heiress, Margaret Ogilvy, to James, earl of Buchan, half-brother of King James II. It remained Buchan property until 1619, when it passed to James, earl of Moray. In 1648 it came into the hands of the earl of Panmure, to return subsequently to the Ogilvies in the person of the earl of Airlie.

5. Balbegno Castle, Fettercairn NO 638 730

In private grounds to the N of the B966 Edzell-Fettercairn road, 0.75 miles W of Fettercairn. A large L-plan tower of exceptional quality, attached to a small, plain 18th-century mansion on the site of its barmkin and out-buildings. The main building carries the date 1569. It rises to four storeys and an attic, with harled walls and the parapets and upper-works finished in fine sandstone ashlar. The stair-tower, formed from the SE angle of the main block, and the jam at the NE, rise one storey higher than the rest of the building and are finished with gabled 'cap-house' carried on a decorative corbel table and provided with round bartizans at the angles covered by the oversailing roof. The S gable is elaborately decorated with heraldic panels and carved work, including the name of the builder and his wife – I Wod (John Wood) and E Irvein (Elizabeth Irvine) – and the date 1569.

The entrance was at ground floor level in the re-entrant, now covered by the 18th-century porch which infills this area. The basement is vaulted and comprises cellarage and the kitchens. A straight stair led to the hall at first floor level, but rises as a spiral above this. The hall is a handsome chamber, groin-vaulted in two bays similar to that at Towie Barclay in Aberdeenshire, with the springers of the vault rising from corbels carved as grotesque heads. The areas between the ribs are painted in tempera with the armorial bearings of prominent Scottish families. There is a private chamber in the jam. The upper floors of the tower contain bed-chambers and domestic accommodation.

Balbegno was granted for life in June 1488 to Andrew Wood, one of the doorwards of the king's chamber. The initial life-grant was later made heritable, for he was succeeded in 1512 by his son, John, by whom the castle was built. Balbegno remained with the Woods until 1687, when it was sold to Andrew Middleton, youngest brother of the Royalist commander, John, earl of Middleton. The castle subsequently passed to the Ogilvies.

6. Balfour Castle, Kirkton of Kingoldrum NO 337 546

At Balfour Mains farm, adjacent to the unclassified road 400m SSE of Kirkton of Kingoldrum. Situated on rising ground, Balfour commands fine, open prospects to the S. The chief survival of the castle is an imposing six storey round tower attached to a large 19th-century farm-house. The tower has a peculiarly angled roof which looks as though it has been sliced off, probably replacing a seventh storey capped with a conical roof. It is massively built and of high quality, the walls divided by three stringcourses, the lowest stepped and the middle one rising to frame a window, and has a distinct taper towards the top. There are numerous gunloops in the lower stages of the walls. The tower may have stood at the SE angle of a Z-plan structure, but 19th-century accounts suggest that it formed the SE element of a courtyard castle, traces of which extend to the N and E.

Tradition relates that Balfour was built by Cardinal David

Beaton for his mistress, Marion Ogilvy, and their children. It was, however, a property of the Ogilvies from at least the middle of the 15th century, and the surviving castle may have been built by Marion's brother, Walter.

7. Ballinshoe Tower, Kirriemuir NO 417 531

On the S side of the unclassified road running E from the A926 Forfar-Kirriemuir road, 1 mile S of Maryton. Ballinshoe, pronounced Benshee, is a rare survival of the fortified houses of the lower ranks of the landed gentry, a class composed perhaps of younger sons of lairds, or their richer tenants. It is a miniaturised version of the traditional Scots towerhouse of the 16th century, comprising a rectangular main block of two storeys and an attic, with a round tower housing a spiral stair at the NE corner, and a turret corbelled out at attic level over the SW angle. The stair tower is reduced to its lowest courses and lies under a pile of its own debris, and the timber floors have gone. There are only two small fireplaces visible in the remaining structure, one at first floor level, the other in the attic bed-chamber, indicating that the kitchen fire must have been in another building. It is probable that additional accommodation was provided in buildings in the enclosure which extends to the S of the castle, as was the case at the slightly more substantial Murroes Castle (45 below).

8. Ballumbie Castle, Duntrune NO 455 344

In private grounds to the E of the unclassified road from Burnside of Duntrune to Ballumbie, to the NE of the Whitfield housing-estate in Dundee. The fragmentary remains of Ballumbie Castle suggest a substantial courtyard castle, possibly dating from the later 14th or 15th century, rather than the over-large L-plan tower which it is sometimes suggested to represent. The ruin consists of the lower stages of two round towers and a linking stretch of curtain wall on an elevated site protected by the deep watercourse of the Fithie Burn. It appears to have been a ruin since the 17th century. The stable block of a later mansion was built to the W and utilises the old wall as the outer face of its courtyard.

Ballumbie was anciently a property of the Lovel family. Association with the Ogilvies and Lindsays in the 15th century saw a steady rise in prominence for the Lovels, capped by the marriage in 1463 of Robert Lovel to Elizabeth Douglas, niece of the earl of Crawford. In 1485 Alexander Lovel was sheriff-depute of Forfar. Close connections with the Douglas earls of Angus brought more property to the family, but by the 16th century their fortunes were in decline. A later lord, Henry Lovel, used the castle as a base for raids on his neighbours – including his own son – and in 1566 a complaint against him was brought before the Queen.

9. Benholm Castle, Benholm
NO 804 705

On private land at Mains of Benholm farm, 1 mile N of Benholm. The imposing tower of Benholm occupied a strong position above a deep ravine in rising ground to the NE of Johnshaven and commands fine views southwards to the sea. In 1992, shortly before the beginning of work on restoration of the tower, which had severe cracking in its walls, half collapsed in a storm. Its remains are attached to the gutted shell of a modern mansion.

The tower was 15th century, square in plan and rose through four storeys to the corbelled parapet which enclosed a garret. The stair rises in the thickness of the SW angle and finishes in a later square cap-house which blocks the original open round at that corner of the parapet. A hall on the first floor, over vaulted basement cellars, was the principal apartment of the castle, provided with mural chambers and a carved aumbry in the wall near the great fireplace. The recessed windows had stone benches. The upper floors formed domestic accommodation.

Benholm was held in the 12th century by a family known by the territorial designation of 'de Benholm'. In *c.*1201 Hugh, son of Hugh of Benholm, had a re-grant of the property from the crown. The Benholms ended with an heiress in the late 14th century, possession passing to the

Lundys, an Angus family. The tower was probably built by John Lundy, who in 1485 had a confirmation of the lordship of Benholm from James III. In the 16th century the lands passed to a cadet branch of the Keith family.

10. Braikie Castle, Friockheim NO 628 509

At Wester Braikie farm 2.25 miles ENE of Friockheim. Until its roof began to collapse through neglect in the 1980s, this was one of the most complete and unaltered late 16th century towerhouses in Scotland. Its importance is increased by the relatively unaltered state, too, of its internal arrangements, with surviving partition walls of wattle and daub. It is to be regretted that when so many towerhouses, often in a more dilapidated state, have been restored, it has been allowed to fall further into decay.

The castle stands on the slopes which lead to Wuddy Law, enjoying a broad prospect to the S and W over the valley of the Lunan Water. It is a tall, imposing L-plan structure rising to four storeys and a garret. There is a small turret corbelled out at the SW angle above the third floor, now lacking its roof. A turret corbelled out in the re-entrant from the first floor carried the stair to the upper levels. The entrance, at ground floor level in the re-entrant, still has its iron yett and is defended by widely-splayed gunloops, and there are shot holes in the sills of almost every window. Over the doorway is an armorial panel with the arms of Fraser impaled with those of Kinnaird, the initials TF and CK for Thomas Fraser and Catherine Kinnaird, and the date 1581.

The main stair rises in the jam to first floor level only, above which it is carried in the turret in the re-entrant. Beneath the stair is a guardroom, while to the left a doorway opens into two vaulted cellars. The hall occupies the first floor of the main block. A stair in the thickness of the wall at its N end leads up to the laird's bed-chamber in the second floor of the jam. The upper floors of the tower contain bedrooms and domestic accommodation.

Braikie was in the hands of the Lovat Frasers by the 15th century, forming part of their lordship of Kinnell. Braikie itself, made up of Easter and Wester Braikie, was occupied from 1407 by the Stirling family as tenants. In 1476 John Stirling of Braikie granted Easter Braikie to his son, George, to be held in feu-ferme. In 1501 Thomas, lord Fraser of Lovat, sold Wester Braikie and other property in Kinnell to his kinsman David Lyon of Balmadies, but it returned to Fraser possession later in the 16th century. Thomas Fraser, the builder of the tower, was a son of the fifth Lord Lovat. Braikie passed from the Frasers to the Grays in the mid-17th century, and subsequently from them to the Ogilvies.

11. Broughty Castle, Broughty Ferry, Dundee* NO 465 304

On the promontory adjoining the harbour at Broughty Ferry, overlooking the mouth of the River Tay. At the core of the present structure lies the original square towerhouse built after 1490 by Andrew, lord Gray. The simple lines of his square keep have been blurred by the extension which clasps its northern side, and further obscured by the 19th-century artillery fortification which encircles the rock on which it stands, but a recent re-harling of the old portion of the tower serves to distinguish it from its 19th-century addition.

The medieval tower was a free-standing, almost square block rising to five storeys and capped with a parapet enclosing a garret. When first built it occupied a tidal rock known as the Partancraig, now joined to the mainland, and was enclosed within a barmkin wall with a round tower on its E side. The original stair rises in the thickness of the SE angle to end in a square, gabled cap-house. The parapet is carried on simple corbels and is provided with machicolated projections over the doorway and at various points around its circuit. The internal arrangements of the tower, and the garret structure, were subject to major alteration for military requirements in the 1860s.

Most of the outer works were swept away in the construction of the gun battery after 1861, but the main enclosure follows the line of the 15th-century wall. The N wing of the keep was added at this time and the building converted into the garrison's barracks. A separate guardhouse to control the drawbridge-defended gate was added to the E. A lower spur of wall was added on the SW to cover the harbour area.

The lands of Broughty belonged from the late 12th century to Arbroath Abbey, and were the site of a hospital for the convenience of pilgrims and travellers over the Tay (see above p.124). In 1490 Andrew Gray of Foulis and Castle Huntly acquired the land and received royal licence to construct a fortalice. This, represented by the surviving towerhouse, was complete by 1514. In 1547, during the so-called Wars of the Rough Wooing, Patrick, fourth lord Gray, surrendered the castle into the hands of the English, who established a garrison there. Broughty was an important English base during the wars, its garrison plundering widely through Angus and terrorising Dundee. Despite the attentions of a besieging force, the garrison survived until 1550 when the castle was retaken by the Scots with French assistance and a force of French troops established in their place. Broughty became one of the strongholds of Mary of Guise, regent of Scotland for her daughter, Queen Mary, until captured by the Protestant Lords of the Congregation in 1559. Following the withdrawal of the French from Scotland in 1560, the castle was partly demolished. Garrisoned by the King's Party in the civil war which followed Queen Mary's enforced abdication and subsequent flight to England, it was captured on the exiled queen's behalf in 1571 by the Fife laird, Seton of Parbroath. Despite traditions of its demolition in 1571, it remained intact and was to be the residence of the Master of Gray into the 17th century. Still entire in 1716, it fell rapidly into ruin thereafter and was little more than a gutted shell in 1821 when it was offered for sale as suitable for restoration as an inn or private house.

12. Careston Castle, Careston
NO 530 599

Set well back in its wooded policies to the N of the A90(T) Forfar-Brechin road, 4.4 miles W of Brechin, Careston occupies a slightly elevated position on south-facing slopes overlooking the valleys of the Noran and South Esk in central

Strathmore. The castle has a complex building-history and the southern show-façade which it presents to the world is an 18th-century screen behind which lurks a much older building.

The nucleus is believed to be a 15th-century tower built by the Dempsters. This was extended in the later 16th century when the bulk of the Z-plan towerhouse which forms the most substantial portion of Careston was constructed by its then Lindsay owners. Much of the superstructure of the four storey tower has been altered, probably at the time of the building of the 18th-century range, but it was clearly a building of refinement with decorative stringcourses, pedimented windows and other carved stonework.

In 1379 Andrew Dempster, lord of a portion of Menmuir, received a heritable grant of his office of 'judex' in the Scots parliament from Robert II. The Dempsters of Careston continued to flourish through the 15th-century, but the disreputable behaviour in the mid-16th century of the fifth laird brought ruin on the family. His son was the last Dempster to hold the property, which passed into the hands of the Lindsays, and then in turn in the mid-17th century to Sir Alexander Carnegie, younger brother of the first earl of Southesk. In 1707 the estate was bought by Sir John Stewart of Grandtully who, in 1714, added the splendid S façade to the castle.

13. Claypotts Castle, Dundee* NO 452 319

In the western suburbs of Dundee, to the SE of the A92 Dundee-Arbroath road at Claypotts roundabout. Barely altered since its completion in the later 16th century, it is one of the finest surviving towerhouses of its kind in Scotland. Unencumbered by later alterations and additions, the tower now stands in stark isolation but formerly would have formed the nucleus of a small ferm-toun community. The steading which replaced this in the 18th century, of which the castle formed the farmhouse, stood a little to the W and was demolished in the 1960s to make way for housing development.

The castle is a Z-plan towerhouse comprising a

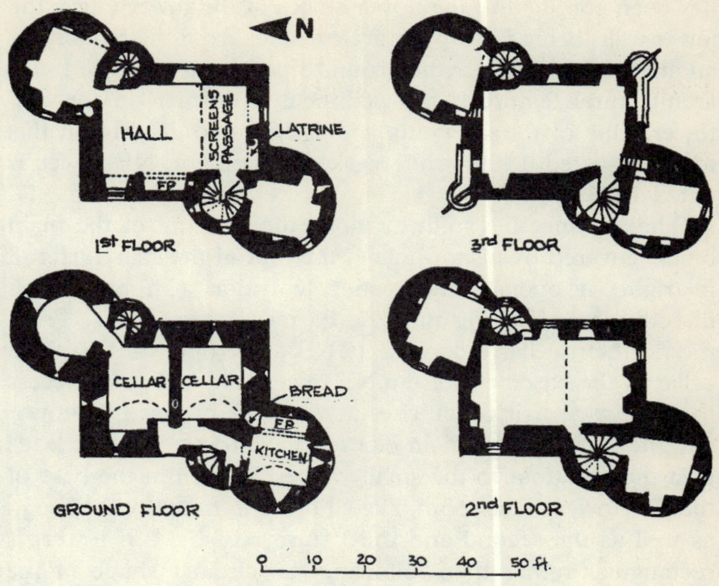

Figure 9. Claypotts Castle.

rectangular central block of three storeys and a garret with four-storey round towers, massively corbelled out into the square, at its NE and SW angles. The adoption of this plan gave greater scope for elaboration of the internal arrangements and provision of additional accommodation, for the angle towers contained not stairs but private chambers, the stairs instead being carried in smaller circular turrets built in the angles between the main block and the towers. It also had defensive merit as gunloops in the corner towers could cover the faces of the central block. The main defences are concentrated in the lower stages of the tower, widely splayed gunloops covering most of the exterior wall surface, but there are short stretches of parapet walk at the SE and NW angles of the main block at garret height. These now lack the parapet walls, but the corbelling of the open round on the angle and the straight length along the gable remain. All the elaboration has been confined to the upper stages of the towerhouse, the lower walls being largely featureless apart from the remains of an armorial panel over the ground-floor entrance. The finest architectural feature is the pedimented dormer on the SW tower. One of the skewputs of the crowstep gabling on this tower is dated 1569, while a skewput on the NE tower is dated 1588.

The entrance lies midway along the W front of the main block, covered by a shot-hole at the foot of the stair-turret to its right. It opens onto a short corridor with two doors directly ahead leading into the barrel-vaulted cellars. From the northern cellar a door in its NE angle opens into a third cellar in the basement of the NE tower, and also gives access to the service stair which rises in the angle between the tower and the E wall of the main block. The entrance passage leads past the stair-foot to the small vaulted kitchen in the base of the SW tower. This room, like all those in the tower above it, as well as the second and third storeys of the NE tower, is rectangular rather than following the circular shape of the towers. It has a slop-drain in its S wall and a massive fireplace with oven opening from it in the E wall. To provide all-round defensive fire over the walls, there was a gun-loop provided in the back wall of the fireplace.

The main apartments were on the first floor. A separate doorway from the principal stair opens into the SE tower room, a large private chamber with wall-presses and a fireplace. A doorway a further quarter turn round the stair leads to what was the screens passage or ante-room of the hall. The screen has gone but scars in the plaster on the walls marks its former position. To the right of the doorway is a recess housing a latrine. The hall proper was a nearly square room lit by two large windows, that in the W wall lighting the laird's table which stood in front of the blank N wall. There is a large fireplace in the W wall, its lintel gone. In the NE angle of the chamber are doorways to the service stair and to the NE tower chamber. This has also been a fine room, lit by large E and W facing windows and provided with fireplace, wall-press and its own private latrine. It probably formed the laird's private chamber. Above the hall in the main block were two chambers divided by a screen wall, over which was a single large garret room. Further private chambers were provided in the upper storeys of the angle towers.

The lands of Claypotts appear to have been given to the abbey of Lindores on the S shore of the Firth of Tay by David, earl of Huntingdon, younger brother of King William the Lion, soon after its foundation in *c.*1190. Claypotts lay within David's lordship centred upon Dundee. Possession was confirmed in 1247 by Alexander II and again in 1365 by David II. By the early 16th century the abbey's lands of Claypotts were tenanted by John Strachan, a cadet of the Angus and Thornton family of Strachan. It was probably his son, also John, who commenced the building of the present castle and whose initials IS appear on one of the skewputs. In 1601, Sir William Graham of Ballunie purchased Claypotts from the Strachans, and in 1620 his son, David, who was perhaps the last owner of the building to live in it, sold it to Sir William Graham of Claverhouse. On the forfeiture of his great-grandson, John Graham, Viscount Dundee, following his death in 1689 at the Battle of Killiekrankie, the lands reverted to the Crown only to be granted in 1694 to the Marquis of Douglas.

14. Clova Castle, Glen Clova
NO 321 734

On an elevated position on the N side of the glen above the unclassified road from Clova to Braedownie, 650m WNW of the Glen Clova Hotel. Plundered for building-stone until the later 19th century, the stump of the round stair-tower and traces of walling from the square main block are the only remains of the towerhouse. Clova was held in the 14th century by the Earl of Mar. In the 15th century it came to the Ogilvies as tenants of the Lindsay earls of Crawford. There is no mention of a castle here in accounts of the young earl of Argyll's raid into N Angus in 1594, which suggests that the structure may have been erected soon afterwards. As an Ogilvy property the castle is believed to have shared the fate of Airlie in 1640 at the hands of the earl of Argyll and his Covenanting army. It was certainly ruinous in 1650 when Charles II, attempting to escape from his over-bearing 'protectors' at Perth in the episode known as 'the Start', fled to the Ogilvies. It being felt that Cortachy was too obvious a shelter, Charles was sent to Clova and found a brief respite before discovery in the cottage then occupied by the laird.

15. Colliston Castle, Colliston NO 611 465

The castle stands in wooded grounds off the A933 Arbroath-Friockheim road, on the edge of the small valley of the Brothock Burn 1mile NE of the village of Colliston. The castle is a Z-plan house of main block and substantial round towers. A massive stair-turret finished with a conical roof, corbelled out from the first floor, rises in the angle between the main block and the SE tower. The NW tower is now finished with a plain parapet supported on simple corbels but was originally of the same form as the SE, which is corbelled out into a square cap-house with gabled roof. This alteration, the reconstruction of the parapet and open rounds which crown the main block, and the dormered garret within it, are all relatively modern. There is also evidence for substantial alterations to the structure in the 17th century.

The colour-washed harling on the exterior masks the evidence for rebuilding, but it is clear that the original concept was not that far removed from the present structure. The main block is of three storeys and a garret, the S front decorated with a prominent stringcourse which is stepped around the second storey windows, while the towers rise one storey higher. There is an ample provision of splayed gunloops round the ground floor, including three to cover the main entrance in the bottom of the SE tower. On first floor level of the stair-turret, which projects partly over the doorway, is an heraldic panel containing the Guthrie and Falconer coats of arms, the initials IG and MF, the date 1553 and the motto Laus Deo.

The main entrance opened originally on the foot of the principal turnpike stair leading to the first floor, but this has been removed and replaced by a squared scale-and-platt stair housed in a projecting block on the N side of the main building. The basement was vaulted and served as cellars, with the kitchen lying at the W end of the range. A service stair, now blocked, led down to the cellars and kitchen from the hall on the first floor. The hall, which originally occupied the whole of the first floor, is a spacious chamber lit by large 17th-century windows. A private chamber opens off the hall in the NW tower, and the upper floors contain private bed-chambers and domestic accommodation.

Colliston belonged to Arbroath Abbey in the Middle Ages. In 1542, Cardinal David Beaton in his capacity as Abbot of Arbroath, alienated the property to John Guthrie, presumably the builder of the present castle, and his wife Isabella Ogilvy. Isabella may have been a daughter of Marion Ogilvy, Beaton's mistress. Sir Henry Guthrie of Colliston sold the castle in 1670.

16. Cortachy Castle, Cortachy NO 398 596

The castle stands in its wooded policies on a low-lying site on the S side of the River South Esk, 3.5 miles N of Kirriemuir on the B955. Situated at the point where the river bursts out of the narrows of Glen Clova into Strathmore, and only 0.5 miles N of the mouth of Glen Prosen, Cortachy occupies a site of great strategic importance for the control of traffic over the Mounth passes.

In its original form, Cortachy was a courtyard castle of the later 14th or 15th centuries of quadrangular form with round towers at each corner. Three of these towers survive, although greatly altered, and portions of the exterior walls of the S and W ranges incorporate stretches of the early curtain wall. The upper storey of the SW tower has been corbelled out into the square in the late 16th or early 17th-century, but the upper works of the two remaining towers and the whole of the wall-head arrangements and parapets are modern. The interior of the building has been subject to considerable alteration over the centuries and owes its present layout to the demands of 19th-century country-house living.

The lordship of Cortachy belonged to the earls of Strathearn in the 13th century. In the reign of Robert I, Malise, earl of Strathearn, settled the property on his wife, Joan of Menteith, who granted it to her son by a previous marriage, John. Before 1409 the property was in the hands of Archibald, fourth earl of Douglas, who in that year resigned it into the hands of Robert, duke of Albany, governor of Scotland during the captivity in England of his nephew, James I, who immediately granted it to his youngest brother, Walter, earl of Atholl and Caithness. Following the forfeiture and execution of Earl Walter in 1437 for his part in the murder of James I, Cortachy was taken into royal hands and subsequently granted by James II to Walter Ogilvy of Oures. In 1473, James III annulled this grant and bestowed the lordship and castle instead on Thomas Ogilvy of Clova. The Clova Ogilvies held Cortachy until 1625 when they sold it to the Earl of Airlie, head of the family. Following the destruction of Airlie Castle in 1640, the earl and his family moved to Cortachy, only for it to be ransacked by Cromwell's soldiers in 1651. The lands and titles were forfeited in 1746 for the support the Ogilvies had given to Charles Edward Stuart, but were restored in 1826.

17. Cowie Castle, Stonehaven
NO 887 874

On the headland E of the old church of Cowie (see above p.131), 1.25 miles NE of Stonehaven. A royal castle here controlled the coastal road to Aberdeen. A headland has been cut off by a broad ditch, behind which rises the remains of what is probably a 13th-century curtain wall 21m long, 2m thick and surviving up to 1.5m high. Although the castle dates most likely from the later 12th century (William the Lion granted property at Cowie to William Giffard between 1196 and 1199), possibly occupying the site of a yet older fortification, the earliest surviving reference to it dates from 1264 when the sheriff of Kincardine accounted for repairs there in his Exchequer returns. In 1292 the forest of Cowie was in the keepership of John Comyn, earl of Buchan. Robert I gave the thanedom of Cowie to Alexander Fraser, and in 1327 gave him the forest of Cowie for making a royal park within the thanage. By that date, however, the castle was probably a ruin.

18. Craig Castle, Montrose NO 703 562

Overlooking Montrose Basin from the south, 1 mile W of Ferryden, Craig is still occupied as a private residence. It is a substantial and extensive structure dating from several periods. It is approached from the E through a massive, but ruinous gatehouse which opens into a large outer court. The gatehouse comprises an arched gateway under corbelled machicolations between two drum towers linked by a length of parapet walk. The whole structure is well provided with gunloops.

The main house is dominated by two small square parapeted towers, probably 15th-century, linked by a high wall to form the S side of a square enclosure. Both towers rise to three storeys with a crowstep gabled garret rising within a corbelled parapet. The parapet of the E tower is plain but provided with open rounds at the angles, while the W is crenellated but has no rounds. It is possible that there were similar towers at the N and S angles also. At the NE angle of the E tower are traces of the gateway which gave access from the outer court into the inner enclosure.

The three-storeyed buildings which form the N and W ranges are later 16th or 17th-century. The N wing has been considerably altered in modern times, but consisted of vaulted cellars and kitchen on the ground floor with hall above. The main private accommodation was originally in the W wing. An original main doorway here has been blocked, but a worn panel bearing the date 1637 in the wall above marks its position. The E side, which closed off the inner court from the outer, has been removed.

Craig appears to have been a property of the de Bosco family – or Woods as they became – by the early 13th century. The property remained with the family until soon after 1617, when it was acquired by David Carnegie, earl of Southesk, who in 1626 settled it on his second son. On his succession to the earldom, it passed to his younger brother and remained in the possession of a cadet line of the Carnegies until modern times.

19. Crathes Castle, Banchory*
NO 734 968

A National Trust for Scotland maintained property set amidst gardens 2 miles E of Banchory, signposted N off the A93 Aberdeen-Banchory road. The substantial L-plan tower which forms the principal portion of Crathes was begun in 1553 to replace the ancient residence of the Burnett family on a crannog in the now drained Loch of Leys 1.25 miles to the WNW. Although L-plan in layout, the E wall of the main block has been massively thickened to accommodate mural chambers and a stair at the SE angle, with the result that the jam scarcely projects more than 3m to the E of the almost square main tower. All corners are rounded, but are corbelled out into the square above the level of the first floor hall. There are bartizans at the S angles and at the NW rising on a decorative, cannon-spouted corbel band above a stringcourse which moves across the wall-face in steps from third to fourth storeys. The lower surfaces of the walls below the stringcourse are plain except for a series of fine heraldic panels, the large window in the S front is a Victorian insertion. Running E from the old tower is an early 18th-century, two-storeyed wing.

The original entrance to the tower, now with its yett restored to its hinges, lies in the E wall of the re-entrant angle. This opened into a passage, off which are two barrel-vaulted cellars in the main block and a kitchen in the jam. The hall, from which a service stair once ran down to the southern cellar, occupies the first floor of the main block and rises a full two storeys in height. To serve the intervening level in the jam, a separate stair rises from this floor in a turret corbelled out at the junction of the N walls of main block and jam. Above the hall are private chambers, four of which contain fine (though restored) late 16th-century painted ceilings which were revealed when later plasterwork was stripped off in 1877. Running east-west over the northern end of the main block and the jam, at garret level, is a superb timber-panelled long gallery.

The Burnetts, a family of Anglo-Norman origin who originally settled in Berwickshire, arrived in Kincardineshire in the 14th century as part of Robert I's introduction of loyal families into a region once dominated by supporters of the Balliols and Comyns. They served at first as royal foresters of the Forest of Drum, an office which was transferred in 1323 to the Irvines. The family was of local importance in the Middle Ages, their comparative poverty accounting for their failure to move to a more amenable residence from their crannog-site in the Loch of Leys. A good marriage by Alexander Burnett in 1543 brought a sizeable dowry composed of former Church lands, revenues from which funded the construction of Crathes.

20. Dudhope Castle, Dundee
NO 394 307

In Dudhope Park, 0.5 miles NW of the City Centre off the A923. The conical roofs and whitewashed walls of Dudhope now form an eye-catching group at the head of the steep embankment on the N side of Lochee Road, but until the 1980s the building was little more than a derelict wreck with an uncertain future. It is now occupied by the Dundee Business School attached to the University of Abertay.

The existing building is the E and S sides of a quadrangular castle begun *c.*1580 as an enlargement of an older towerhouse at the N end of the E range. It is not certain whether W and N ranges were ever planned, but an enclosing wall survived here into the late 18th century. There are round towers at the SW (which has a separate stair turret rising in the re-entrant angle on the S front above the second storey), SE and NE angles, the northern tower being built as late as *c.*1700 following the demolition of the old towerhouse to form a symmetrical façade balanced on either side of the central gateway. The gate, which leads through a pend into the courtyard, is itself flanked by a pair of shallowly-projecting D-shaped towers whose conical roofs form part of the modern restoration work. Between these, at wall-head level, is a small pedimented gable supported on plain corbels and surmounted by a bellcote, added when the castle was converted into a barracks. The whole wallhead of the building was raised in 1799 to form a full extra storey, having originally been finished with pedimented dormers. This makes the towers and gate-turrets, which were not heightened, appear rather squat. Most of the original windows have been altered or enlarged – one still bears a pediment dated 1660 – and many more inserted in the 18th and 19th centuries. The stair turret which rises from the first floor towards the E end of the S wall of the courtyard is a modern restoration, the whole structure except for the corbelling at its foot having been removed in the 18th century.

Internally, Dudhope was massively altered and little remains in its upper levels of the original layout. The main stair, which served all floors, is reached through a moulded doorway immediately to the left of the entrance pend. There is a wide spiral stair in the SW tower running down from the private rooms which once occupied the first and second floors of the S range to a doorway at the foot of the tower which opened into the pleasance, or gardens, which ran down the S slopes from the castle. The basement of the S range is the least altered, comprising a series of vaulted cellars reached by a vaulted corridor which runs along the courtyard front. At the W end of the range is the kitchen with massive fireplace.

The lands of Dudhope and the office of Constable of Dundee were conferred in 1298 on Alexander Scrymgeour, a loyal lieutenant of William Wallace. The massive extension of the original towerhouse reflected the rise to prominence of the family in the later 16th and 17th centuries. Sir James Scrymgeour (*c.*1550-1612) was probably responsible for the rebuilding of the castle. Banished briefly in 1583 for his involvement in the Ruthven Raid, in which James VI had been held for ten months by members of an ultra-Protestant faction led by the Earl of Gowrie, Sir James was to serve as provost of Dundee in 1588. In 1617, on his sole return visit to Scotland after his accession to the English throne, James VI stayed at Dudhope. Charles I created Sir John

Scrymgeour Viscount Dudhope in 1641 but in 1644 the 2nd viscount was killed at Marston Moor fighting against the king. His son, John, was created Earl of Dundee in 1661, but on his death in 1668 the title lapsed and the lands passed out of Scrymgeour possession. Possessed briefly by Charles Maitland, third earl of Lauderdale, it was sold in 1684 to John Graham of Claverhouse, Viscount Dundee, who was killed fighting for the cause of James VII at the battle of Killiecrankie. The third and last Graham viscount was forfeited in 1690 and the property was granted in 1694 to the second Marquis of Douglas. Dudhope ceased to be used as a residence in the early 1760s and in 1792 the castle was converted into a woollen mill. The mill, however, went bankrupt in 1793 and by 1799 it had become a government barracks.

21. Dunnottar Castle, Stonehaven*
NO 882 839

Access via footpath from car park on the A92 1.5 miles S of Stonehaven. Dunnottar, once the stronghold of the Keith Earls Marischal of Scotland, is one of the most dramatically-sited of all Scottish castles. It's cliff-top ruins form a striking landmark on the coastline S of Stonehaven, their scale more akin to those of an abandoned village rather than a castle. The level summit of the promontory which they occupy may have been settled since the Early Medieval period, a fortress of Dunnottar being on record in the 7th century AD. Recent excavation work, however, failed to produce any evidence for occupation of that date, and fieldwork on Bowduns – the next headland to the N – has led to speculation that the early Dunnottar lay there and that the name was transferred to the present site at a later date (see above p.80).

The castle consists of a series of elements dispersed round the summit and approaches to the promontory, representing a complex building-history spanning the later 14th to mid 17th centuries. The approach to the castle is via a track which descends to the shoreline of Castle Haven, bringing visitors under the commanding defences of an outwork on the neck of the narrow isthmus which connected the headland to the mainland. The isthmus, a mere razor-backed strip of land, has been quarried away to remove any threat of attack from that quarter, but the area nearest the castle, known as the Fiddlehead, was crowned by a low parapet from which the access path could be covered. The path runs NE past the Fiddlehead then swings round to the SE to approach the main entrance in the re-entrant between the isthmus and the main promontory.

A flight of steps leads to the main gate, reduced to a square lintelled opening within the infilled archway of the older portal. The approach is commanded to the right by three tiers of flanking gunloops in the lower storeys of the structure known as Benholm's Lodgings. This soars for five storeys up the face of the cliff, its lower floors forming barrack accommodation carved partly out of the rock face. Over these was a suite of vaulted apartments and above that a final floor of accommodation, re-floored and re-roofed as part of a scheme of consolidation work at the castle earlier this century. The gate proper pierces a screen wall 9m high and

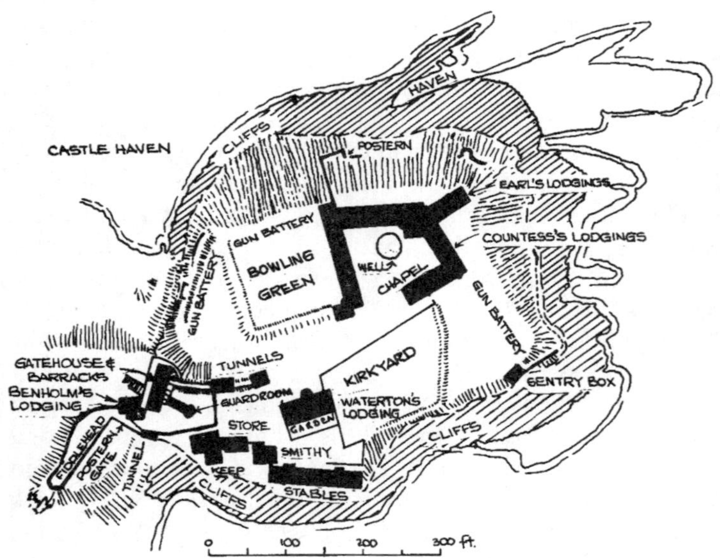

Figure 10. Dunnottar Castle.

2.2m thick crowned by an open walk carried flush with the face of the wall. Behind this was a vaulted magazine under a barrack room, with a second chamber over the gate pend from which the portcullis mechanism was operated. Facing the entrance is the guard-chamber, a long room carved partly out of the rock and fronted by a door and a wall pierced by what looks like four large gunloops arranged in a square, but serving more probably as a menacing-looking window. The whole entrance structure probably dates from *c.*1575, with some remodelling of the upperworks of Benholm's Lodgings in the early 17th century.

From the entrance pend the main approach turns at right angles to the NE behind the barracks. A path round the N wall of the barracks leads to the parapet over the gate, from which a stair carries up round Benholm's Lodging to the Fiddlehead and ultimately to the Keep. The main access, however, turns again to the SE and continues within a walled gully, roofed into two stretches of tunnel, to emerge roughly in the centre of the castle complex. The whole of this approach is overlooked from the parapet of the Keep which stands at the SW angle of the castle rock. This is a self-contained L-plan towerhouse of the 1390s which, showing no concern for the defensive capabilities of its design, has its re-entrant facing SW towards the cliff edge and its entrance in the long E wall. The main block, which lies E-W, measures 12.3m by 7.8m. The jam projects from the E end of the S wall and is 5.7m wide by 5m deep.

The entrance to the keep opens into a lobby in the thickness of the wall. Directly ahead is a vaulted cellar under the main block, converted at a later date into a kitchen. A door in its SE angle leads to a second vaulted cellar in the jam, from which also opens a small prison in the thickness of the E wall. From the lobby the main stair rises to the left of the entrance in a straight flight, which then turns into a spiral stair built into the thickness of the wall between the main block and the jam. The hall occupies the first floor of the main block. It has been a fine chamber with recessed windows with stone benches in each wall, a fireplace at the W end and a latrine in the thickness of the S wall. At the E end are two mural chambers, one in the NE angle, the other opening from the E window recess and provided with an aperture from which the stair could be watched. In the wing at this level was the original kitchen, converted later into a private chamber. The fireplace in the S wall has a bread oven opening from it. On the third storey, the main block contained the private hall of the lord, while there was a bed-chamber in the jam. Above this was a gabled attic contained within a corbelled parapet walk. The parapet wall has gone, but the corbelling survives.

To the E of the keep are three detached blocks of domestic buildings. That nearest the keep contained servants' accommodation over two vaulted cellars. The middle block contained a smithy, of which the large fireplace and chimney are the main survivals. The long E range contained stables with accommodation on the upper floor for the grooms and two chambers at the E end for the livery masters. The whole range was unvaulted and access to the upper floors, which were lit originally by dormer windows, was via external timber stairs. A doorway from the upper livery master's room opened onto a timber gallery built out from the S wall of the range. This may have contained a privy, but more likely was a platform from which the S face of the castle rock could be commanded. The range appears to date from the early 17th century and contains much re-used material in its stonework.

Across the stableyard to the N is Waterton's Lodging, named after Thomas Forbes of Waterton, a 17th-century laird often in attendance on the Earl Marischal. This was a two storey structure, probably built in 1574 as accommodation for the newly-married son of the 4th Earl, with living rooms and private chambers on both floors. Most of the S wall and gables have been demolished, leaving only a circular stair tower in the centre of the N wall rising to almost full height. It is corbelled into the square above the second storey to form a small gabled cap-house, reached via a slender turret corbelled out in the NE re-entrant. There was an enclosed garden on the S of the house, while to the E was the large kirkyard. A single gravestone with the inscription *A BAIRN OF NYN YEARS LYES HERE 1685* remains visible. To the

E of the kirkyard is the site of one of the 17th-century gun batteries, commanding the seaward approach to the castle, while at the foot of the long slopes which fall toward the lower crags at this side stands the shell of a sentry box. Portions of a curtain wall can be seen extending E from the box and can be traced in various places along the E and NE faces of the headland.

N of the kirkyard stands the ruins of the Quadrangle, a complex of buildings of various dates which comprised the main accommodation of the Keiths in the 17th century. Its S range is formed by the chapel, portions of the S wall of which date from the 13th century. Most of the remainder was built in stages between 1581 and 1623 by George, fifth Earl Marischal. The oldest of the domestic ranges appears to be the W. This comprises a long block of seven chambers on the ground floor, each with their own doorway, forming the private accommodation for various of the senior household officials. At its SW angle is a square tower containing a scale-and-platt stair giving access to the upper storey. In its NW re-entrant is a circular turret providing access to a private chamber in the top storey of the stair tower known as the Silver House, this probably being where the Keiths stored their plate. An external timber stair from the first floor landing of the scale-and-platt stair leads to the bowling green to the W of the block The first floor over the seven chambers contained a long gallery measuring 34.5, by 4.5m. Descriptions of the castle in the late 17th century present this as a magnificent chamber with a superb oaken roof and rich furnishings. At its N end was a private chamber with a balcony to the N overlooking the sea.

The N and E ranges have been added at a later date. At the W end of the N range is a pend secured by doors at either end. This, the so-called Watergate, led to a path down the steep northern slopes to a postern in the outer curtain which gave access to a long inlet in the headland with a shingle beach onto which small boats could be drawn. The remainder of the ground floor of the N range contained cellars and a kitchen. Along the S wall from the kitchen extended a service passage which gave access to a vaulted cellar under a NE wing appended to the main complex – known as the Whig's Vault on account of its use as a prison for Covenanters in the late 17th century – and to the ground floor of the E range, which contained a cellar, bakehouse and brewery. A fine scale-and-platt stair in the re-entrant between N and E ranges (replaced by a modern concrete stair) gave access to the principal private accommodation of the castle. At the W end of the upper storey was a drawing room with doors leading to the gallery and private room at the N end of the W range. This chamber was re-roofed by Lady Cowdray during consolidation work in the castle in 1927. The central chamber was the dining room, entered from the head of the main stair, a fine chamber measuring 16.76m by 6.1m. At the E end, entered from the dining room only, was a private retiring room. From the stairhead a door to the left opened into a turret providing access to a room over the stairway, while to the right a door opened into the lobby of the private suites of the earl and countess.

The Earl's suite forms the upper floor of the NE wing appended to the NE angle of the main quadrangle. Completed in 1645, it contained a large private chamber or study with a bedroom opening from it in the E end of the block. Over the fireplace in the bedroom is a fine pediment bearing the arms and mottoes of the seventh Earl Marischal and his wife. The Countess's suite occupied the upper floor of the E range, but the structure here is very badly ruined. Access was provided from the lobby at the N end, but also via an external timber stair at the S end supported in part upon the stone dome of the bakehouse oven. The suite contains a bedchamber at the N end with a dressing room and wardrobe in the S. A gallery in the E end of the chapel was entered from the dressing room. In the courtyard enclosed by the quadrangle is the so-called well, in reality a large circular cistern supposedly fed by lead pipe from the mainland.

To the W of the complex is a levelled area 36.58m square bounded by terraces on its W and S sides. This formed a bowling green. To its N is the embankment of the North Battery, a gun emplacement of the 17th-century which covered the Castle Haven. The embankment which continues down the NE face of the rock and ends in the area known as the Mount overlooking the main gate of the castle was for long thought to lie on the line of the probable defences of the Pictish fort. Excavation in the 1980s showed this, too, to be earthen defences built to cover an artillery battery. The Mount may represent the truncated remains of a motte, but there is no evidence to support this belief.

While it is certain that there were also secular buildings on the site, the oldest datable structure at Dunnottar is the chapel. This was the parish church of Dunnottar, consecrated by William Wishart, bishop of St. Andrews, in May 1276. In 1296 the rock of Dunnottar was seized and garrisoned by Edward I of England on his triumphant progress through northern Scotland following his victory over the Scots, but in 1297 it was stormed by William Wallace and the English garrison burned alive in the church. In March 1335-6 Edward III of England commanded Sir Thomas de Roscelyn to proceed by sea to garrison Dunnottar as part of his campaigns in support of Edward Balliol. Sir Thomas, however, was killed soon after in the course of a raid on Aberdeen, and Dunnottar was captured and destroyed by the Scottish Guardian, Sir Andrew Murray.

In March 1346 King David II granted Dunnottar, with licence to build a fortress there, to his brother-in-law, William, earl of Sutherland. No buildings of this date survive. At some date before 1390 possession passed to Sir William Lindsay, but soon after that year he quitclaimed his interest in favour of Sir William Keith, Marischal of Scotland. Keith probably began work on his tower soon afterwards, building a new church for the parish some miles inland. Despite this, however, he was excommunicated by the bishop of St. Andrews for what was regarded as seizure of Church property, and it took an appeal to the pope before absolution was secured. Sir William's descendants remained in possession of Dunnottar, which became their chief seat, until the forfeiture of the tenth Earl Marischal in 1715.

Despite the formidable gatehouse, the castle was easily captured in 1592 by an officer of the rebel Earl of Huntly. It was, however, regarded as one of the chief fortresses of the realm, and in 1643 it was garrisoned by the Marquis of Argyll and used as his headquarters in the course of his campaign in the NE against the Royalist Marquis of Huntly. In 1645 the Marquis of Montrose attempted unsuccessfully to persuade the Earl Marischal to join the Royalist cause but, lacking the strength to storm the castle, resorted to a systematic devastation of the farmlands round about. By 1650, however, the Earl Marischal had joined the supporters of Charles II and entertained the king at Dunnottar as he headed S to his coronation at Scone. Following Charles's defeat at Worcester it was to Dunnottar that the Scottish regalia were taken for safe-keeping, together with the king's plate, furniture and private papers. Under the constableship of George Ogilvy of Barras, with a garrison of sixty-nine men and forty-two guns, the castle was by May 1652 the last stronghold in Scotland to fly the royal standard. Besieged by Cromwell's troops under General Overton from September 1651, the castle had little to fear until the arrival of heavy ordinance in the spring of 1652. By then, however, the regalia and papers had been smuggled from the castle and the crown, sword and sceptre hidden beneath the floor of nearby Kinneff Kirk (see below). On 24 May 1652, after bombardment by the heavy guns of the besieging army, Ogilvy surrendered.

The castle was restored after the Restoration in 1660. Descriptions of it made in the late 17th century show it to have been one of the most sumptuous noble residences in Scotland, boasting fine furnishings and an outstanding art collection. In 1715, however, the tenth Earl Marischal joined the Jacobite Rebellion and guns from the castle were used by the rebel army. On the collapse of the Rising the forfeiture of the Earl was confirmed and his properties seized, Dunnottar in 1718 being sold to the notorious York Building Company, who systematically looted the buildings for all salvageable materials.

22. Edzell Castle, Edzell*
NO 584 691

Signposted N of the unclassified road from Edzell to Glen Lethnot, 1 mile W of Edzell. The core of the castle is the substantial early 16th-century L-plan towerhouse built by the Lindsay earls of Crawford, onto the N of which later in the century was added a spacious mansion arranged round a central courtyard. On the S of this complex a great pleasance, or walled garden, with out-buildings was built in 1604. Although the mansion is heavily ruined, this ensemble of tower, courtyard extension and pleasance is one of the finest late 16th-century groups to survive in Scotland.

The tower consists of a rectangular main block 13.4m by 10.4m, with a projecting stair wing at the N end of the NW wall. This is 4.8m long and extends 2m beyond the wall of the main block. The doorway, at ground level, is placed off-centre in the NW wall of the main block, and opened into a passage giving access to the vaulted basement cellars and the stair. The cellars are provided with gunloops and there is a further gunloop looking NW in a small chamber under the stair. The N cellar has a service stair leading to the hall. This was a splendid chamber with a large fireplace in the NW wall and large windows in the SE and SW. In the W angle is what appears to have been originally a bed-chamber in the thickness of the wall, converted into a spacious cupboard at a later date. The N end of this floor was screened off from the hall to form a service area into which both the main stair and the stair from the cellar opened, and provided with its own latrine and a small fireplace. It was roofed at a lower height than the main hall chamber, the space above serving as a minstrels' gallery. Over the hall were two storeys of private rooms, each provided with privies and mural closets, with parapet and garret above. The parapet wall has gone, but the chequer-moulded corbelling which carried the walk, with open rounds at the angles and in the middles of the walls, survives.

In *c.*1580 the outbuildings which adjoined the tower were swept away and replaced by a great quadrangle, roughly 34m square, of which the tower formed the S angle. It was intended to have ranges of buildings on all sides, but only the SW (forming the show front) and the W half of the NW ranges were completed. Working from the S end of the SW range, where it abuts the towerhouse, on the ground floor there was an ante-room or hallway giving access from the courtyard to the tower. Opening from this was a kitchen to serve the tower, replacing earlier service arrangements. Immediately to the N is the entrance pend, still closed by its original wooden doors, and with stone benches on both sides. Over the gateway are four empty niches for armorial panels. N of this are two chambers, the northernmost possibly serving as a guardroom. In the courtyard angle between the SW and NW ranges was a circular stair tower. In the SW range the upper floor was occupied by a drawing-room and parlour. The basement of the NW range contains vaulted cellars and a kitchen at its northern end, the latter with a massive fireplace and bread-oven. On the first floor was a large hall. Projecting from the NW angle is a cylindrical tower furnished with gunloops at ground floor level, and with its own stair, also serving as a service stair from cellars and kitchen to the hall, rising in a turret in the N re-entrant.

Onto the SE side of the courtyard, Sir David Lindsay constructed the finest early 17th-century walled garden to survive in Scotland. Coats-of-arms over the NE door into the garden display the arms and initials of Sir David, his second wife Isobel Forbes, and the date of completion, 1604. The exterior is otherwise featureless, but the inner walls are divided into compartments by pilasters, each made of a shaft of two sections separated by richly carved bands and with sculpted heads and bases. The shafts, sadly, have long since been removed. The wall-head over these is finished with a heavy coping, into which are set round-headed niches, probably to contain busts. There are no niches on the W wall, reflecting economies forced on Sir David by mounting debts. The wall surface has been treated in various ways. The square recesses were intended to contain flowers and formed a floral representation of part of the Lindsay arms. The most striking features, however, are sculptured panels displaying the Planetary Deities, the Liberal Arts and the Cardinal Virtues, based on engravings made in 1528-9 in Nuremberg.

At the E angle of the pleasance is a two-storeyed summer-house, its upper floor serving as a small museum. There are two non-communicating rooms in the ground floor, one entered from the garden the other from outside. The garden room has a fine ribbed and groined vault and has a stone bench running round the walls. A door in its northern wall opens into a stair turret giving access to the upper storey, which contains a single room with a closet in an angle turret at the E corner. At the S angle of the garden was another substantial out-building, now reduced to foundations, which formed a bath-house. At the Mains farm, on the right hand side of the track leading to the castle, is a fine 17th-century doocot provided with sawn-off turrets, corbelled out at opposing angles and covered by the oversailing roof of the main chamber.

After gaining control of the lordship of Glenesk from the Stirlings in 1357, the Lindsays continued to reside at the ancient motte of that family to the S of the present castle. In the early 16th century work began on the towerhouse which forms the core of the existing complex. Most of the building is attributed to Sir David Lindsay, Lord Edzell, second son of the 9th earl of Crawford by his second wife. David succeeded as a child to Edzell in 1558 and had a brilliant career as a Lord of Session and member of the Privy Council. Widely travelled and a man of culture and education, he sought to improve his estates by a policy of planting and through development of mine-workings in Glen Esk, using his experience from Continental travelling to bring skilled German mining engineers to Scotland. Despite such attempts to improve his finances, however, he left a crippling burden of debt for his family when he died in 1610. The Lindsays retained Edzell until 1715, when they sold the estate to the Earl of Panmure. He was almost immediately forfeited for his part in the Jacobite rebellion of that year and the property came into the hands of the notorious York Building Company, who plundered the estate and began to strip the castle. In 1764 the Company was declared bankrupt and, to meet the demands of creditors, its properties were ruthlessly stripped of any materials of value. At Edzell this saw the felling of the beech avenue leading to the castle and the stripping out of floors, roofs and windows, reducing the building to a gutted shell.

23. Ethie Castle, Inverkeilor NO 688 468

Ethie Castle stands in private grounds 2.5 miles SE of Inverkeilor, off the unclassified road from Cotton of Inchock to Boghead. The existing mansion is a complex structure which may incorporate portions of a late medieval property which belonged to Arbroath Abbey. Despite traditions that the oldest recognisable element of the building, an L-plan block which now forms the SW corner of the castle, was the residence in the 1530s and 1540s of Cardinal David Beaton who also held the abbacy of Arbroath, it is more likely that it post-dates the transference of the estate from the Church to the Carnegie family in 1549.

The original house has a long main block measuring 12.8m by 7m, with a square jam which houses the stair projecting from the W end of its northern side. This stair tower has been carried up in modern times to be finished with a flat roof contained within a balustrade, its upper stages reached by a stair contained in a smaller turret corbelled out from its NW angle. It is possible that the original design similarly ended in such a lofty belvedere from which to view the pleasance around the house. The main block has three vaulted cellars on its ground floor, the easternmost serving as the kitchen prior to the construction of the late 16th or early 17th-century wing immediately adjacent to the E. From the westernmost cellar a straight service stair leads up to the first floor hall.

The eastern extension consists of a second L-shaped block rising to three storeys and a garret. The basement of the main block contains the kitchen, with massive fireplace, and a well, while the jam is occupied by a staircase. A new main doorway, replacing the older entrance in the re-entrant of the old tower, opens directly to the foot of this stair. The tower is off-set into three stages by two bands of continuous corbelling. There are later extensions to the N and W which occupy the site of the barmkin and incorporate portions of its wall and angle towers. The present main entrance to the castle lies in the W range, surmounted by a defaced armorial panel, and possibly represents a development from the original gateway through the barmkin.

The estate was alienated from Arbroath Abbey in 1549, being granted to Sir Robert Carnegie of Kinnaird. His grandson, Sir John, younger brother of the first Earl of Southesk, received the castle and lands in 1596. He was created Lord Lour in 1639 and Earl of Ethie in 1647, but in 1662 he exchanged those titles for those of Baron Rosehill and Inglismaldie and Earl of Northesk. The property remained in Carnegie hands until the early 20th century.

24. Farnell Castle, Farnell
NO 624 555

In private grounds to the W of Farnell village, occupied as a private house. The eastern half of the long main block is the towerhouse built in the early 16th century for the bishops of Brechin. It consisted of a rectangular tower of three storeys and an attic, with a courtyard to the S. On the E gable are the corbels, wall-plate and water-table of a timber gallery at third-storey height, and at the E end of the N wall are latrine projections on the second and third storeys. The crowsteps of the E gable are finished with 'ecclesiastical' gablets and the northern skewputt have the letters I.M. (Jesus Maria) and a crowned M. In the later 16th century the house was doubled in length and a round stair tower built on the S side at the junction of the two portions. The main doorway is in the foot of the tower. The wall-head of the tower is corbelled out into the square, but there is no garret chamber.

Farnell is referred to in 1512 as 'palatium nostrum' by Bishop William Meldrum of Brechin, and remained a property of the bishops until 1566, when it was alienated and granted to the earl of Argyll, passing subsequently to the countess of Crawford. Farnell eventually became a Carnegie property and remains in the possession of the family.

25. Fiddes Castle, Stonehaven
NO 805 813

Off the A90(T), 5.25 miles SW of Stonehaven. Restored in the 1960s as a private residence, Fiddes stands to one side of a modern farm-steading, which serves to convey a better impression of its original role as a laird's house than examples where the towers survive alone, shorn of their ancillary buildings. It consists of a main block of three storeys over a vaulted basement, with a northern jam of similar size rising four storeys over the vaulted kitchen. On the SE and NE angles of the main block two turrets rise the full height of the building. The SE serves as the head of the straight service stair from the cellar to the 1st floor hall, and carries the stair to the bed-chambers in the upper floors of the main block. The NE turret contains the main staircase to the hall and the re-entrant between it and the northern jam has been infilled to form an entrance chamber at ground floor with small rooms above. The top of the tower was re-instated with a flat roof in the modern reconstruction, while the SE tower is corbelled out into the square and finished with crowstep gables and a saddle-back roof. There are bartizans corbelled out from the third storey on the northern angles of the jam and SW angle of the main block, while a secondary stair is corbelled out from the hall level at the NW of the main block.

The lands of Fiddes are on record in the 12th century, when William the Lion excluded them from the lordship of Kinneff which he had granted to William de Montfort. It is believed that they passed subsequently to the Arbuthnott family, but in 1439 they are recorded as the property of one John de Rate. In 1506 the property formed part of the lands of Sir James Arbuthnott, and remained with his descendants until the 17th century. The present castle is the work of Andrew Arbuthnott, who was given a charter of the lands in 1553.

26. Finavon Castle, Finavon
NO 497 566

Occupying an elevated site amongst trees on the Finavon estate, 8 miles WSW of Brechin off the A90(T), are the shattered ruins of the chief castle of the Lindsay earls of Crawford. The centrepiece of the castle was a substantial rectangular towerhouse, measuring 17.2m by 10.4m with walls 3m thick, possibly dating from the late 14th or early

15th century. Only the N wall, which is abutted by later buildings, survives above foundation level. The basement of the tower, which was unvaulted, had loop windows in either end gable, contained a well, and was entered from the N through a (possibly later) passage. In 1590 a large tower measuring 9.4m by 9.2m was added to the NE angle of the old tower, and a long block containing a scale-and-platt stair rising over a vaulted prison built into the re-entrant. This portion, too, is much ruined, but the E and N walls, rising to some 26.5m, still tower over the lower ruins of the rest of the castle. It consisted of four floors of private rooms over a vaulted cellar provided with splayed gunloops. Each room was lit by large windows protected by external grilles, and was provided with its own fireplace. Running N from the NW angle of this tower is a short stretch of curtain wall with gunloops, while what appears to have been an older and thicker wall can be traced running W from the early tower.

Finavon was resigned into the hands of David II in 1370 by William, earl of Ross. It was granted by Robert II, along with the office of keeper of the Forest of Platar, to David Annandale, but in 1375 the king granted it to Sir Alexander Lindsay. David, third earl of Crawford, died here in 1446 from wounds received in the Battle of Arbroath. His brother-in-law, Ogilvy of Inverquharity, who had been wounded in the same fight while on the opposing side, had also been brought to Finavon and was smothered with a pillow by his own sister following the earl's death. The eighth earl was imprisoned in his own castle for 13 weeks in 1530 by his son, known as the Wicked Master, who was eventually disinherited in favour of his cousin and ultimately died on the knife of a Dundee cobbler in the course of a drunken brawl. His son became tenth earl and restored the fortunes of the family with a huge dowry brought by his wife, a bastard daughter of Cardinal Beaton. In the later 16th century the castle was held by Lord Lindsay of the Byres, who built the NE tower in 1590, but returned to the earl of Crawford in 1608, only to be sold in 1629.

27. Forter Castle, Glen Isla NO 183 646

At Meikle Forter of the B951 in Glen Isla, 2.25 miles N of Brewlands Bridge. A gutted shell since its burning in 1640, Forter has recently been restored as a private residence. It consists of a rectangular main block 11.8m by 8m with a substantial 6.2m square tower, or wing, at the SE angle. The ground floor of the main block originally contained two cellars entered from a service passage along the S side which led to the kitchen at the W end. Two loops in the passage provided cover for the entrance, which lay in the re-entrant on the W wall of the wing. This contained a wide stair leading to the first floor hall. This was a fine chamber with a large fireplace in the S wall, and a privy opening from it in the SW angle formed by the projecting flue of the kitchen chimney. Access to the bed-chambers and private rooms on the upper floors of main block and jam was by a spiral stair contained in a turret corbelled out in the re-entrant angle. There are conical-roofed corbelled bartizans at the angles of the main block.

The lands of Forter were acquired by the Ogilvies of Airlie from the monks of Coupar Angus abbey. Soon after the 1560 Reformation, James Ogilvy began construction of the present castle. This was destroyed by the Earl of Argyll in 1640 during the descent of the Campbells and their Covenanting army on the lands of the Royalist Earl of Airlie. A report of this destruction made in 1661 appears to be a masterly piece of over-stated insurance claim on behalf of the Ogilvies, for it implies a comprehensive demolition of the castle. There is nothing in the present building to indicate that it is the product of a major 17th-century rebuilding.

28. Gardyne Castle, Friockheim NO 574 488

In private grounds 1.25 miles SW of Friockheim. Much of the present structure belongs to the later 17th and 19th centuries, long after the property had passed out of the hands of the Gardynes of that Ilk, but the E end of the main block is formed by a tower of *c.*1560 and there is a reset stone bearing the date 1568 and the defaced arms of the Gardynes. The tower was originally a simple rectangular structure of three storeys and an attic with a stair tower at the NW angle, corbelled out into the square at attic level of the main block. Its upper storey is reached by a separate stair-turret in the NE re-entrant. At attic level of the E gable are two highly unusual corbelled bartizans capped with conical roofs of stone contained within mock crenellations and provided with dummy dormers. Internally the tower is little altered, having a hall on the first floor over vaulted cellars and private chambers above. The summit chamber of the stair tower is decorated internally with some fine cable mouldings. To the W of the old portion is an extension dating probably from soon after 1682, when Gardyne passed to the Lyells of Dysart, which contains some fine pine-panelling.

Gardyne throughout the Middle Ages belonged to the family of Gardyne of that Ilk. Disputes with their Guthrie neighbours (see below) were to be settled through the marriage in 1558 of the laird of Guthrie to the daughter of the laird of Gardyne, but the murder of the son of that marriage by a Gardyne cousin reopened the feuding. In 1578 Patrick Gardyne of that Ilk was murdered by William Guthrie of that Ilk, who was in turn killed by the Gardynes in 1588. Following the subsequent murder of the then Gardyne of that Ilk, James VI stepped in to end the feud and forfeited both families. The Guthries recovered their property, but the Gardynes failed to do so and disappeared from the ranks of the local gentry.

29. Glamis Castle, Glamis*
NO 387 481

Lying at the heart of its extensive wooded policies immediately to the N of the village of Glamis. There is a fantasy quality about the profusion of conical-roofed turrets, balconied gables, wrought iron roof-ridges and decorative stonework which make Glamis one of the most-photographed castles in Scotland. Casual observation would suggest that the core of the castle is formed by the tall 15th-century L-plan tower which dominates its profile, but the oldest portion is in fact the lower, three-storey SE wing. This was built in *c.*1400 as a rectangular main block with a large round tower at its SE angle. Originally, it contained a hall at first-floor level over vaulted cellars and a kitchen, but has undergone considerable alteration in the 17th century and later.

The massive L-plan towerhouse was added in the mid-15th century as a free-standing block. The main section is 21.3m long by 11.4m wide and has a large jam 8.8m wide and projecting 6.3m at the E end of its S side. Its vaulted basement held kitchen and cellars. The original entrance to this tower was at first floor level on the W end of the S front, now converted into a window. It was flanked by two small guard-chambers and opened into what would have been a common hall measuring 15.5m by 6.4m. The stair to the upper floors lay in the re-entrant and was reached from this hall. The large circular stair tower which now fills the re-entrant, entered by the new main doorway at its foot, was added in 1608. The main hall of the castle lay on the second floor of the main block. This was a magnificent vaulted chamber measuring 16.45m by 6.4m, with a dais in front of the fireplace in its western wall, large recessed windows furnished with benches, and a private stair to the upper floors in the NW angle. There were originally latrines in the thickness of the NE angle at first and second floor level, but these have been broken through to form access passages into the later wings adjoining the tower.

Between 1528 and 1542, when the castle was in royal hands, the gap between the early building and the L-plan tower was bridged by a narrow block of chambers. The conversion of the castle into a sumptuous residence began in 1606 when the old tower was heightened and its skyline re-modelled with the provision of round chimney-stacks, conical-roofed bartizans, balustraded gables and a grand new stair-tower in the re-entrant. Further work between 1677 and 1695 saw the construction of a NW wing to balance the old SE block, which had its roof lowered and large new windows provided.

Glamis was an important royal thanage in central Strathmore but, despite Shakespearean tradition has no link with either King Duncan I or Macbeth. The lands were used by the crown throughout the 12th and 13th centuries as a source of revenue (the church of Glamis was granted by William the Lion to Arbroath Abbey, while the second teinds of the thanage went to Restenneth Priory). In the 14th century David II granted the thanage to Marjory, countess of Wigtown. The thanage passed out of royal control in 1372 when Robert II granted it to John Lyon of Forteviot. Lyon was a rising star under the early Stewart kings, serving as Chancellor to Robert II, and in 1376 married the king's daughter, Joanna. His rise, however, was resented by his neighbours, particularly the Lindsays of Crawford, and in 1382 he was murdered by Sir James Lindsay. The earliest portion of the castle was built by his son, another Sir John, soon after he attained his majority in 1400. His son, Patrick, was created first Lord Glamis in 1445, and was to be a loyal servant of James II. The castle was seized by James V after the death of the sixth Lord Glamis in 1528 in pursuit of his vendetta against the Douglases. The widowed Lady Glamis, a Douglas, was condemned for witchcraft and burned in Edinburgh. The property was restored to the seventh Lord Glamis in 1542. Patrick, ninth Lord Glamis, accompanied James VI S in 1603, and in 1606 was created Earl of Kinghorne. The second earl's loyalty to Charles I saw the plundering of house and estate by the Covenanting army under the Earl of Argyll in 1640, damage which was repaired by the third earl only in the 1680s. The castle is still in the hands of the (Bowes-)Lyon family.

30. Glenbervie House, Glenbervie NO 769 805

In private grounds at Glenbervie, off the A90(T) 7 miles SW of Stonehaven, the castle is still occupied as a private residence. The castle occupies a promontory site at the confluence of the Water of Bervie and Pilkettie Burn. The original block of the present structure, a long rectangle measuring 22m by 9.5m, lies across the neck of the promontory, cutting off the easy approach from the E. Built shortly before 1500 by Sir William Douglas of Braidwood, it is furnished with flanking round towers provided with cross loops with bottom roundels in their vaulted basements from which to cover the approach. The long central block contained three vaulted cellars over which was a hall, and a vaulted kitchen with private chamber above. The cellars and kitchen are linked by a service passage along the W front. A modern entrance has been cut through the northernmost of the three cellars. The house was considerably altered and extended in the 1850s, but the battlements on the SE tower which were built at that time have been removed and replaced by a conical roof to match that on the NE tower.

Glenbervie belonged to the Melvilles in the 13th century. It passed through the marriage in the 1460s of the heiress, Egidia Melville, to Sir Alexander Auchinleck. In 1492 Auchinleck's heiress married Sir William Douglas, a younger son of the Earl of Angus, builder of the castle. In 1572 it was besieged during the absence of the then laird by forces loyal to Queen Mary commanded by Sir Adam Gordon. Glenbervie remained in Douglas hands until 1675, when it was sold to Robert Burnett of Leys. It was sold on in 1721 to the Nicholsons of Mergie, with whose descendants it remains.

31. Guthrie Castle, Guthrie
NO 563 505

In private grounds to the N of the A932 Friockheim-Forfar road, 2 miles WNW of Friockheim. Forming the core around which a large, modern mansion has developed is a fine late 15th or early 16th-century rectangular towerhouse, rising to three storeys and a garret. In the basement are two cellars and a straight stair rising in the thickness of wall from the ground-floor entrance. Above is the hall, from which the stair rises in a spiral in projecting turret to finish in a cap-house now crowned with a modern pyramidal roof. Over the hall is a bed-chamber with further domestic accommodation in the garret. The parapet is carried on a fine corbel table with provision for rounds at the angles, but the crenellated parapet itself is a modern reconstruction.

The castle was occupied from the time of its construction until comparatively recently by the Guthries of Guthrie. It is believed that the tower may have been built by Sir David Guthrie of Kincaldrum, Treasurer to James III, who in 1466 received the lands of Guthrie from the crown, or by his son, Sir Alexander, who was killed at Flodden in 1513. Sir David's grandson married the daughter of the neighbouring Gardyne of that Ilk, and the murder of their son by one of his Gardyne cousins sparked years of feuding which saw the murder of the heads of both families and resulted ultimately in the forfeiture of both families for disturbing the peace. While the Guthries recovered their property through a junior branch, the Gardynes failed to regain theirs.

32. Hallgreen Castle, Inverbervie NO 832 721

Recently restored from near-dereliction and again serving as a private house, Hallgreen stands among trees overlooking Bervie Bay on the southern edge of Inverbervie. Occupying the site of a castle which may date back to the 14th century, the oldest part of the present structure appears to be an L-plan house of the late 16th century onto the N and W of which has been grafted a more modern mansion. The main block is 12.6m long by 7.6m wide and contains two vaulted cellars linked by a passage running along its W side. The jam extends from the S end of the W front and measures 5.4m wide and projects for 4.2m. It is unvaulted and may originally have contained a wide stair leading to the hall on the first floor of the main block. Above the hall are private chambers with pedimented dormer windows in the garret. The basement is provided with wide splayed gunloops on its S and E fronts, those on the E having double apertures. There are round, conical-roofed bartizans at the angles.

Hallgreen was originally part of the Dunnett properties of Inverbervie, but in the reign of James III the line ended with heiresses and their lordship was divided among the husbands of the various portioners. In 1478 Alexander Menzies, burgess of Aberdeen, granted his ninth portion of the lands of Inverbervie, 'known as le Hawgrene', in feu-ferme to his 'cousin', David Rait, another of the portioners of the estate. In 1488, however, Menzies resigned his rights to the crown, who granted superiority of the lands to Robert Arbuthnott of that Ilk. Hallgreen remained an Arbuthnott property into the

17th century, when it passed by marriage to the Halls.

33. Hatton Castle, Newtyle
NO 302 411

Rescued from complete ruin in the late 1980s, Hatton has been restored as a private residence. It lies on the lower slopes of Hatton Hill, at the SE edge of the village of Newtyle on the B954 Dundee-Meigle road. The castle is of Z-plan form, consisting of a rectangular central block with square towers at the NE and SW corners. The central block measures 18.3m long by 7.2m wide and contains two vaulted cellars at its W end and a kitchen at the E, linked by a service passage along the S front. The vaulted basement of the NE tower, approximately 6m square, opens from the kitchen, while a service stair to the upper floors rises in a turret in the re-entrant on the N. The western of the two cellars has a straight stair in its W wall leading up to the hall. The entrance, covered by two loops in the service passage, is in the E wall of the SW tower. The doorway opened into a small lobby with doors into the cellars and L-shaped guardroom under the wide scale-and-platt stair which leads to the upper floor. The upper storeys were reached above first floor level by a spiral stair built into the NW re-entrant, but this was removed probably in the 17th century.

The first floor of the main block contained the hall in its western three-quarters. This was a substantial chamber with a large fireplace in the S wall, service stairs leading down to the cellar at its W end and down to the kitchens and up to the laird's private rooms via the stair turret entered from the room's NE corner. The E end of the block was occupied by a withdrawing room with a privy formed in its SE corner. The upper floors of the NE tower provided the private accommodation for the laird and his family, reached by the spiral stair in the turret in its re-entrant, while the upper floor and garret of the main block and SW tower contained domestic accommodation.

The lands of Hatton were granted in the early 14th century to Sir Walter Oliphant and his wife, Isabella Douglas, but the early lords probably occupied the now-vanished Balcraig

Castle a little to the S. The present castle was constructed in 1575 for Patrick, fourth Lord Oliphant. In 1627 the estate passed to the Halyburtons of Pitcur and was garrisoned in 1645 by the Earl of Crawford in the Covenanting interest against Charles I. Later in the 17th century the castle passed to the son of the Lord Advocate Sir George Mackenzie of Rosehaugh, nephew of the Earl of Seaforth, notorious as a prosecutor of the Covenanters under Charles II.

34. Hynd Castle, Kirkbuddo NO 505 416

Lying in a plantation of trees on the southern edge of agricultural ground to the S of the unclassified road between the B978 and A958 1.25 miles S of Kirkbuddo. The shattered remains of the castle occupy the level summit of a low mound which may be a motte. The structure appears to have been a simple tower 9.1m square, possibly of the 14th or 15th century, with a splayed loop in its northern wall. It has been extensively plundered for stone, leaving only the massive angles of the unvaulted basement upstanding. There is no record of its early owners or history.

35. Inglismaldie Castle NO 644 669

In private grounds overlooking the gravel terraces above the River North Esk, 4 miles SW of Laurencekirk off the A90(T). The core of the mansion is a tall L-plan towerhouse of the late 16th century. Rising to three storeys and a garret, the present turreted roof-line represents modern restoration. The jam, which contained the original entrance, has largely been replaced by a modern wing, and a modern entrance cut through the S wall of the main block. A band of label moulding runs round the main block above the first floor windows of the hall, and similar label corbelling supports the bartizans at the angles and midway along the S side. The conical roofs of the bartizans are modern reconstructions, the turrets having been cut down and covered by the oversailing roof of the main block.

Inglismaldie was originally Church property. In 1588 the

lands were granted by James VI to John Livingstone of Dunipace, who built the towerhouse soon after receiving possession. The lands passed in 1635 to John Carnegie, earl of Ethie, and were sold on in 1693 to David Falconer of Newton and remained with the Falconer family until the beginning of this century.

36. Invergowrie House, Dundee NO 363 304

In the grounds of Ninewells Hospital in the western suburbs of Dundee overlooking the Tay. Invergowrie House is a large, rambling pile that has been altered and extended considerably over the centuries. The oldest portion of the house carries the date 1601 on a panel over the entrance, but it is probable that building commenced soon after 1560 when the lands of Invergowrie, formerly a property of Scone Abbey, came into the possession of Sir John Carnegie. At the core of the structure there may be the remains of an L-plan house, but the clearest early fabric is the long rectangular block which runs N-S at the W end of the house. This rises to three storeys, the basement being vaulted as cellars and with the kitchen in the southern extremity of the range. The doorway lies at the northern end of the W front and is defended by a shot-hole in the stair turret which is corbelled out to the S of it from first floor level. There is a single original bartizan, conical roofed and furnished with shot-holes, at the SW angle. All the window openings have been enlarged, and the large oriels in the W and S walls at first floor level, plus the pediments of the second floor windows, belong to a major reconstruction of the house in 1837. Some early 17th-century pediments bearing the arms of Gray and Napier and the initials PG and AN for Patrick Gray and Agnes Napier, mottoes and the date 1601, are reused in the modern N porch.

The royal lands of Invergowrie, where the notoriously unreliable 16th-century historian Hector Boece claimed King Edgar (d.1107) had built a stone castle, were granted to the abbey of Scone by King Alexander I (*d.*1124). At the Reformation the estate passed to Sir John Carnegie, who in

1568 sold it to Sir Patrick Gray, builder of the house. Gray was implicated in the Gowrie House Conspiracy of 1600 against James VI, and the estate was forfeited and the newly-completed house given to David Murray, first Viscount Stormont. In 1615 Murray sold the property to Robert Clayhills of Baldovie, with whose descendants it remained until the 20th century.

37. Invermark Castle, Glen Esk NO 443 804

On an elevated site immediately to the N of the River North Esk, on the promontory formed by the confluence of that river with the Water of Mark at the head of the unclassified public road up Glen Esk. The round-angled tower of Invermark, now standing in splendid isolation but formerly possessing a barmkin and out-buildings on its S side, rises to four storeys and an attic. The barrel-vaulted basement, lit by two horizontal gunloops and accessible only by a newel stair in the thickness of the SW angle, the hall above, and the second storey bed-chamber reached by a stair in the NW angle date from the early 16th century. Traces of a corbelled parapet show that the upper storey, SE angle turret and attic, the latter lit by windows which pierce the tall chimney stacks in the N and S walls, were added in *c.*1600. The entrance to the tower is at first-floor level in the S side and is still protected by its original yett. Access was by ladder or removable timber stair.

Invermark formed part of the Stirling lordship of Glenesk which came into the hands of the Lindsays in the mid-14th century. Although isolated, it was a strategic location which controlled the Mounth Road from Glen Tanar in Aberdeenshire and the southern routes into Glens Clova and Lethnot, and probably also functioned as a hunting-seat. The ninth earl of Crawford died here in 1558.

38. Inverquharity Castle, Kirriemuir NO 411 579

In private grounds 3 miles NE of Kirriemuir off the B955. The castle, a ruin since the 18th century, was restored in the

1960s and serves once again as a private residence. The lands of Inverquharity formed a portion of the lordship of Kirriemuir which were held before 1420 by Walter Ogilvy of Lintrathen from William Douglas, earl of Angus. In that year Walter granted Inverquharity to his younger brother, John. The present castle was probably begun by his son, Alexander, who in 1444 received royal licence to fortify his house and defend the entrance with an iron yett. Inverquharity remained with this branch of the Ogilvies until the early 18th century.

The tower was of L-plan, consisting of a main block 13.4m long by 10m wide with a jam 8m wide. The jam was demolished in the 19th century to provide stone for a farm-steading and has been replaced by a modern three storeyed extension. The entrance to the tower, defended at the wall-head by an overhanging machicolation, opened directly into the vaulted basement. Corbels at the point where the vault begins to spring from the walls shows that there was a timber floor dividing the chamber into two levels. The lower probably served as storage and possibly as a byre, while the upper may have formed accommodation for servants. Both levels are poorly lit by slit windows. There appears to have been a service stair at the N end, leading up to the hall, but the principal access was via a spiral stair built into the thickness of the wall at the re-entrant angle. This did not open directly into the hall, but opens instead onto a passage which through the thickness of the E wall between the main block and jam, turns through a dog-leg and enters the hall through a doorway in the N wall. The hall is a fine, lofty chamber which rises 6.3m to the apex of the vault. A window high up in the S gable suggests that this level, like the basement, may have been divided into two by a timber floor. The hall has mural chambers in the N and W walls, and in the NW angle there is a strange porch-like projection which may originally have covered the head of the now removed service stair. The dais stood at the S end in front of the large fireplace and is flanked to E and W by recessed windows provided with stone benches. The jam at this level was divided into two floors – possibly a kitchen with the laird's room above – strengthening the suggestion that the hall itself may have been so divided. The top storey lies partly within the gabled roof contained within the parapet. Fireplaces at either end suggest that this was divided into two bed-chambers.

The parapet walk is carried on a finely moulded corbel table and has large open rounds at the angles. This appears to be a remodelling of the original wall-head undertaken in the 16th century. At parapet level there is also a large cap-house, entered from the wall-walk, positioned over the stair-head.

39. Kelly Castle, Arbirlot*
NO 608 402

In private grounds overlooking the Elliot Water, 0.4 miles SE of Arbirlot. The castle occupies a rocky site, protected on the N by the deep channel of the Elliot Water. It consists of a 16th-century four-storey and attic L-plan tower attached to a courtyard surrounded by lower ranges of domestic offices. Entrance to the courtyard is through a gabled pend protected by shot-holes in a flanking squat, cylindrical angle tower. The buildings which are ranged round the interior of the courtyard are largely 19th-century. The towerhouse itself is massively-built of coursed red sandstone rubble. The main block contains vaulted cellars and a kitchen at courtyard level, with pine-panelled hall on the first floor and private chambers above. The doorway is in the re-entrant and opens on a wide staircase in the jam which leads to the hall. The upper floors of the jam, which rises a full storey and garret higher than the main block, are private chambers. There are two bartizans, one round and corbelled out above the fourth storey, the other square and corbelled out above the third. This latter, which bears close similarities to the early 17th-century example at Amisfield in Dumfriesshire, rises two storeys above the height of the main block and is finished in a gabled cap-house. Its upper storeys are reached by a stair in a turret corbelled out in the re-entrant.

Kelly was a property of the Mowbray family, forfeited by Robert I for their adherence to the English in the Wars of Independence. King Robert granted the estate to Robert

Stewart, and confirmed it in the possession of Walter Stewart in the 1320s. In 1444 William Ochterlony acquired an interest in the estate, which by 1466 had been renamed Ochterlony. The lands appear to have remained with the Ochterlonies until 1614, when they were sold to Sir William Irvine, who was probably responsible for the enlargement of the house and construction of the square bartizan. Irvine ruined himself fighting in the Royalist interest and Kelly was sold in 1679 to the Earl of Panmure for £11,000 Scots. It was given in 1681 to Harry Maule, brother of the then earl, who was to become one of the most capable of the Jacobite commanders in the 1715 Rising. The Maule brothers fled abroad after the collapse of the rebellion, never to return, and their properties were forfeited. Kelly was allowed to decay, but came eventually into the hands of the Maule-Ramsay earls of Dalhousie, who restored the building in the 19th century.

40. Kincardine Castle, Fettercairn NO 671 751

On the summit of a tree-crowned hillock immediately to the W of the unclassified road between the B966 and B974 1.75 miles E of Fettercairn. The overgrown remains of a large courtyard castle are all that survives of what was once one of the most important royal fortresses in NE Scotland. A regular residence of both William the Lion and his son, Alexander II, Kincardine was a favoured hunting-seat of the Scottish kings in the 13th century (see below). The walls have been stripped of their facing stones and reduced largely to footings, but can be seen to have been 2.2m wide above a broad plinth, and to have formed an enclosure roughly 34m square. Traces of a 7m-wide range on the E side may mark the position of the hall block, while a narrower range along the N side probably housed the main private chambers. Towards the western end of the S wall are the badly-robbed remains of the main entrance between two rubble-choked towers. The only feature recognisable is a pair of latrine chutes in the W wall of the western tower.

It was to the young King Alexander II at Kincardine in

1215 that Ferchar MacTaggart, lord of Applecross, sent the heads of the defeated McWilliam rebels. In 1296 the first stages of the abdication of John Balliol to Edward I of England were performed within the castle. Despite its decline in popularity as a royal hunting-seat after 1296, it remained a royal castle in the custody of the Woods, the builders of nearby Balbegno. A community which had grown up in the shadow of the castle was in 1532 created county town, but the removal of the courts to Stonehaven during the reign of James VI marked the beginning of a process of decay which led to the ultimate disappearance of the village.

41. Lauriston Castle, St. Cyrus NO 759 666

The castle occupies a commanding position overlooking a deep den to the W of the B9120, 1.75 miles NE of St. Cyrus. Lauriston is a complex structure of several phases, all now in a sadly advanced state of decay. The earliest surviving portions appear to be the remains of a courtyard castle of the 15th century, the large SE tower having formed its main residential element. This tower has undergone a major reconstruction *c.*1600, when it was transformed into a fine L-plan residence. A stair is carried in a turret at its SW angle, corbelled out from the first floor. The building is in a very unstable condition and much of the interior has collapsed, but the basement contains two vaulted cellars, one roughly 2m deeper than the other, from which it is reached via a short flight of stairs. This may have formed the prison of the 15th-century tower.

Until comparatively recently the SE tower was connected to the square tower at the SW angle of the castle by a surviving length of the original curtain wall, complete with parapet and wall-walk. This has now collapsed, leaving the tower standing in isolation. The tower rises from the rocky lip of the den, its vaulted basement containing a shaft which descends to the foot of the ravine. Above this sub-level the original tower rises for three storeys, but has suffered the addition of an ugly modern superstructure of a further three storeys. The original parapet, carried on simple corbels and with plain rounds at the SW and SE angles, survives on the S side.

Lauriston was held from the 1240s by the Stirling family, who were succeeded in the late 14th century by the Straitons. Alexander Straiton was one of the Lowland casualties in 1411 at the battle of Harlaw in Aberdeenshire. The family held Lauriston until 1695 when the estate passed to Sir James Falconer of Phesdo.

42. Logie House, Kirriemuir NO 392 521

In private grounds 1 mile S of Maryton, off the unclassified road from Maryton to Mains of Ballindarg. The main part of the house is a simple rectangular towerhouse of the 16th century with a circular stair tower at its NE angle, built for the Wisharts. The whole building has undergone considerable reconstruction in the late 17th or 18th century when it had come into the hands of the Kinlochs of Kilrie, at which time the wall-head has been altered and the upper stages of the stair tower cut down and covered by the over-sailing roof of the main block. The building has also been extended to the W at that time. The upper storeys have been remodelled, but the basement contains a vaulted service passage which links two vaulted chambers, one a cellar the other the kitchen. A dormer pediment bearing the date 1688, presumably removed at the time of the re-fashioning of the wall-head of the tower, is built into the wall of the yard. Various low buildings abut the N side of the main block.

43. Mains Castle, Dundee* NO 401 330

Overlooking the Den o' Mains in the northern suburbs of the city. Mains, for so long a derelict, vandalised and gutted ruin, has recently been restored. Although it is likely that there was an earlier structure on the site, the oldest portions of the present castle date from the mid-16th century. The main buildings occupy the N, E and S sides of a central courtyard, the W closed by a high curtain wall. This is pierced halfway along its length by the main gate, a high archway above which is the massive corbelled base of a bartizan. There is the corbelled base of a second bartizan at the NW angle. The superstructures of both, together with the linking parapet, were relatively complete as recently as the 1960s, but disappeared at the hands of vandals in the 1970s.

The main accommodation lies in the N range, originally an L-plan house of *c.*1560 with its main block lying E-W and a massive stair-tower projecting from the W end of its S front. A later extension, 1m narrower than the main block, has been built onto its W end into the NW angle of the courtyard. The entrance lies in the re-entrant at the foot of the stair-tower, which is the most striking feature of the castle. The tower rises through six storeys and is finished with a corbelled-out cap-house with gables on all four faces. This final stage, designed as a watch-chamber to look out over the rapidly rising ground to the S of the castle, is a 17th-century addition. The main block comprised a vaulted basement of two compartments, with a hall above and private rooms in the garret.

The E range bears the date 1582 and contained a kitchen on the ground floor at its N end. A wide stair leads up to the first floor from a finely-detailed Renaissance doorway at its S end, suggesting that the first floor rooms in this block superseded those in the N range as the main public chambers of the castle. The S range has been demolished with the exception of the courtyard wall to the full height of its ground floor. Blocked windows in the S end of the W wall show that a late range of buildings stood here, but no trace of these survives on the interior.

Originally the Mains of Claverhouse, a property of the Earls of Angus, Mains was acquired in 1530 by John Graham of Balargus, a cadet of the Stirlingshire Grahams of Fintry. His son, Sir David, changed the name of the property to Mains of Fintry and built both main elements of the existing structure. Sir David was executed in 1593 for his involvement in the conspiracy known as the Spanish Blanks, but the Grahams retained the property. Passing subsequently to the Erskines, it was sold in 1913 to Sir James Caird, one of Dundee's great industrial magnates and a notable benefactor of the city, who handed it and its grounds over to the then Dundee Corporation for use as a park. The castle, sadly, was allowed to decay until the 1970s when the first steps were made to protect and consolidate the ruins, and in the 1980s Dundee District Council undertook an excellent programme of restoration and refurbishment.

44. Melgund Castle, Aberlemno NO 546 564

At Mains of Melgund farm, 2 miles NE of Aberlemno off the B9134. Excavation and consolidation of the stonework is being undertaken currently in advance of the restoration of the castle as a private residence. Appearances are deceptive at Melgund, for what looks at first to be a double-stepped L-plan tower of *c.*1500 onto which a later 16th-century hall block has been grafted is in fact all of one build of *c.*1540. The tower rises to four storeys and a garret contained within a parapet with rounds at the angles carried on a rich corbel table. The long block to the E rises to two storeys and an attic, the wall-head on the S side finished with the same rich corbelling and parapet. There is a small round tower at the NE angle, gunloops in the lower floor of which provided covering fire along the main N front and E gable of the castle. The castle is provided with numerous gunloops in the basement and first floor, but the first floor windows are large and do not appear to have been covered by grilles. The large windows in the S wall of the lower block lit the hall at first floor level, two having high sills so that large pieces of wall furniture could be positioned below them. The whole structure measures 31m long by 12.5m wide for most of its length, narrowing to nearer 9m at the 'towerhouse' at the W end.

The entrance was in the now missing N wall of the wide portion, opening into a service passage running E-W along the building and linking the main stair in the 'jam' of the tower to a service stair at the E end of the block. Although it was an internal doorway, the entrance from the passage to the foot of the main stair could be closed with a stout timber door with a drawbar, effectively turning the W end of the building into a self-contained towerhouse. Opposite the foot of the stair is a recess for the porter. A narrower passage continues to the W, forming the 'step' within the re-entrant between the main tower and the stair jam. This leads to two vaulted cellars under the tower, the E having a service stair to the first floor, the W having two recesses in its outer angles provided with gunloops. Immediately to the E of the tower was the kitchen, with oven and fireplace in the W wall. The chimney flue was carried in the thick E wall of the tower, but this has collapsed and carried with it the vaulted ceiling of the kitchen. E of this again are vaulted cellars. The polygonal vaulted room in the basement of the NE tower is reached along a short passage in the E end of the service corridor.

On the first floor doorways from the main stair opened into a large private room in the tower, into the hall, and into the western of three private chambers in the missing N range over the service corridor. The laird's room in the tower was a splendid chamber, occupying the entire floor. It was provided with fine large windows with stone benches in the W and S walls, a rather small fireplace, two recesses in its outer angles with gunloops, and a private latrine with closet opening from it in the step in the re-entrant. The hall, 11m long, has a fine large fireplace in its N wall, three windows in the S – the two western with high sills, the eastern with stone benches – and a service stair rising from the cellars in its SW angle. A door at the E end of its N wall leads to the middle of the three rooms in the N range. Adjacent to it in the E wall is a doorway leading to a large withdrawing room. The attics of the low block and the upper floors of the tower contained bedchambers.

The castle is believed to have been built by Cardinal David Beaton, tradition recounting that it was here that he kept his mistress, Marion Ogilvy. After Beaton's assassination in 1546 it passed to his kinsman, David Bethune. In the 17th century Melgund passed to the Gordons of Huntly, and subsequently to the Maules and Murrays before eventually descending through marriage of an heiress to the Elliots of Minto, the heir to the earls of Marchmont still bearing the title of Viscount Melgund.

45. Murroes Castle, Murroes
NO 461 350

Overlooking the valley of the Sweet Burn in Murroes village, off the B978 Broughty Ferry – Kellas road. Restored and occupied as a private residence, the castle is clearly visible from the main road through the village. The castle appears to have originated as a simple rectangular towerhouse of the 16th century, but has been lengthened and probably lowered in height in the early 17th century. As it stands, it is a long two-storeyed block, lying N-S, with a semi-circular stair-turret projecting midway along its W side. There are numerous gunloops and shot-holes in the walls, and the original windows have finely-moulded surrounds. The steeply-sloping ground on which the castle is built has resulted in a number of peculiarities of lay-out, the most notable being that the turret, which rises from ground-level externally is supported internally on corbels placed 1.54m above the floor of the kitchen. There is some fine panelling in the upper rooms, brought to Murroes from Fotheringham House, the demolished chief seat of the Fotheringham owners of Murroes.

46. Old Panmure Castle, Muirdrum
NO 544 376

In the middle of the Panmure estate, lying to the N of the A92 Dundee-Arbroath road 1.5 miles NW of Muirdrum. The ruins occupy a position of great natural strength on a promontory which projects from the N into the valley of the Monikie Burn, 1 mile SSE of the site of the demolished 17th-century palace of the Maules.

This site is more fragmentary and overgrown than many included in this gazetteer, but it is a ruin of great architectural importance. From descriptions of the remains made in the 17th century and confirmed largely by 'excavations' by the earl's gardener in the 19th century, it is clear that Panmure was a stronghold of some scale. The ruins are those of a quadrangular castle measuring 34.1m NS by 36.2m EW, provided with square towers at all four angles. The NW tower appears to have been the 'great tower' or keep. This was in ruins in the early 16th century and was replaced in 1530 by a cylindrical tower, but the lower stages of the older work survive. Clearance of the ruins in the 19th century revealed a series of structures ranged around the interior of the N, E, S and southern end of the W walls, identified from the 17th-century account as a hall range to the N (across the original entrance) with domestic accommodation to the E. The chapel lay at the SE angle, S of the later main gate. To the N of the castle, heavily overgrown with trees, is an extensive outer bailey with prominent earthen bank and water-filled ditch across the neck of the promontory.

Although it is clear even from the scanty ruins which remain that the castle has undergone rebuilding in several periods, it is probable that the original quadrangle is of 13th-century date and bears close similarities to other early castles such as Kinclaven, Kincardine (see above), and Tarbert. The lands of Panmure were held in the later 12th century by Philip de Valognes, chamberlain of William the Lion, who confirmed them in 1198 x 1200 in the possession of his son, William de Valognes. The earthwork remains, and possibly the earliest phases of stone building, may belong to the time of Philip (d.1215) or William (d.1219), both of whom were influential men of standing. In 1224 Panmure passed via William's only daughter, Christina, to the Maules, with whom it remained until recent times. The castle was occupied by the English during the first phase of the Wars of Independence, and was held during the second phase by Richard Talbot, one of the chief supporters of Edward Balliol. It was captured in 1335 by Sir Andrew Murray, Guardian of Scotland. The castle was still occupied in the 16th century, but was little more than a shattered ruin in the early 17th century, probably having been plundered for stone to build the Maule's magnificent new house of Panmure, itself demolished in 1955.

47. Pitcur Castle, Pitcur
NO 252 370

In the farmyard of Pitcur farm, off the A923 Dundee-Coupar Angus road, 3.5 miles SE of Coupar Angus. The substantial towerhouse at Pitcur may represent two separate phases of building, with a projecting wing having been grafted onto the N side of a large rectangular block which measures 13.5m by 8m with walls 1.4m thick. The eastern wall of the jam is not flush with the E wall of the tower, being stepped back to the S by some 1.2m, and with a larger re-entrant on the NW it forms a T-plan rather than L-plan house. The stair is carried from the ground floor in a circular turret in the NW re-entrant angle. The entrance, a round-headed archway defended by a yett, is in the N wall of the jam. Over the door is a vacant recess for an armorial panel. The basement of the jam contained the kitchen, the vault of which has fallen in, while there are two vaulted cellars under the main block. On the first floor of the main tower was the hall, a large chamber with a fireplace flanked by two narrow slit windows in the E wall and two large recessed windows in the S wall. The W end of the chamber may have been partitioned-off as a screens passage. Opening off the hall in the wing is what was probably the laird's private chamber, provided with a privy contrived in a dog-leg passage in the thickness of the N wall of the main block. Above the hall were at least two storeys of private chambers. At some stage after the abandonment of the castle the upper works have been remodelled with all trace of corbelling or parapet removed and the walls capped instead with flat coping, presumably to stabilise them and prevent masonry from collapsing into the farmyard.

Pitcur belonged to a branch of the Chisholms in the 14th century. On the death of Alexander Chisholm the estate was divided between his two daughters, the eldest, who in 1432 married Walter, younger son of Sir Walter Haliburton of Dirleton, receiving the castle as caput of the lordship of Pitcur. On the extinction of the main line of the Haliburtons in 1505, the Pitcur branch became heads of the kindred.

48. Pitkerro Castle, Dundee NO 453 337

In private grounds 0.25 miles NE of the crossroads of the B961 and B978, 1.2 miles N of the Claypotts Roundabout. Pitkerro was originally a small towerhouse of the late 16th century, but it has been greatly enlarged and elaborated in the first decade of the 20th century to plans by Sir Robert Lorimer. The old house comprised a long two-storeyed block with a circular tower containing the stair and the main doorway – with the date 1593 and initials ID and IF (for James Durham and his unidentified wife) carved on the lintel – in its S re-entrant projecting from its eastern side. The stair tower is corbelled out into the square and rises one storey higher than the main block, the stair turret giving access to its upper level being carried on a squinch arch over the S re-entrant. The bartizan at the SW angle of the main block was reinstated by Lorimer. The interior has been greatly altered, but the basement, which was never vaulted, can be seen to have comprised a kitchen and three cellars. Pitkerro was by 1534 in the hands of James Durham, younger son of Durham of Grange of Monifieth. The castle would appear to be the work of his son, also James.

49. Powrie Castle, Dundee
NO 421 346

Powrie, or more correctly Wester Powrie, lies on gentle S-facing slopes looking over Strathdichty to the E of the A90(T) Dundee-Forfar road on the northern outskirts of the city. The castle now consists of two detached portions: a large Z-plan towerhouse and a long two storey block. The towerhouse is the earlier of the two buildings, dating from the later 16th century. The lower storey of the main block may belong to an early 16th-century plain rectangular tower onto which the round angle towers have been grafted, its massively thick walling (nearly 2m, while the walling of the upper levels is considerably thinner) being unique among surviving Z-plan towers. There is, however, no firm evidence to support this suggestion. The towerhouse, which bears close similarities to nearby Claypotts and was probably designed by the same mason-architect, is a complete ruin, its SW tower destroyed and its upper storeys above the first-floor great hall gone. What survives shows it to have been a building of some refinement. The entrance is positioned in the centre of the N wall of the main block, and is defended by a shot-hole in the foot of the main stair turret which rises to its E in the NW re-entrant with the NE tower.

The entrance opens into a short passage which leads eastwards past the foot of the main stair into the square, vaulted kitchen in the circular NE tower. Two vaulted cellars open from the passage immediately inside the main door, the W having a doorway in its SW corner that led into the basement of the now vanished angle tower. The main stair appears to have risen the full height of the building to serve all storeys. There is no sign that there was a service stair connected to the SW tower. The hall, with its high barrel-vault, occupied the whole first floor of the main block. It has been a magnificent chamber with a large fireplace in the N wall and five large recessed windows. The NE tower contains a private room with fireplace.

The detached block lies slightly to the NW of the towerhouse. It consists of a long main block measuring 22m by 6m, with a conical-roofed round tower at its NW angle and a square two-storeyed porch off-centre in its S wall. This is a fine building with several features of quality, notably the pilasters which flank the windows in its upper storey. Over one of the porch windows is the date 1604. The basement contains a kitchen at the E end, a bakery at the W, and cellars in between. Access to the upper floor was via a timber stair to the doorway in the projecting porch. The laird's room lies to the W, with a private room opening off it into the NW tower.

The lands of Powrie were granted, together with those of Ogilvy and Kilmundie in Glamis, by William the Lion before 1174 to Gilbert, son of the earl of Angus, from whom the Ogilvies may be descended. While the Fotheringhams acquired the lordship of Powrie by marriage in 1412, in 1428 James I confirmed a charter of Alexander Ogilvy of that Ilk ratifying a grant to Walter Ogilvy of the lands of Wester Powrie. Wester Powrie, however, subsequently also passed into Fotheringham ownership. The old castle was burned in 1492 by the Scrimgeours and again in 1547 by the English garrison of Broughty Castle (see above).

50. Redcastle, Inverkeilor NO 688 510

On an elevated mound overlooking Lunan Bay at the mouth of the Lunan Water, reached by a footpath from the unclassified road from Inverkeilor to Lunan Bay, 2.25 miles NE of Inverkeilor. The rich red sandstone ruins of Redcastle are in an advanced state of decay, a further portion of the structure having fallen in the course of storms in the winter of 1994-5. The remains of the castle form two distinct portions: a high curtain wall to the E, with NE angle and part of the N return surviving, and the N gable and parts of the E and W walls of a towerhouse. The towerhouse, a rectangular structure originally 13.5m by 10m, dates from the late 15th century, and has been a fine structure of dressed sandstone ashlar. It rose to four storeys with a garret enclosed within a corbelled parapet with open rounds at the angles. Externally, the northern wall is blank, but on the interior there are fireplaces in the hall at first floor level and in the third floor room, while there is a mural closet opening to the NE in the second floor. The basement does not appear to have been vaulted, and there are the mutilated remains of slits with wide internal splays in its E and W walls. There are the remains of large recessed windows in the hall and second floor, looking out over the bay, and in the third floor looking W.

Opinions differ on the dating of the curtain wall. It has recently been suggested that this is also 15th-century, contemporary with the building of the towerhouse. Its relationship with the tower, however, points rather towards it being an earlier feature into which the tower has been inserted, and it is probable that it should be dated to the 13th century. Excavations to the NW of the castle in the early 1980s demonstrated the presence of an outer ditch and earthen rampart of medieval date, possible contemporary with the earliest phases of defence at the site in the 12th century, and also vestigial traces of still earlier fortifications.

The lands of Inverkeilor were granted by William the Lion to Walter de Berkeley, the royal chamberlain. On Walter's death in *c.*1194 his lands passed, via his daughter, into the hands of a branch of the Balliol family, the probable builders of the first stone castle on the site. At the end of the 13th century the lands appear to have passed, again through heiresses, to the Umfraville and Percy family, and remained divided thereafter. Both families were forfeited by Robert I during the Wars of Independence and the portions of the lordship of Inverkeilor were thereupon granted to Donald Campbell and Hugh, earl of Ross, Campbell apparently receiving the castle. In 1367 Andrew Campbell sold the lands to Robert Stewart of Schanbothy, and Redcastle remained with his descendants, the Stewarts of Innermeath, builders of the towerhouse.

51. Thornton Castle, Laurencekirk NO 688 718

In private grounds to the W of the B9120 Laurencekirk-Fettercairn road, 3 miles NW of Laurencekirk. This is a well-preserved L-plan towerhouse of *c.*1500 with lower extensions of various dates from the 16th century to more modern times. The towerhouse rises to four storeys and garret, the latter being a modern restoration, with a crenellated parapet with open rounds at the angles carried on a rich table of chequered corbelling. There is an additional corbelled half-round in the middle of the parapet on the E side of the main block to carry the walk round a large chimney. The doorway was in the re-entrant angle at the SE, but this has been infilled by a single storey structure in more recent times. The two storeyed range which extends E from the tower and then returns S to form two sides of a square, probably lies on the site of ranges grouped round the interior of a barmkin wall. There is a large four storey cylindrical tower at the NE angle of these ranges. Internally the towerhouse has undergone considerable alteration, but the basement vaults survive, as does the wide newel stair in the jam. The hall on the first floor is now panelled, but traces of tempera painting have been found behind the woodwork.

Held by the Thorntons of that Ilk in the 13th century, Thornton was confirmed in the possession of one Valentine Thornton in the reign of Robert Bruce, despite the tradition that it passed by marriage early in 1309 to Sir James

Strachan. The Strachans, however, appear to have gained possession in the course of the 14th century and held it down into the late 17th century. It was bought back by the family in 1893 and is still their private residence.

52. Tilquhillie Castle, Banchory NO 772 741

In private grounds looking NE towards the River Dee 2 miles SE of Banchory off the unclassified road between the B974 at Bridge of Feugh and A957 at Blairydryne. Although complete and roofed, Tilquhillie stood derelict for many years until recently restored as a private residence. It is a tall but plain-looking Z-plan house of four storeys, but a number of unusual features lend it some character. The angles of main block and jams are all rounded from ground level to within 1m of the wall-heads, where they are corbelled out into the square and finished with crowsteps on the gable ends. The entrance is placed in a straight stretch of wall built diagonally across the re-entrant between the main block and SW jam, which then rises as an angled stair tower to a level mid way between the fourth and fifth storeys. A second service stair, corbelled out from the second storey, also rises in a turret formed by a length of straight walling built across the re-entrant. Over the doorway there is a much worn heraldic panel.

The entrance opens into a curious passage which goes through one and a half turns round the stair – which rises in a straight flight immediately to the left of the door – into a vaulted kitchen in the SW jam. The E wall of the kitchen is provided with three gunloops which cover the entrance. A doorway immediately to the right of the entrance leads into a vaulted cellar under the E end of the main block, from which access is gained to a further vaulted cellar in the basement of the NE tower. A later doorway has been cut through the N wall of the first of these cellars. A second doorway in the N side of the entrance passage opens into a cellar under the W end of the main block, from which a straight service stair in the N wall leads up to the hall at first floor level.

Tilquhillie was Church property in the Middle Ages, being

a possession of Arbroath Abbey. It was probably before 1560 that it passed into the hands of the Ogstouns, possibly by a grant in feu ferme, before passing by marriage to David Douglas, son of the laird of Lochleven. It was his son, John, who in 1576 built the present castle. The Douglases of Tilquhillie supported Charles I and suffered the privilege of having their house garrisoned by the Covenanters. In 1665 the estate passed by marriage to the Crichtons of Cluny.

53. Vayne Castle, Noranside
NO 493 599

On the N side of the Noran Water in agricultural land on Vayne farm, 2.25 miles SE of Noranside on the unclassified road from Noranside to Careston. The shattered ruins of Vayne show it to have been a building of some sophistication and architectural pretensions. It was a Z-plan structure consisting of a rectangular main block measuring 12.4m by 7.7m, with a tower 7m square at the NE angle and a round tower 6.4m in diameter at the SW. There is a round stair-turret in the re-entrant between the NE tower and the E gable of the main block. The entrance, with moulded surround, is in the E side of the round tower, defended by a double-mouthed horizontal gun-loop beneath the sill of the adjacent window in the main block. Corbelling in the re-entrant above the doorway shows that the stair to the now largely vanished upper floors was carried in a turret in this position. Most of the building above basement level has collapsed, but the high-standing masonry of the gables show it to have been of three storeys with an attic. There is no trace surviving of a courtyard, but it is probable that the 30m wide terrace S of the castle, which ends abruptly at the steep embankment down to the Noran, was formerly enclosed by a barmkin.

The doorway has opened onto a wide stairway in the round tower leading up to the first floor hall, while a door to the right of the entrance has opened into a service passage along the S side of the building. Opening from this was a cellar in the W end of the main block, provided with its own service stair to the hall above. The E end was occupied by a kitchen, from which a door in the NE opened to the foot of the service stair in the turret and into the basement of the NE tower. The fireplaces in the gables show that above the hall the main block was occupied by private chambers, while the upper stages of both jams also contained private rooms.

Vayne was a Lindsay property built probably in the 1550s or 1560s, rather than as late as 1580-1600 as has recently been suggested. The Lindsays held the lordship of Vayne until the 17th century, when it was sold to the Carnegies of Kinnaird. Robert Carnegie, third earl of Southesk, appears to have undertaken a refurbishment of the castle in the 1670s, a tympanum from one of the windows in the upper storeys which bears his initials and the date 1678 is reused as the lintel of a gate in the garden of the nearby farm.

Burgh Defences

1. The Wishart Arch or Cowgate Port, Dundee NO 405 306

One of only two remaining medieval town gates in Scotland – the other is the West Port of St. Andrews – the Wishart Arch stands isolated on the N side of the inner ring road at the E end of the Cowgate. It is not entirely clear whether or not the gate stands in its original position, but the structure is believed to date from at least the early 16th century. In 1544 it was said to have served as a preaching platform from which the Protestant martyr, George Wishart, addressed the victims of the 1544 plague. Dundee possessed a circuit of walls until their destruction in the course of General Monck's siege in the early 1650s, but if the wall at the gate is in any way representative of its general form, it can hardly have offered a substantial deterrent to determined attackers. Indeed, the thin-walled gate, provided with high central arch for mounted and vehicular traffic, and lower side arch for pedestrians, more likely served as a commercial barrier from which goods entering the town for sale in its regulated market could be checked for tolls. The parapet walk appears to be part of the original scheme, but the bold crenellations and screen wall appear to be 19th-century.

Hunting Parks

1. Arnbarrow Hill (King's Deer Park), Clatterin' Brig NO 632 772 – NO 662 777

On the slopes of Arnbarrow Hill, to the W of the B974 Fettercairn-Banchory road. The hunting of deer was, in the Middle Ages, the exclusive preserve of the king and favoured nobles to whom grants of land 'in forest' had been made. Often, to ensure a good day's hunting and a guaranteed bag, large tracts of land were emparked – enclosed within a substantial boundary – and stocked with a captive herd of deer. The crown maintained such parks on its estates round Scotland, several being grouped in the NE, such as that at Drum near Aberdeen which Robert I had Alexander Burnett construct for him. One of the best-preserved, however, is the early great park of Kincardine. The presence of this hunting preserve surely accounts in part for the popularity of Kincardine Castle (above p.192) as a residence by the early kings of Scots. Although its construction is often attributed to William the Lion, references in the Exchequer Rolls to the making of the 'New Park' of Kincardine in 1266 implies that the surviving earthwork may belong to the time of his grandson, Alexander III.

The boundary of the park is still visible in a number of places as a substantial earthwork. This took the form of an earthen rampart crowned by a timber palisade, or pale, the earth being excavated from a ditch on the inside of the enclosure, thereby effectively doubling the height of the obstacle which the deer would have to leap to escape. The rampart, which has slumped and spread with time, measures between 3m and 4.5m wide and stands up to 1.5m high over the largely silted ditch. The ditch measures between 2m to 3m wide. The surviving earthwork is best-preserved on the N side of Arnbarrow Hill, where it runs for over 2 miles across the moorland. A short stretch can be seen running S from Clatterin' Brig for 0.25 miles, while a similar length lies N-S in woodland 0.25 miles N of Crichieburn farm. A separate northern enclosure can still be traced on the N side of the Back Burn of Arnbarrow, 1.5 miles WNW of Clatterin' Brig. The quickest approach to the earthwork is via an indistinct footpath which climbs the steep slopes behind the tea-room at Clatterin' Brig, then along the N side of the forestry plantation. The ditch and bank can be seen clearly emerging from the NW angle of the plantation and striking out to the W over the hillside. This stretch of the bank can be seen clearly from the B974 0.5 miles NW of Clatterin' Brig.

2. Dunlappie Dyke, Edzell
NO 555 681 to NO 589 665

This linear earthwork begins on the S side of the West Water on the steep slopes below the NW flank of Lundie Hill. It runs from there in a long arc which turns S and E to Cairndrum farm, approximately 2 miles from its starting point. Well-preserved sections can be seen at NO 558 677 in the col between Lundie Hill and the Brown Caterthun, at NO 578 666 on the N side of the farmtrack to Chapelton and Cairndrum farms S off the unclassified Menmuir-Edzell road, and NO 558 665 just to the W of Cairndrum farm. It may once have extended as far as Auchenreoch (NO 600 656) just to the W of Inchbare on the B966 Brechin-Edzell road. It probably formed the E boundary of the royal forest of Kilgarie, on record by 1319.

3. Durward's Dyke, Lintrathen
N0 257 545 to NO 259 548

This well-preserved bank-and-ditch earthwork runs across the eastern slopes of Knock of Formal, the prominent hill which rises on the E side of the B954 Alyth-Dykend road, between the road at Bridge of Craigisla and the Loch of Lintrathen. It formed part of the boundary of the medieval deerpark of Lintrathen – the loch bounded it to the E. The lands of Lintrathen belonged to Alan Durward in the first half of the 13th century and formed a hunting estate, positioned like Kincardine and Kilgarie on the edge of the Highlands. The earthwork remains of the Peel of Lintrathen, the Durwards' residence which lay at Peel farm (NO 263 540) 0.5 miles SE of the Dyke, have been obliterated by agricultural action, but a cropmark enclosure immediately S of the present farm may mark its site.

THE POST-MEDIEVAL PERIOD

*c.*1600 to the Present

The Reformation of 1560 did not, despite popular traditions, bring an overnight transformation in the character of Scottish society. Processes of change which can be traced back into the later Middle Ages continued, and the more obvious religious implications of the official breach with Rome were to take over a century to settle down finally into the pattern which lasted until this century. Moreover, it must be remembered that Reformation did not bring religious – or political – unity, and that in some cases the old local rivalries between families were deepened by the added colour of religious difference. Angus, however, where influential lairds like John Erskine of Dun were early converts to Protestantism, and where the burghs, especially Dundee, which had strong trading links with Lutheran Germany and the Low Countries, was a major bastion of Protestantism.

Reformation did bring major changes to the landscape. The great monasteries, apparently already in terminal decay by the early 16th century, were its most significant casualties. With a few notable exceptions, such as the friaries in and around Dundee, the death of the monasteries was protracted. There was no Dissolution of the Monasteries as in England, simply the recruitment of new monks and canons was prohibited and, where the monks refused to embrace the new faith, the communities died slowly and withered away over time. The destruction of the buildings, again with the exceptions of the friaries in Dundee in particular, was a consequence of Reformation. It was often, however, not simply a case of vandalism, or the fires of the new reformed faith obliterating all trace of the old Church, but a coldly economic decision. The ruin of *Arbroath Abbey* was not accomplished by Protestant zealots in the 16th century, but by the hands of townsfolk with an eye to a handy source of good-quality building-stone.

At parish level, the physical changes were often more superficial. Most of the churches were simply converted to

Protestant worship by shifting the focus from the altar in the E end to the pulpit centrally-placed against the S wall of the nave. Few buildings required complete reconstruction, but were instead altered to accommodate the new forms of worship. New and larger windows were cut through old masonry to flood with light the dimly-lit, mystery-inducing interiors of the medieval buildings, and galleries were inserted in either end of the former naves to accommodate the swollen congregations who clamoured to hear the Word of God pronounced by the new ministers. Indeed, many of the small, plain kirks which dot the countryside of Angus and the Mearns, usually labelled as 16th- or 17th-century, are simply the renovated medieval buildings, as for example at *Eassie* or *Inverkeilor*.

Although some churches were built from new in the 17th century, it is not until the 18th century, as fashions and ideas began to change, that rebuilding became widespread. Often, it was the upper class ideals of the ministers which led to the replacement of the old buildings, as taste demanded the new, classical refinements in architecture and design. Long, low, narrow-bodied churches were replaced by high, wide-bodied buildings. *St. Andrew's Church* in Dundee was one of the first of this kind, a wholly new building constructed on a virgin site. Elsewhere, as at *Tealing* or *Aberlemno*, parts of the old fabric were retained at the core of the new building, but extra space was provided by the addition of large N aisles, converting the old churches into spacious T-shaped structures with galleries arranged round three sides of the central amphitheatre which held pulpit and communion table. But it was not simply a question of taste which fuelled the 18th-century era of rebuilding, it was the growing prosperity of the land and the new confidence of the great men of the parish – who often paid for the new buildings – which stimulated this investment in their spiritual future.

Rising levels of prosperity in the 16th century had seen the emergence of the merchant-burgess and lairdly classes as influential groups in the new society of post-Reformation Scotland. Their wealth was reflected in the increasing sophistication of their residences, seen in the later 16th century in castles like *Claypotts* and *Powrie*, and in the 17th century in houses such as *Flemington*, *Pitkerro* or *Gagie*. The increased confidence and wealth of these classes was perhaps most clearly to be seen in the burghs, especially in Dundee, where the later 16th and early 17th centuries saw a major expansion and the building of fine town residences by the rising merchant-princes and the newly-influential county lairds. Sadly, the sack of Dundee in 1651, town centre redevelopment in the 19th century, and the profit-driven semi-official vandalism of the early 1960s has all but destroyed every vestige of the prosperous burgh of the early 17th century. Only the much altered town house of the *Gardyne's*, tucked away down a city centre close, survives to give an impression of the burgh landscape of that super-confident period.

Despite the sack of the burgh in 1651 and the destruction of its old harbour by a storm in 1658, Dundee established and maintained a local hegemony which it has preserved to the present day. Commercial dominance was soon to be followed by the physical expansion of the old town beyond its medieval boundaries, until it had outstripped in size all its old local rivals. By the 18th century, Dundee's prosperity had returned and its revived vigour was marked in the construction of the first of a series of fine public or commercial buildings in the town centre. At a time when most other Scottish burghs were simply restoring their old, medieval tolbooths, Dundee's council opted for construction of a wholly new building which could be the embodiment of their civic pride. The result was the superb Town House of 1731, designed by William Adam as a classical temple to house the burgh's great and good. Sadly, however, this was to be one of Dundee's first casualties to 'improvement' being swept away in the 1930s, against popular feeling, to make way for the cold austerity of the City Square. Other burghs, however, followed Dundee's lead later in the 18th century, and the fine Town House at Forfar is one of the best examples of its kind.

Dundee's rapid commercial and industrial expansion in the early 19th century was eventually to see the loss of much of its late medieval and early modern townscape, other than its street-plan, which survived largely unaltered until the 1960s. Lucky survivals, like the *Exchange Coffee House and Reading Rooms*, one of the meeting-places near the harbour of Dundee's commercial leaders, offer us a glimpse of what disappeared in the 1870s as the city sought to open up its medieval heart and give the centre of the burgh a more open and 'dignified' layout. The demolition of the Trades and Union Halls, which faced each other across the central part of the High Street at the foot of Reform Street, deprived the city of two of its finest late 18th-century public buildings. The result is that much of the 'old' heart of the city dates only from the late 19th and early 20th centuries, but even still some snatched glimpses can be had of the city's formerly rich architectural heritage. In the Nethergate in particular, late 18th century speculative tenements, such as Miln's Building, or the wonderful *Morgan Tower*, preserve the flavour of the pre-19th century townscape. The fragments of 18th-century and earlier Dundee seem still more tragic when compared to Montrose. Here, the full plan of the medieval burgh with its wide, centrally-placed rectangular market area, is preserved intact, but the buildings which enclose it are largely of the late 18th and 19th centuries.

The upsurge in the prosperity of Dundee, and the other Angus burghs, was largely a product in the later 18th century of the twin driving-forces of the Agricultural and Industrial Revolutions. Angus, with the exception of Dundee, can hardly be classed as an industrial zone, but within the burghs there was a rapid expansion of the industrial base from the last decades of the 18th century onwards. Textiles lay at the heart of this expansion. At first it was the production of linen, and this remained the main product in towns such as Kirriemuir, Forfar and Arbroath – there are excellent museum displays on the flax-spinning industry in the Meffan Institute (Forfar Museum) in Forfar, the Signal Tower Museum in Arbroath, and on the cottage side of the industry in the *Angus Folk Museum* – but in Dundee the production of coarse jute fabrics ultimately fuelled the city's 19th and early 20th-century prosperity. Few of the earliest mill-buildings survive. The best, until recently, were to be seen along the line of the Dichty Burn on the N fringe of Dundee, where the soaking ponds and bleachfields of the old linen works survived into the 1970s. The last remaining bleachworks, Claverhouse, is currently undergoing redevelopment. Here, however, something can be seen of the old mill village, now overshadowed by Dundee's Trottick and Claverhouse housing estates. A single row of 18th-century cottages stands on the N side of the road opposite *Mains Church*, while to their E stands the Claverhouse Bleachfield Offices, a two storey structure of 1835–40 with a central bellcote housing the work's clock and bell for signalling shift changes.

Within the city, there are few mill-buildings surviving from before *c.*1850, the grim-looking '*Coffin Mill*' of 1828 being one of the earliest to remain. The massive industrial temples of the Baxter, Cox and Gilroy dynasties still dominate the city skyline, but many are now either derelict or converted to other uses, usually housing or student residences. The great classically-pedimented façade of the Tay Works, the mill of the Gilroys, built around 1860, still forms a massive screen on the W side of Lochee Road, but the most potent symbol of the domination of Dundee by its jute lords is Cox's Stack, the towering brick-built chimney, designed in the fashion of an Italian campanile, which soars over the remains of the Cox Brothers' Camperdown Works in Lochee.

There are few other traces of early industrial development in Angus and the Mearns. What do survive, however, are several fascinating ruins of speculative commercial ventures floated by local lairds who saw the opportunity to boost their fortunes through industry. The most striking are the remains of the Scott brothers' developments at *Boddin* and *Usan*, which can best be described as rural industrial complexes. The saltpans at Usan had a short commercial life, their high-cost product eventually priced out of a market flooded with cheap supplies of Cheshire rock-salt, but in their day, they met a substantial proportion of local demand. It was local demand, too, which saw the development of the Boddin limekiln, the Scotts of Dunninald having the good fortune to have on their lands one of the few local outcrops of limestone from which the lime demanded for improving agriculture in the 18th century could be obtained.

The basis of much of the visible fabric of the agricultural society of the Mearns and Angus was laid at the end of the 18th century, but most dates from after the period under consideration in this book. What can be seen of the earlier, underlying systems, is often to be found on the peripheries of the areas of modern agriculture, especially along the S fringes of the Mounth. There is often more here than meets the eye, and the few sites detailed below are intended simply to offer a taste of what remains rather than to provide a comprehensive overview. It would give an improper image, however, to concentrate solely on the great houses of the lairds, or the humble dwellings of the agricultural workers, for the full picture of the rural society of the 17th and 18th centuries requires the mills, inns, trackways, doocots, bridges, churches and chapels to be included too. But a society is made by more than just the bricks and mortar with which it encloses itself, being rather a subtle interplay between the land and the people who inhabit it. In Angus and the Mearns the land created one of Scotland's more distinctive regional, rural societies, a culture which lingers yet in more than just folk memory and tradition. Its physical flavour can be seen, preserved as it were in aspic, in the *Angus Folk Museum* at Glamis, or the excellent little Glenesk Folk Museum, which provides a contrasting image of life in the Angus Glens as opposed to the arable farms of Strathmore, but its emotion and personality can now only largely be reached through literature. Perhaps the best representation of this is to be found in the fiction of Lewis Grassic Gibbon, whose trilogy *A Scots' Quair* records the changes in Scottish society, focused on the agricultural society of the Mearns, or in David Adams' superb studies of bothy life and culture in the early 20th century.

Fishing has always played a vital part in the economy of the region. Our earliest records concern the salmon fishings granted to, amongst others, the monks of Arbroath in the late 12th century. The salmon industry remained important throughout the Middle Ages, but the early development of

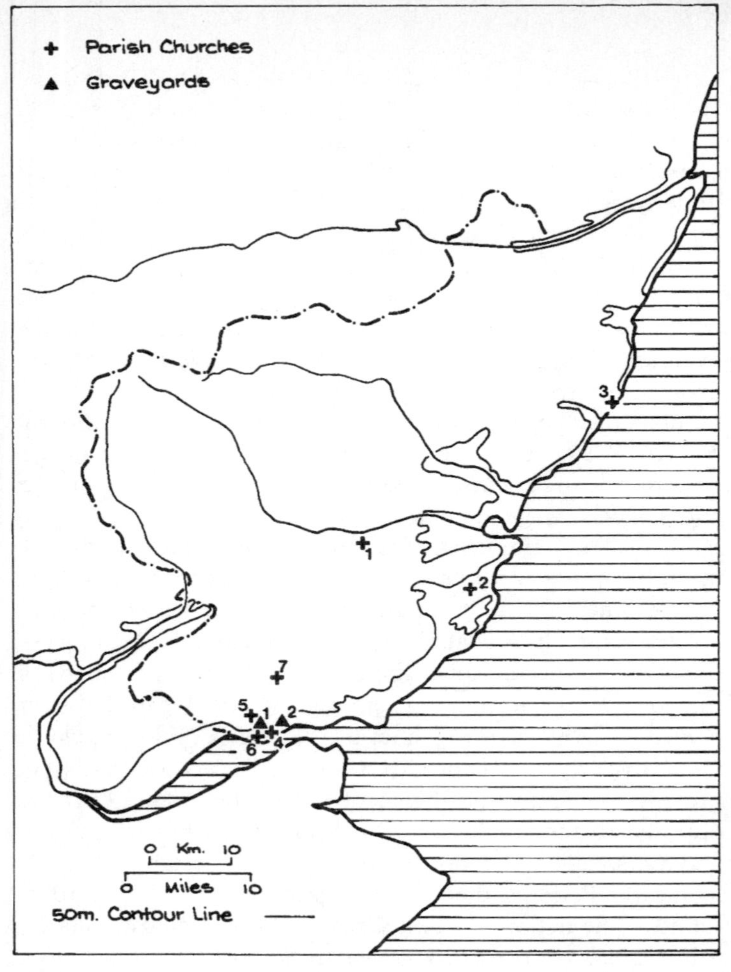

9. The Post Medieval Period – parish churches.

the herring fisheries should not be overlooked. Fisher touns are recorded all along the coasts of Angus and the Mearns in the medieval documents, lordship over them being an important factor in the economies of several estates. Commercial salmon fishing began to develop rapidly in the late 18th and early 19th centuries, when the fish, packed in ice, was transported in bulk to the London and S English market. Important fisheries developed around the Tay estuary, mainly in NE Fife, but the South Esk and North Esk salmon stations were hardly insignificant players. The great icehouses at *Fisherhills*, or the converted saltpan building at *Usan*, are testimony to the scale of the venture.

The fishing communities along the coast have largely reverted to, at most, involvement in inshore fishing, with only Arbroath and Stonehaven preserving a larger scale industry. Although many of the communities, such as Inverbervie, are of undoubted antiquity, their present character is largely the product of the substantial development of the trade in the 19th century. Catterline, Gourdon, Johnshaven, St.Cyrus and Auchmithie all, to greater or lesser extent, reflect the rise and fall of the herring fisheries. As with rural society, most of their story lies outwith the scope of this present study. Excellent museum displays are to be seen in the Signal Tower Museum at Arbroath.

Post-Medieval Monuments

Parish Churches

1. Aberlemno Church, Aberlemno
NO 522 555

At Aberlemno, to the E of the unclassified road between the B9134 Forfar-Brechin road and the B9113 Forfar-Montrose road. This fine early 18th-century church was erected in 1722 on the site of its medieval predecessor, whose foundations are probably for the most part followed. It is a large T-shaped structure with a range of dignified, simply-traceried windows along its S side. The bell-cote is crowned with a miniature spire.

2. Inverkeilor Church, Inverkeilor NO 664 496

At the N end of the village, on the E side of the main road. The general 19th-century image presented by this church is quite deceptive. Despite major reconstructions undertaken on two occasions in the mid-19th century, the main body of the fabric may be largely that of the medieval church. Certainly, the main structure occupies the site of the earlier church, the Carnegie loft and Northesk burial aisle at the E end probably incorporating the remains of the chancel. There are some fine heraldic panels in the S wall of the burial aisle, which also bears the date 1636. The N aisle was slapped through the wall of the nave in 1735, luckily missing two fine 17th-century panels, that at the NE retaining some of its original paint. The laird's loft in the former chancel is fronted by a superb gallery containing good 17th-century panelling.

3. Kinneff Old Kirk, Kinneff NO 855 748

At Kinneff, E off the unclassified road from the A92 approximately 1 mile N of Inverbervie, to Catterline. The tall, harled and whitewashed church represents a 1738 rebuilding of the 17th-century and earlier structure where the Scottish regalia were concealed from 1651 – when they were smuggled out of the besieged castle at Dunnottar – until 1660. It is a large T-plan structure, the main block lying on the line of the pre-Reformation building and the leg, added in 1876, projecting on the N side. The interior is well-lit and airy, illuminated by a range of six fine pointed windows with simple Y-tracery along the S side. There is a plain belfry with a tiered cap on the apex of the W gable. The chief features of note internally are the monuments to Rev James Grainger, minister of Kinneff, who hid the 'Honours of Scotland' beneath the floor of his church and, with his wife, dug them up once every three months to air them, and that of George Ogilvie of Barras, commander of the garrison of Dunnottar during its siege by Cromwell's army.

4. St. Andrew's Church and Glasite Chapel, Dundee NO 404 306

To the E of the Wellgate Shopping Centre, at the Junction of King Street, the Cowgate and St. Andrews Street. St. Andrews, built in 1774 for the Incorporated Trades of Dundee to designs by Samuel Bell, was the first post-Reformation suburban church to be built in the burgh. It is a fine rectangular preaching church, the Palladian detailing of its S side reflecting the internal arrangements. Two large Venetian windows flank the pulpit in the middle of the wall, while two tiers of round-headed windows with Classical detailing to E and W mark the position of the S ends of the elongated U-shaped gallery which extends round the N side of the building, providing lighting for the spaces above and below the gallery. The two doorways in the S wall open into the aisle around the communion table. Above the Venetian windows are carved swags flanking an oval panel. At the W end is a tall tower rising in three stepped stages and capped by a slender stone spire. The churchyard to the S was originally laid out as a formal garden and is entered through a pair of contemporary gates.

To the SE of the church and now linked to it by a modern extension, is the Glasite Chapel or Kail Kirk of 1777. This is a fine octagonal building with a pyramidal roof and two storeys of round-headed windows. It was built for the Rev John Glas, founder of the Glasite sect. Between services the congregation ate communally in a now-demolished refectory on the NE side - their kail broth winning it the name of the Kail Kirk from Dundonians. The building was gutted earlier this century when it was converted to commercial uses, but it has been restored and now forms part of the halls of St. Andrews church.

5. St. Ninian's Church (Lochee Old), Dundee NO 378 316

At the junction of Methven Street and Lochee High Street. Standing almost at the gates of the former Cox's jute mills – the Camperdown Works – Lochee Old represented the spiritual heart of the community which had grown up under the paternalistic regime of the mill owners. Built in 1829–30 to designs by David Neave, it is a plainly utilitarian box given a few neo-Classical features to relieve its dullness. The main (S) gable is graced with shallow pilasters and is crowned with a plain pediment pierced by an undecorated oculus. Above this rises a squat, square belfry with paired pilasters at the angles, flanking small round-headed openings. The still dumpier upper stage of the tower is octagonal, as is the stone spire which completes it. All the windows are undetailed.

6. St. Peter's Church, Dundee
NO 390 297

In St. Peter's Street off the N side of Perth Road, 0.75 miles W of the city centre. Built in 1836 to serve the rapidly-expanding western residential and industrial suburbs of Dundee. This is a fine rectangular preaching church of Classical design. At its E end is a fine tower rising in three stages, the upper two bearing strong Classical detailing. The upper stage has pedimented gables, above which rises and octagonal stone spire with three tiers of circular lucarnes.

7. Tealing Parish Church, Tealing
NO 403 379

In Kirkton of Tealing, to the S of the unclassified road from Tealing/Balgray to Auchterhouse. The pre-Reformation church of Tealing was massively remodelled in 1806 and given its present box-kirk form with internal galleries on the N, E and W walls. Several fragments of carved stonework from the older building, however, are incorporated within the structure. These include portions of a sacrament house, a 14th-century slab, and a splendid high relief mural monument dated 1618. Sadly, this church which only became redundant in recent years, has been subject to vandalism and some of its fine early 19th-century fittings have been destroyed.

Graveyards

1. The Howff, Dundee
NO 401 304

In the angle formed between Ward Road on the N and Barrack Street on the W is the splendid old burial ground of the city, known to generations of Dundonians as the Howff. The ground was formerly occupied by the gardens of the Franciscan Friary, whose buildings lay to its SW (see above p.125), which were granted in 1564 by Queen Mary to the burgh Council as a new burial ground outside the town wall to replace the overcrowded and insanitary St. Clements kirkyard in the centre of the old burgh. The name is derived from its use as the open-air meeting-place of the Incorporated Trades of Dundee from the 16th century until the building of the now demolished Trades Hall in 1776. The Howff contains a magnificent collection of tombstones and monuments dating from the 16th to 19th centuries, surpassed in Scotland only by those in Greyfriar's Kirkyard in Edinburgh. The high screen wall on the W side, lined on its inner face by deeply-recessed blind arcading, was built in 1601. Numerous fine monuments fill its recesses. The epitaphs on the slabs, of all dates, are a classic record of wry Dundee humour.

2. Roodyards Burial Ground, Dundee

On the S side of Broughty Ferry Road, E of the city centre. The burial ground began its life as a plague cemetery in 1561, but most of the surviving monuments date from between 1820 and 1860. It is dominated, however, by the massive ashlar, late 18th-century mausoleum of the Guthries. This is a square Classical box surmounted by a hemispherical stone dome. All four sides are treated in identical fashion, with a central archway - blind on three sides and containing the doors on the fourth - flanked at the angles by paired flat Ionic pilasters. There is also a series of linked semi-subterranean burial lairs.

Houses and Mansions

1. Arbuthnott House, Inverbervie NO 795 750

In private grounds overlooking the Bervie Water S of the B967 Inverbervie-Fordoun road, 3.5 miles E of Fordoun. Outward appearances can be deceptive, for what seems at first to be a large laird's house with attendant outbuildings of the late 18th century on closer inspection can be seen to conceal much earlier origins. This rambling collection of harled and whitewashed buildings of various ages has grown up on a strong defensive site occupying a promontory near the confluence of the Bothenoth Burn with the Bervie. It is possible that the much-altered early 15th-century hall block on the S incorporates some 13th-century stonework from the hall-house of the early Arbuthnotts of that Ilk. This block contained a first floor hall over an unvaulted lower chamber, had a screens passage at the W entered via external stone steps, and had a vaulted kitchen with laird's room over it in a slightly narrower E extension. This group underwent major expansion in the later 15th century with the construction of a second block to the W of the original hall, further buildings to the N and the erection of a curtain wall with central gate-tower across the W approaches. Much of this is now incorporated within the large U-shaped house which dominates the W end of the site today, the product of a major remodelling undertaken in the 1750s and completing the transformation of the medieval stronghold into a comfortable private residence which had begun in the 17th century.

2. Baldovan House, Dundee NO 395 348

In private grounds off Old Glamis road on the N outskirts of the city. Currently derelict and prone to the attentions of vandals. The coldly austere house of the Ogilvies of Baldovan was built in the 1750s and altered in the early 1800s, but remains largely true to its severely Classical planning. It is a plain rectangular box of three storeys – the principal entrance and apartments being on the second storey – extending to nine bays across the N and S fronts, the three central bays of

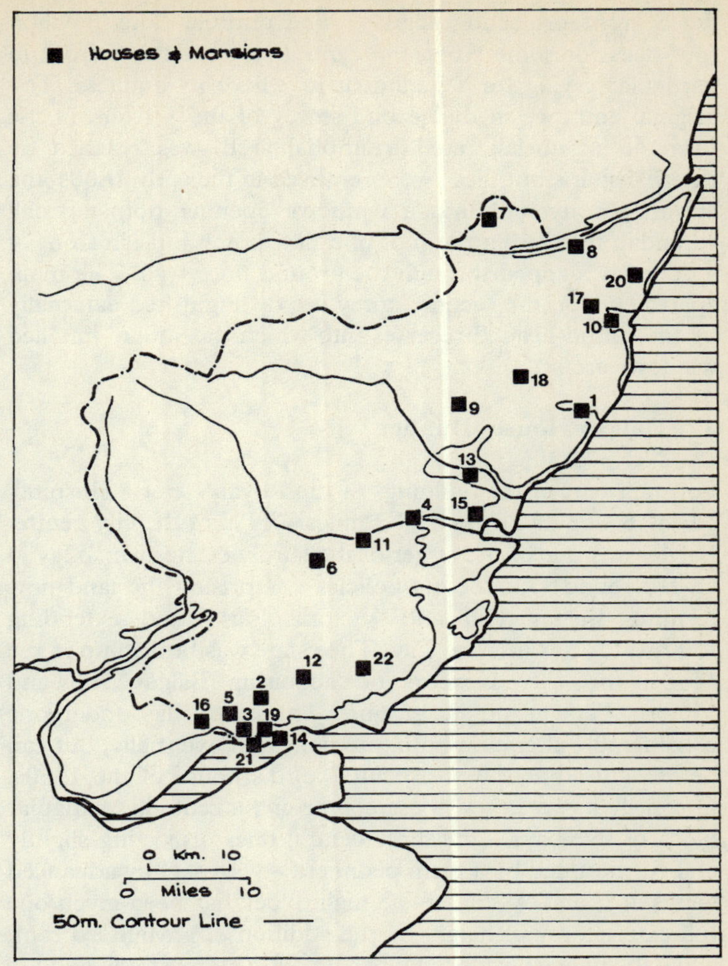

10. The Post Medieval Period – mansions and houses.

the S front projecting slightly. The unpretentious pavilion roof begs for some relief, the central stage of the S front in particular crying for a pediment to relieve its dullness. The original entrance in the second storey of the S front, in the form of an unelaborated triumphal arch, was reached by external stairs, but these were removed in the early 1800s, the entrance converted into a windows opening onto a small verandah formed on the roof of a new porch built in front of a doorway slapped through the ground floor wall. The main apartments on the second storey are distinguished externally by the round-headed recesses into which the square-lintelled windows are set.

3. Balgay House, Dundee NO 375 306

Forming part of the buildings of the Royal Victoria Hospital, on the S side of Balgay Hill 2 miles WNW of the city centre. Balgay was one of the larger of the lairdly estates which lay in an arc round Dundee, its policies comprising the land now forming Balgay Hill and Victoria Parks and extending southwards towards the Tay. The estate was broken up in the 1870s, the City Corporation acquiring Balgay Hill and Victoria Park as public ground. The house has undergone considerable alteration both internally and externally, but can be recognised as a well-executed laird's house of the 1760s. Originally a two storey house comprising a central rectangular block of five bays – the three central ones projecting slightly and surmounted by a plain pediment – with slightly advanced wings at E and W ends. The main block has been given one full extra storey of height by the addition of a Mansard roof, while the wings have been given an extra stone storey and are now capped by ogee-shaped roofs.

4. Brechin Castle, Brechin NO 597 599

In private grounds on the W outskirts of Brechin, the castle occupies a site of great natural strength high on a crag overlooking the River South Esk. There was a castle here by the 13th century, but this was largely destroyed in the course of the Wars of Independence. Brechin passed in 1378 into the hands of Walter Stewart, youngest son of King Robert II, but on his forfeiture and execution in 1437 for complicity in the murder of his nephew, King James I, it was taken into the royal demesne. In the 16th century it passed to the Erskines, Earls of Mar from 1565, and it is probable that the vaulted cellars under the present building date from that period. In 1634 the Maules, created Earls of Panmure in 1646, who had held the property in the 13th century, purchased the estate from the Erskines. In *c.*1700 the fourth earl built a new show front across the western neck of the promontory on which the castle stands. This is a splendid piece of symmetrical planning in a plain Classical style, yet given a curiously medieval feel by the cylindrical towers which project boldly at the angles. These towers may represent earlier fabric incorporated into the new structure. This is a long rectangular block of three storeys, divided into eleven window bays, the three central being placed in a projection crowned with a pediment framing an armorial panel. The entrance is at the ground floor, with the principal apartments on the second storey. The earl was forfeited for his part in the 1715 Jacobite Rebellion and the castle and estate taken over by the York Building Company. Unlike many others placed in its hands, Brechin escaped major damage and in 1764 was purchased by William Maule, a kinsman of the former earl, who was also created Earl of Panmure. Under his direction three ranges were built around the irregular-shaped courtyard to the rear of the 1700 block, all unpretentious late Georgian structures. On his death the estates passed to his kinsman the Earl of Dalhousie, whose descendants still occupy the castle.

5. Camperdown House, Dundee*
NO 358 329

In Camperdown Park, signposted from the A923 NW of the city. The house was built in 1824 to designs by William Burn for Admiral Adam Duncan, first Viscount Camperdown. It is one of the finest neo-Classical mansions in Scotland. Much of the design appears to have been influenced by William Wilkins' more famous house, the Grange, in Hampshire.

This is seen particularly in the E front, formed from one of the narrow ends of the main rectangular block of the house, which is screened – all bar single bays at the N and S – by the massive portico of six Ionic columns supporting a high entablature and pediment. This allowed the main front, facing S across the park towards the Tay, uninterrupted views from the windows of the suite of principal rooms arranged along that side. The S front is simply modelled, its 'portico', positioned off-centre to the W, having undetailed square pilasters. Strangely, the private apartments of the Duncans were placed in the single storey range on the N side of the house, which looks rather as though it should have contained the domestic offices. The interior contains excellent panelling and good plasterwork, but its chief ornament is the grand entrance vestibule. This rises the full height of the two storey house, and is lit from above by a stained glass dome supported on elliptical pendentives built out from the angles of the rectangular chamber below.

6. Carse Gray, Forfar
NO 464 538

In private grounds on the S side of the long ridge extending WSW from the Hill of Finavon, 1.5 miles NNE of Forfar. The large and rambling E-shaped house of the 18th century developed out of a smaller 17th-century laird's house. The building now consists of a long main block lying E-W, with wings running S at both ends. The E end, however, can be seen to have developed out of a two storey and garret T-shaped house of the early 17th century. The only embellishment in this building is in the wing, formerly the stairtower, whose upper storey is corbelled out slightly to N and S. It appears to have done so on the W also, but this wall is now carried up flush with the lower floor. The moulded doorway is in the northern re-entrant, and above it in the N wall of the first floor is an empty niche for an armorial panel. The interior has undergone considerable alteration, but the 17th-century stair still rises to the first floor. The lands of Carse were formerly the possession of the Rynd family, and the original house was probably the work of William Rynd or his grandson, John, who succeeded him in 1621. In 1648 the Rynds sold out to Francis Ruthven, and in 1741 it was bought by Charles Gray, a member of a cadet line of the Lords Gray, under whose ownership the house was greatly enlarged and the name of the estate changed to Carse Gray.

7. Cluny Crichton, Banchory NO 686 997

In agricultural land on Cluny farm, 3 miles N of Banchory on the A980 Banchory-Torphins road. Looking like a much older towerhouse, the ruined L-plan castle built in 1666 for George Crichton of Cluny incorporates medieval principles with Classical symmetry. In plan it is an equal-armed L composed of three square rooms, all unvaulted, rising to three storeys. A square stair tower rises in the re-entrant.

8. Durris House, Durris NO 799 968

In private grounds E of the unclassified road to Denside, S off the B9077, 2 miles E of Kirkton of Durris. It is probable that the present towerhouse of *c.*1600 occupies the site of, or incorporates portions of the structure of, the medieval stronghold of the Frasers which replaced the motte 1.25 miles to the W. Certainly, the vaults below the house possibly date from the 14th or 15th centuries. Of the upstanding structure, the oldest portion is a four-storeyed, formerly L-plan towerhouse standing at the S end of the later mansion. The tower originally consisted of a main block with a smaller stairtower rising one storey higher, crowned by a cap-house carried out slightly wider on a course of individual, plain corbels. Later in the 17th century the re-entrant has been infilled, the roofline of the main block altered to provide the infill with an oversailing roof, and the whole harled to conceal the join. There are rather curiously-shaped bartizans on the W angles, possibly representing the built-up remains of the open rounds from an open parapet walk. Internally the house has undergone considerable alteration. The old entrance is now an interior feature, opening into the unvaulted ground floor, beneath which there is a vaulted subterranean basement. The hall, with two fireplaces, occupies the first floor, and there are bedrooms above. The cap-house is reached by a tiny stair in the thickness of wall from the stairhead below.

The Frasers held Durris from its grant to them by Robert I until the late 17th century, when it passed through an heiress to Charles Mordaunt, Earl of Peterborough. In 1706 his daughter married the second Duke of Gordon, and Durris passed ultimately into Gordon hands before being sold on in 1834.

9. Fasque House, Fettercairn* NO 648 755

Signposted off the B974 Fettercairn-Banchory road, 1 mile N of Fettercairn. Although most of the interior fittings and decor are of the late Victorian and Edwardian eras, the house itself is a superb example of an early 19th century country house. Fasque was built in 1809, possibly to designs by John Paterson of Edinburgh, executed in unpretentious and unfussy late Georgian Gothic style. It consists of a three storey rectangular main block, flanked by turrets at the angles and with a bold four storey tower projecting from the centre of the S front. The Doric portico which covers the main entrance in the foot of this tower was added in 1829 for John Gladstone, who had recently purchased the property on the proceeds of his lucrative trade in supplying grain to the industrial towns of NW England. Extending to E and W of the main block are lower wings, again with angle towers, the whole producing a pleasingly symmetrical stepped effect. To the N are ranges of domestic offices. Much of the ground floor of the main block is occupied by service accommodation – kitchens, scullery, servants' hall etc. – while the main apartments are on the first floor. These are reached by a magnificent staircase, cantilevered out from the walls, and lit from above by an oval glazed cupola.

The house has strong associations with the Victorian prime minister, William Ewart Gladstone, the younger son of John, who lived here from 1830–51. The library in particular is largely the product of his collecting interests. The rest of the house, however, is largely a monument to the style of country living which died with World War I, typified by Gladstone's nephew, who, with seven of his friends, once shot over 3000 pheasants in one day in 1905 on the moors to the N.

10. Fetteresso House, Fetteresso NO 843 855

In private land overlooking the valley of the Carron Water from the N, 1.5 miles W of Stonehaven off the unclassified road from Stonehaven to Glenbervie. A roofless ruin until recent restoration as flatted accommodation, Fetteresso House forms an extended L-plan with a large staircase in the re-entrant and an outer screen of offices forming three sides of a courtyard built across the re-entrant. The oldest portion of the structure is the S range, a 35.5m-long block containing six vaulted cellars and a kitchen at its E end, all linked by a service passage along the N side. A boldly projecting turret on the S side carries a service stair from the cellar W of the kitchen to the apartments on the first floor. This represents the only survival of the fine 17th-century house built by the Keiths, burned by the Marquis of Montrose in his harrying of the Earl Marischal's estates in 1645. Fetteresso was rebuilt in 1671 and it was there in 1715 that the then Earl entertained the Old Pretender on his march to Perth. For his part in the Jacobite Rebellion of 1715, the Earl was forfeited. Fetteresso passed to the Duffs, who between 1782 and 1808 massively extended the existing structure and altered the layout of the old S range. The main development was the construction of the great octagon at the E end of the S range and the long block extending N from that, all in a rather pallid Gothick style. A new grand staircase was built in the angle between the blocks, rising within a domed rotunda. During WWII, the house was occupied for military use, a fate which here, as in so many other cases, resulted in severe damage and neglect leading ultimately to abandonment and dereliction after the stripping of its furnishings in 1954.

11. Flemington House, Aberlemno NO 527 556

The sadly dilapidated ruin of Flemington stands adjacent to the modern farm, 0.25 miles E of Aberlemno off the B9134. Of late 16th- or more probably early 17th-century date, Flemington consists of a large rectangular main block with a smaller wing at the N angle, forming an L-shaped house with inner and outer re-entrants. The main block and wing are both of three storeys. Stair turrets rise in both re-entrants, that in the external being a flat-faced structure corbelled out from the first floor and giving access only to a second floor bed-chamber in the wing. The other, in the inner re-entrant, is also corbelled out from the first floor, but rises the full height of the rest of the building. Under it is the entrance leading to the foot of the main stair in the wing – which rises to the first floor hall – and to two vaulted chambers. The S chamber was the kitchen. The hall occupied the first floor of the main block, but was later subdivided. The upper floors contained bed-chambers.

Flemington formed a portion of the royal thanage of Aberlemno in the Middle Ages. Portions of the thanage, plus revenues from Flemington, were granted in 1365 by David II to Sir William Dishington for the service of one archer, amplifying an earlier grant by Robert I. William's son, Sir Thomas, received the lands of Flemington from Robert III. Nothing more is known of the history of the estate until the 18th century, when it was in the hands of the Ochterlonys. John Ochterlony, episcopalian minister of Aberlemno, continued to hold services in Flemington House after his ejection from his charge, until in 1742 he was appointed Bishop of Brechin.

12. Gagie House, Kellas NO 448 376

Amongst trees in its private grounds, approximately 1.5 miles NNE of Kellas. This is a beautiful little laird's house of the early 17th century, doubled in size in later years into a roughly T-shaped plan. The oldest part of the house forms the leg of the T. This is a two storey structure with conical roofed bartizans at its S angles. The lands of Gagie were bought in 1610 by William Guthrie, younger son of Alexander Guthrie of that Ilk, who built the house for himself and his wife, Isabella Leslie of Balquhain. There is an heraldic panel on the W wall bearing her initials and the Leslie arms, while on the summer house in the walled garden are the Guthrie arms and the date 1614.

13. Gallery House, Logie Pert NO 673 657

In private grounds overlooking the River North Esk, 1 mile NNE of Logie Pert. A symmetrically-planned house of exceptional quality, built in the late 17th century for the Fullartons. Gallery consists of a substantial rectangular main block of three storeys with a steeply pitched roof, and projecting hipped roofed wings at either end of the entrance front producing an inverted U-shape. The date 1680 appears on the finials of the main block. Centrally positioned on the ground floor is the main entrance, a finely moulded example with good Classical detailing, over which is a very large heraldic panel bearing the Fullerton arms. The principal apartments of the house are on the first floor, the drawing-room in particular containing excellent plasterwork. To the S of the house is a well-preserved complex of domestic and ancillary buildings, including barns and stables.

14. Gardyne's House, Dundee NO 403 304

In Gray's Close behind Nos 70–73 High Street. This is the last visible survivor in Dundee of the substantial town houses of the Angus lairds which were largely swept away in the 19th-century redevelopment of the burgh's central area, an unfortunate process repeated for most of the remaining pre-1800 buildings in the 1960s. Probably dating from around 1600, it is a much-altered L-shaped block – now fronted by a plain 18th-century tenement – with the short wing towards the street and a long extension running down the property behind it, all rising to five storeys. The interior was drastically remodelled for commercial purposes in the 19th century, but development work revealed fine tempera ceilings with poems and mottos painted on the timbers.

15. House of Dun, Dun*
NO 670 598

Signposted from the A935 Brechin-Montrose road. Plans for the house, designed as a replacement for the medieval towerhouse of the Erskines, whose site can still be located in the gardens of the mansion, were drawn up by William Adam in 1723, but building commenced only in 1730. It is a rather severe-looking composition, its design based around a plain rectangular block. The entrance is in the central bay of the seven bay N front, set back in a monumental archway which rises the full two storeys of the house. This archway is flanked by plain pilasters to form a triumphal arch three bays wide which forms a shallow projection in front of the main façade. The heavy entablature was formerly relieved somewhat by a balustrade surmounted by urns, but the removal of these has made the structure appear more squat. The windows of the main apartments on the first floor have round heads, while the upper storey windows have flat lintels. In contrast to the rather dour exterior, the interior of the principal suite is a masterpiece of ornate Baroque plaster-work, now restored to their former magnificence under the care of the National Trust for Scotland.

16. House of Gray, Liff
NO 337 321

In private grounds to the E of Mains of Gray, 0.5 miles SE of Liff village. The recent history of the House of Gray has not been a happy one, having suffered at the hands of both architectural thieves who have targeted its rich interior fittings, and failed would-be restorers. Built in 1716 to designs by Alex McGill and John Strachan for the twelfth Lord Gray, it is a masterpiece of early Scottish country house architecture, Classical in concept yet distinctively Scottish in its execution. It consists of a rectangular central block of two main storeys over a basement, with symmetrical N and S façades of seven bays, the central three slightly advanced and elevated above the walls to either side and crowned with a triangular pediment. This contains a richly-sculpted armorial panel flanked by a pair of oculi. The quoins of the central bays and angles of the main block project boldly. There is a rounded, sculptured pediment over the main entrance, and three elaborate swags over the second-storey windows of the central portion. At either end of the main block are ogee-capped stairtowers with bold quoins, flanked in turn by shallow wings housing offices and domestic buildings. The eaves of the towers and main block project well clear of the face of the walls.

17. Mergie House, Rickarton
NO 796 886

Overlooking the Cowie Water on private land S off the A957 Stonehaven to Crathes road, 5.5 miles NW of Stonehaven. This fine oblong laird's house appears to date largely from the 17th century, but may incorporate portions of a 16th-century towerhouse. A stair tower projecting from the middle of the S side is certainly an addition, while it is possible that the three storey main block represents two main phases of building. A stair turret is corbelled out from the first floor in the centre of the N wall, but all its decorative features, windows and shot-holes have been harled over. Its head, along with the whole wall-head of the house, has been altered at a late period. The interior, too, has been subject to much alteration. The ground floor was unvaulted, containing stores and a kitchen. The first floor may have held a hall, but is now divided into three panelled rooms with a lobby. Bed-chambers occupy the upper floor.

18. Monboddo House, Laurencekirk
NO 744 783

Lying some 1.25 miles W of the A90(T) off the unclassified road to Auchenblae, Monboddo has recently been saved from a state of terminal decay through restoration as the centrepiece of a private housing development. The 18th- and 19th-century portions of the once-sprawling mansion have been demolished, leaving the original early 17th-century house. This is a simple rectangular building of two storeys and garret. The roofline and wall-head has been altered, probably in the 18th century, but the rather heavy-looking bartizans at the N angles are original. In the W gable is an heraldic panel containing the arms of Douglas and Irvine and the date 1635. The house has, understandably, been much altered internally over various phases, but the layout is clear. The unvaulted basement contained cellars, with a kitchen at the W end, over which were hall and private chamber respectively.

Monboddo formed part of an extensive estate granted between 1189 and 1195 to Humphrey, son of Theobald, ancestor of the Barclays. By the late 16th century it was Strachan property, passing from them to the Irvines – who built the present house – and subsequently to the Burnetts. In 1714 James Burnett, Lord Monboddo, prominent advocate and a Lord of Session, was born here. Monboddo was described by Boswell in his *Journal of a Tour to the Hebrides* in 1773 as '...a wretched place, wild and naked, with a poor old house...'.

19. Morgan Tower, Dundee
NO 399 299

Forming Nos 135-139 Nethergate, the Morgan Tower, although apparently dating from only 1790, is a poignant reminder of the striking character of the Dundee street architecture which has been obliterated by development in the 19th century and again in the 1960s. Forming the centrepiece of a block of mansion flats, it is a boldly projecting five storey bow crowned by a slated saracen's cap roof with crescent moon finial. The four upper stages are broken by crude, but pleasing, Venetian windows. The massively thick walls include large blocks of red sandstone at the rear, which, together with the presence of a well and the remains of a U-shaped building adjacent, has led to the suggestion that an earlier group of buildings – possibly of the 16th century – may lie at the core of the 18th-century redevelopment.

20. Muchalls Castle, Muchalls*
NO 892 908

In private grounds occupying an elevated site on S-facing slopes to the W of the A90(T), 0.5 miles W of the village of Muchalls. This is one of the finest early 17th century laird's houses to survive in NE Scotland, being both of exceptional architectural quality and having been little altered since its construction. Earlier work is incorporated in the building, but the character of Muchalls is entirely that of a major rebuilding operation undertaken between 1619 and 1627 by Alexander Burnett of Leys and his son, Thomas.

The house is a substantial L-plan which forms ranges on the N and W sides of a small courtyard. A small SE wing extends down the E side from the N wing, but the remainder is closed by a curtain wall, pierced in the middle by a high gateway with a segmental arch. There are triple gunloops on either side of the gate, and the wall-head has been provided with corbelled rounds. Conical roofed bartizans are corbelled out above the second storey at the N angles and at the SE and SW angles of the W range, and an elaborate band of corbelling on the S front of the SE wing carries out the gable of the small watch-chamber formed in its third storey. It is clear from the gables of both ranges that the wall-head has been lowered, probably through the removal of an attic storey.

The main doorway is in the foot of the SE tower, opening to the foot of the principal stair leading to the first floor apartments. A vaulted passage runs along the S front of the N range, providing access to the range of groin-vaulted cellars and the kitchen at the W end. A service stair from the kitchen rises in a turret in the main re-entrant. The hall occupies the first floor of the main block. This is a magnificent chamber with a painted plaster ceiling and a grand fireplace with a carved and painted over-lintel. To the W of the hall was the original laird's bedroom with a 'lug' or aperture in a mural chamber for eavesdropping on conversations in the hall, while in the W wing are two further magnificent rooms with fine plaster ceilings, the withdrawing room and laird's study. The upper floors contain bed-chambers.

21. Nethergate (Provost Riddoch's) House, Dundee NO 399 298

No. 158 Nethergate was built in 1790, possibly to designs by Samuel Bell the burgh architect, as the private house of Provost Alexander Riddoch, one of the most notorious of Dundee's political 'godfathers' who held the office of provost from 1788 to 1819. Set back from the street front in a small garden formed from its original carriage-way, it is curiously out of place amongst the tenements of this part of the Nethergate, looking more like the residence of a country laird than the townhouse of a powerful burgess. It is a symmetrically planned house of two storeys over a basement, with single storey wings or pavilions to E and W. The doorway is framed by simple Ionic pilasters with a plain entablature. It is now occupied as a bank.

22. Panmure Castle, Muirdrum (Lost) NO 537 387

In the Panmure estate, at the head of the E drive, off the B9128 1.75 miles NNE of Muirdrum. The demolition of Panmure Castle in 1955 must rank as one of the greatest acts of officially-sanctioned vandalism of its type in Scotland. The 'New' Castle of Panmure was begun for the second Earl of Panmure in 1666 to plans by John Mylne, the Royal Master Mason in Scotland and designer of Charles II's Holyroodhouse, and completed after Mylne's death in 1667 by Alexander Nesbit. What was constructed was a splendid Renaissance palace, conceived as a quadrangle with substantial towers at the four angles, crowned with cupola'd turrets after the fashion of Heriot's Hospital in Edinburgh or Drumlanrig Castle in Dumfriesshire. The ranges round the quadrangle rose to three storeys and a dormered garret over a deep basement level which contained the service accommodation, while the towers rose to four storeys. In 1852 the then Earl of Panmure and Dalhousie had the house substantially enlarged and embellished by Sir David Bryce, who, influenced by Thirlestane Castle at Lauder, added ogee-shaped roofs to the angle towers and built a massive turreted central tower on the W front overlooking the gardens. Some service buildings survive, as do the walled gardens to the SE of the castle site. Much of the estate, which is currently owned by Commercial Union Insurance Company, is given over to forestry, but in clearings amongst the trees are various pieces of formal architecture which graced the grounds of the house, including a peculiar ecclesiastical-style ruin, built as a folly, roughly 0.25 miles NW of the castle.

Travel and Communications

1. Bridge of Dye, Strachan
NO 651 860

Carrying the old main coach route S across the Cairn o' Mount between Fettercairn and Banchory (now the B974), 6.25 miles S of Banchory. The building of this bridge in 1680 marked the beginning of the opening up of this part of the NE to larger and more regular traffic, the road by the early 19th century having become the main coach route from Moray through Mar to Strathmore. Spanning the deep channel of the Dye in a single archway, ribbed on its underside, the bridge is the lineal descendant of a bridge-building tradition characterised by the more famous medieval Brig o' Balgownie over the Don at Old Aberdeen. It is an unsophisticated structure, designed to withstand the spates of the Dye rather than for architectural pretensions, and is provided with refuges for foot traffic at SE and NW only.

2. Bridge of Dun, Bridge of Dun
NO 662 584

The bridge carries the unclassified road from Bridge of Dun village over the River South Esk to Bankhead. Bridge of Dun is one of the finest pieces of bridge architecture in the region, built between June 1785 and January 1787. For what has always been a relatively minor crossing place, however, it is an unusually sophisticated piece of design executed in late Georgian Gothic style. The carriageway is carried over the river on three main spans supported by two piers with sharp cutwaters. Over the cutwaters are refuges for foot traffic, supported on slender columns composed of bundled shafts.

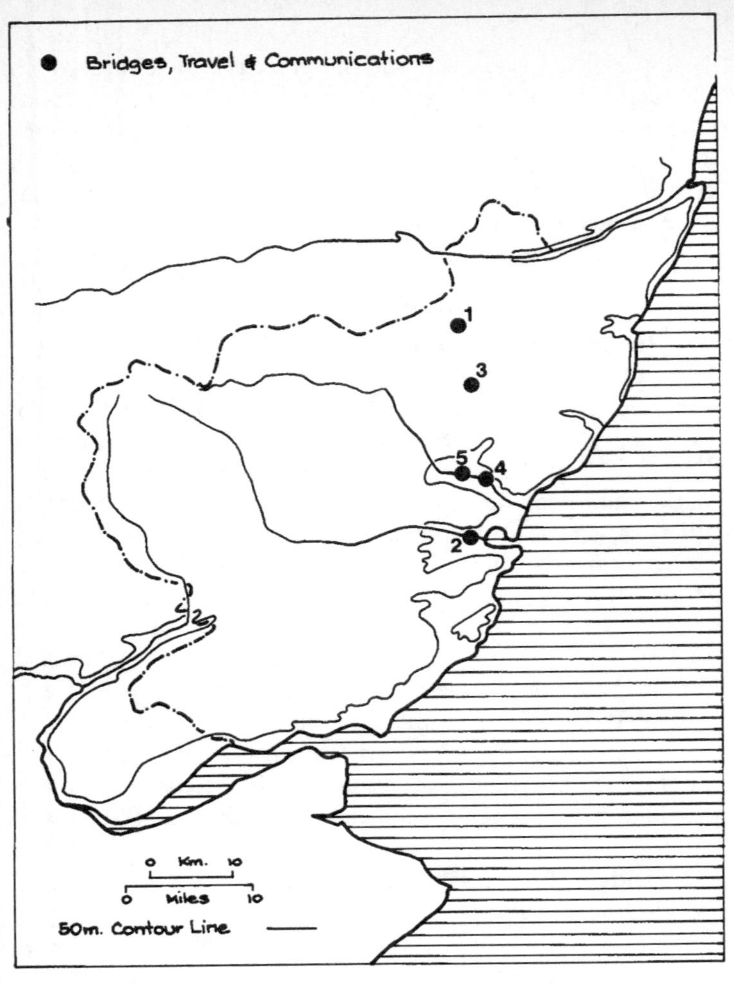

11. The Post Medieval Period – bridges and communications.

While the parapet of the carriageway is carried on a course of decorative corbelling, those of the refuges rise from a cornice over the columns decorated with a band of quatrefoil designs. The parapet of the approach road has some mock castellated features, including blind cross-loops and more corbelling.

3. Knowegreens Inn, Clatterin' Brig NO 659 787

The crumbling remains of what appears to be an abandoned cottage on the S side of the B974 Fettercairn-Banchory road as it climbs the shoulder of Redstone Hill towards the Cairn o' Mount, 0.3 miles NW of Clatterin' Brig, are in fact those of the former Knowegreens coach inn. Built between 1789 and 1807, the inn served traffic on the recently-established coach route between Moray and the lowlands. Substantial traffic on the route diminished in the later 19th century as the railways developed, and the inn was abandoned before 1900.

4. Marykirk Bridge, Marykirk NO 686 650

This fine bridge, built in 1813 to designs by John Smeaton, carries the A937 from Montrose to Marykirk across the River North Esk. Crossing the river in four round-arched spans of equal size, it has simple Classical features, such as the round oculi in the spandrels over the piers, the massive voussoirs of the arches, and the elegant lines of the parapet. Smeaton's design included a toll-house at the SW (Angus) end of the bridge, a simple one storey house, again with Classical detailing.

5. Old North Water Bridge, Bridgend NO 652 661

Now redundant, by-passed by the new concrete bridge carrying the A90(T) over the River North Esk, from its completion in 1539 until comparatively recently the North Water Bridge was the main river-crossing for traffic on this route between Aberdeen and Forfar/Brechin. It is a classic example of Scottish late Medieval bridge design which continued to influence bridge-building in Scotland down to the late 17th century, with ribbed archways carried on wide piers provided with sharp cut-waters on the upstream (W) side. The bridge has been widened in modern times to cater for increased and more bulky traffic, resulting in the loss of the original parapets and refuges over the piers.

Agriculture and Fishing

1. Angus Folk Museum, Glamis*
NO 395 468

In Kirkwynd in the centre of the village. Part of the Improvement of the Glamis estate in the late 18th century saw the provision of better-quality housing for estate-workers and tenants by the Earl of Strathmore. Building was very much an estate-run enterprise, all the materials used being drawn from local sources. There were several quarries on the Strathmores' property, and the grey slate with which the cottages were roofed, and the ridge stones, came as part of the rents paid by the tenants. The estate also owned a brickworks at Haugh of Cossans, N of the walled policies, supplied from claybeds locally. The row of six cottages occupied by the Museum were built in 1793 and remained in use as estate houses until well into this century. They were presented to the National Trust for Scotland in 1957 and developed to house the Angus Folk Museum collection which had been built up by the Maitlands of Burnside.

Various rural interiors from different parts of the county have been reassembled in the Museum. These include a kitchen, a Victorian farmhouse parlour, a 19th-century laundry and a schoolhouse. Also on display are looms for the weaving of damask linen, representing an important 'cottage industry' which developed in the later 18th century. In a separate gallery across the road from the cottages are a series of agricultural displays, including a reconstructed smiddy from nearby Eassie, and a farmworkers' bothy.

2. Arnbarrow Hill, Clatterin' Brig
NO 646 778

The farm track which runs from Arnbarrow farm NW across the flank of Arnbarrow Hill is on record from at least the late

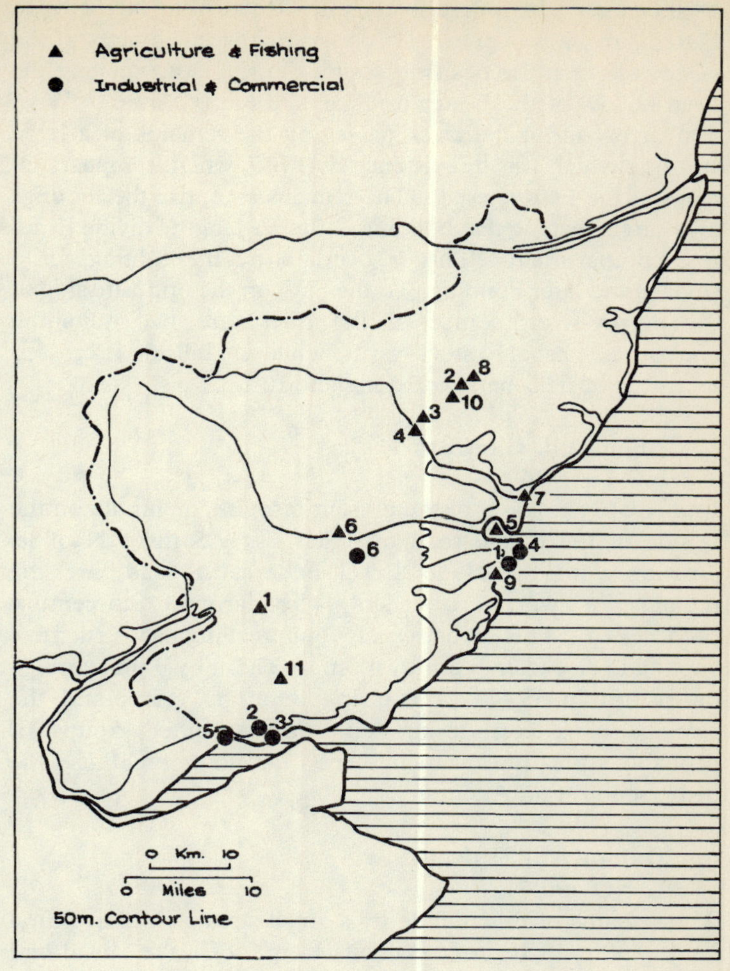

12. The Post Medieval Period – industry, commerce, agriculture and fishing.

18th century when, described as the 'Road from the Moss to Fettercairn', it was presumably used by the inhabitants of the village to reach the peat mosses on the ridge overlooking the deep hollow of the Water of Charr. About 0.3 miles NW of Arnbarrow farm, the track passes by the remains of a large steading which was in existence by 1789, when it appears on maps of the Fasque estate. The remains comprise the footings of a large rectangular building, 40m in length, divided into five compartments. This is overlain by the footings of a smaller and later building. To the SW, on the opposite side of the deeply-worn course of the track, are two adjoining enclosures, probably stock-yards, while the hillside is crossed by traces of field-banks of stone and turf.

3. Auchmull, Glen Esk
NO 584 744

Immediately to the S of the present farm of Auchmull, on the E side of the public road up Glen Esk 2.5 miles N of its junction with the B966 Edzell-Fettercairn road, are the remains of what is probably the farm's 18th-century predecessor. This consists of four rectangular structures varying in size from 8.8m by 4.6m to 22.3m by 3.9m, a mill – on record in 1794 – measuring 8.3m by 6.5m, and the remains of a corn-drying kiln. Several other groups of probably pre-Improvement era farming buildings lie dispersed around Auchmull.

4. Dalbog Mill, Edzell
1. NO 590 718

The remains of this mill lie by a small stream in agricultural land 250m ESE of Dalbog farm, off the dead-end unclassified road from Gannochy Bridge 1 mile N of Edzell, to Dalbog and Tullo. The mill stood on a platform on the N side of the burn measuring 10m by 5m, and 20m to the E of a dam constructed from large, water-worn boulders.

2. NO 593 719

The ruins of this mill stand on the W bank of the North Esk 600m E of the steading at Dalbog. The buildings, which comprise four rectangular structures ranged round three sides of a yard, have been reduced to little more than wall-footings. Some 40m to the SE a circular kiln is set into the riverbank. Prior to its collapse and the robbing of its stones, the mill-house bore the date 1681.

5. Dronner's Dyke, Montrose Basin
NO 687 577 to NO 699 578

This peculiar monument, visible at low tide in the muddy flats in the centre of Montrose Basin, represents the remains of a late 17th-century attempt to reclaim some 2000 acres in the northern half of the basin. Dutch expertise was imported to advise on its construction, but it was soon breached by the tides and the venture was abandoned.

6. Finavon Doocot, Oathlaw*
NO 491 570

Immediately to the W of the A90(T) at Milton of Finavon, entry via the unclassified road from the A90(T) to Oathlaw from Milton. Restored in 1979, this is believed to be the largest double-chamber lectern type doocot in Scotland. The chambers are entered through low doors in the S front, the division internally being marked at roof level by a third band of crow-steps. The N wall is finished with ball finials at either gable end and over the central partition wall.

7. Fisherhills Icehouse, Kinnaber
NO 729 621

On the S bank of the River North Esk, to the E of the A92 2.5 miles N of Montrose. Erected as part of a commercial salmon fishery at the mouth of the North Esk, the Fisherhills icehouse has the largest ice-chamber known in Scotland, measuring 12.5m by 7.24m and rising 7.58m to the crown of the barrel-vaulted roof. The embankment of earth heaped over the chamber was designed to allow carts to be manoeuvred to the top of the vault and ice carried in them discharged directly into the chamber below.

8. Knowegreens, Clatterin' Brig NO 658 757

On the S slopes of Redstone Hill, just 70m W of the ruins of Knowegreens inn (see above) on the S side of the B974 Fettercairn-Banchory road, are the remains of the late 18th-century farmstead. This was in existence by 1774, when it appears on estate plans, and fell into disuse in the later 19th century. The remains consist of the footings of three rectangular buildings, one incorporating a corn kiln. To the N of the farmstead are the remains of a slurry-pit or pond, and 35m to the ESE are the footings of a small square structure.

9. Lunan House Ice House, Lunan Bay NO 689 517

To the S of the access road to the public car-park at Lunan Bay, behind the remains of the domestic complex of Lunan House. The barrel-vaulted icehouse is built into the side of a bank beside a small pond from which ice would be taken in winter, its turf-covered main chamber forming a distinctive rounded hummock. Unusually, its entrance has been covered by a small square porch which rises into a low tower, ornamented with prominent quoins at the angles and a corbelled mini parapet. The icehouse was built to store fish caught by the commercial salmon station in Lunan Bay.

10. Shank of Cardowan, Fettercairn NO 631 778

On the E spur of the hill, adjacent to the W line of the bank enclosing the King's Deer Park (see above p.208), roughly 1 mile NNW of Crichieburn farm, are the remains of the farmstead of Todholes. These comprise of the lower footings of two rectangular structures lying at right angles to each other, a corn-drying kiln, and a number of adjoining enclosures. To the E of the buildings is a large area of rig-and-furrow cultivation. The property is on record in 1606, but it is unlikely that the existing ruins are that early, occupation apparently having continued into the early 19th century.

11. Tealing Doocot, Tealing*
NO 412 381

Signposted from the A90(T) Dundee-Forfar road, access via track from Tealing Home Farm. This well-preserved structure is one of the few survivors of the ancient house of the Maxwells of Tealing, although traces of old stonework and reused stones can be seen in the buildings of the farmyard. Built in 1595 by David Maxwell of Tealing, it is an unusual example being neither of beehive type nor of the still more common lectern-roofed variety, instead having a conventional pitched roof. It is a single-cell structure with nesting boxes running from floor to wall-head internally. Externally, it has a broad ledge running all the way round the walls roughly 2m above ground level, this being designed to prevent vermin from entering the doocot via the pigeon-holes. The doorway, with chamfered jambs and lintel, the latter carved with the monogram DM HG, is in the middle of the S wall. On the SE skewputt of the crowstep gables is the date 1595 and an octagonal design containing a saltire and the initials DM.

Industrial and Commercial Buildings

1. Boddin Limekilns, Boddin
NO 713 533

On Boddin Point, at the foot of the steep trackway from Boddin at the S end of the unclassified road from Dunninald. The substantial kilns at Boddin are the largest to survive in Angus, and their scale and appearance has seen them likened to an old Moorish fort rising from the coastal rocks. There are two main blocks remaining, erosion having recently carried off the S wall and the upper third of the stonework has also collapsed, but in the 1770s the structure consisted of one draw kiln and four 'ordinary' kilns. The kilns belong to the era of agricultural improvement in the later 18th and early 19th centuries, when lime was used to improve the fertility of the soils of Strathmore. There is little limestone available in Angus, most lime therefore being recovered from marl beds in the shallow lochans which dotted the pre-Improvement landscape, or carried inland from coastal sites like Boddin. The limestone outcrop here is reported to have been worked since 1696, but the present kilns appear to date from 1771 and were apparently the work of Archibald Scott of Usan.

Coal to fire the kilns had to be imported, sloops of a maximum of 40 tons' burden braving at high tide a 30-foot channel which held only 1 ft of water at low tide. Any swell or strong winds prevented a landing, rendering the fuel supply prone to the vagaries of the weather. In 1783 Archibald's brother, David Scott of Dunninald, constructed a wharf to render landings easier. The remains of this appear to be incorporated in the surviving slipway used by the salmon boats. With coal supply eased, and further encouraged by the repeal of the duty imposed on coal transported N of the Red Head in 1793, production soared and peaked at 40,000 bolls of lime annually. Rising expenses and the depletion of the limestone reserves led to abandonment in 1831.

The row of largely derelict cottages on the N side of the promontory housed the lime quarriers and fishermen involved in a local salmon fishery. The S house is still used as a salmon bothy, but was once the salmon gaffer's house. The icehouse in which the catch was stored is built into the steep slope leading down to the headland.

2. Coffin Mill (The Logie Works), Dundee NO 391 304

At the junction of Brook Street and Horsewater Wynd, S of Lochee Road. Rarely known to Dundonians by its official name of the Logie Works, this is one of the oldest surviving mill buildings in the city, dating from 1828. Its popular name, 'the Coffin Mill', is actually derived from the ground plan of the building, which occupies a tapering, wedge-shaped site, but mill tradition developed a rather gruesome tale of a female mill-worker whose hair became entangled in the machinery and dragged her to her gory death.

The building has undergone considerable alteration over time, especially since its demise as a jute works in the 1960s. The chimney at the W end of the main block has been removed to allow a new road into modern development on the N side of the mill to be built, but the position of the main engines powered by the boiler whose furnace vented up the stack can be seen clearly marked by the tiers of venetian windows in the SW wall of the main block. The remainder of the windows are plain rectangular openings. At the NW angle there is a large, seven storey tower capped by a low, pyramidal roof. At the time of writing the mill building is undergoing restoration.

3. Exchange Coffee House, Dundee NO 404 302

At the junction of Castle Street and Shore Terrace, now overshadowed by the approach roads to the Tay Road Bridge. Now divided up for various commercial uses including a public house and a stationer's store, this grand building was once one of the principal centres of Dundee's commercial life. Built in 1828 to designs by George Smith, it was a neo-classical palace fronting on to the city's main harbour area, frequented by the mercantile community. It is essentially a large rectangular box of two storeys, the ground floor with squat Doric pilasters divided into retail units to either side of the main entrance in the W side, the upper storey with soaring Ionic columns and pilasters. All the principal rooms were on the upper floor: Coffee House, Assembly Rooms, Merchant's Library and Reading Room, each lit by large windows with finely detailed architraves.

4. Fishtown of Usan, Icehouse and Saltpan, Usan NO 725 545

On the coast 1.75 miles S of Ferryden by unclassified road. While the fishing community of Usan is only on record from 1548, the estate in which it lies first appears in documentary sources in 1245. The main development of the community, however, appears to have been a late 18th and early 19th-century phenomenon, when the estate owners turned their attentions to the commercial possibilities of their coastal properties. Early maps show Usan to have been a straggling, dispersed community, but in 1822 the whole of this was swept away and replaced by the then laird, George Keith, by a single row of 28 cottages built of stone and lime and with slate roofs. The bold square tower with its pairs of high arched windows and crenellated parapet was built as a landmark for shipping, but from 1835 was leased to the coastguard service, along with the four houses at the E end of the row. These were larger, provided with additional attic rooms, and were intended for the guards and their families. The remainder of the houses were tenanted by fisher families, by those employed in the saltworks, and by the customs officials who monitored the taxable manufacture and trade in salt.

The main expansion of Usan began in the late 18th century. In 1787 there were 22 households in the community, a total of 61 persons, of whom the majority were fisher families. By 1791 there were 16 fishermen, some 20 families, and a population of 100. This was swollen after 1794 by the arrival of several dozen saltworkers, plus a full-time Salt Officer and Officer of Excise, posts which survived until the closure of the pans in the mid-1820s. By the mid 19th century the peak of fishing activity had been reached, with 39 fishers and 80 folk employed in the related occupations of curing, selling etc. Alongside these, however, there was also a sizeable population employed in agriculture on the farms in the hinterland, plus several families of Coastguards. A peak seems to have been reached in 1855, from when a long, slow decline set in. Part of the cause was a drift towards Ferryden, where the Usan men tied up their boats in winter, but cessation of involvement in herring fishing led to a rapid drop in numbers. Vacant houses were increasingly let to folk from Montrose as holiday cottages, or used to house estate workers. By 1910 12 of the houses had been let in this way and out of the remaining villagers only 10 men were involved in fishing. By 1920 that number had dropped to 5.

Although there appears to have been a major salmon fishery here since at least the 17th century, it seems to have been a secondary commercial development to the saltworks. This was established in 1794, the year following the abolition of the tax on the carriage of coal N of the Red Head which had rendered prohibitive the cost of fuelling such a major industrial venture in this part of the country. It is interesting to note that one of the main agitators for the repeal was David Scott of Dunninald, MP for Forfarshire, whose brother Archibald was laird of Usan at that time, and it is clear that the Scott brothers aimed to create a local monopoly in salt supply for themselves.

Of the saltworks, only one of the three pan houses survives, converted into an icehouse following the collapse of the Scottish salt industry in the 1820s. This is a large, stone-built structure standing on the foreshore, overlooking the table-rocks to the E of the village. Before the history of the saltwork at Usan was fully researched it was believed that this was simply another commercial icehouse, albeit with unusual features. Internally, it is a stone barrel-vaulted chamber divided into two compartments at the ratio of one to three instead of the more standard one to two. Externally, on its seaward gable it has a masonry projection described formerly as a buttress, flanked by two blocked windows, and in the foot of the gable, below high-water mark, there is an inlet. The 'buttress' is in fact a chimney stack, reduced in height after 1823 to the same level as the remainder of the building, while the windows formed ventilators and the inlet admitted sea-water to the pump which carried it up to the evaporating pan. The smaller of the two internal chambers appears to have been originally of two storeys, while to the S of the vaulted structure are the remains of an L-plan two storey structure with fireplaces and windows which formed a courtyard, open to the S, abutting the pan structure.

Running to seaward of these buildings is a clearly man-made channel cut through the rocks. Although this was later used as a shelter for fishing boats, its original purpose was to carry water to the inlets in the pan building. Water was collected on the flat area of rock to its N, contained within a slight rim which bounded its surface to form a lagoon some 5–10cm deep. This probably formed the first stage in the salt-producing process, natural evaporation increasing the salinity of the trapped water before it was discharged into the channel and pumped up into the boiling pans. At the seaward end of the channel are grooves which contained the mountings for a sluice gate. Scott hoped to produce 9,000 bushels of salt annually, supplying one third of local consumption, but even the building of a third pan in 1798 only raised annual output to 3,700 bushels.

5. Kingoodie Quarry and Piers, Invergowrie NO 347 295

Off the unclassified road from Invergowrie to Kingoodie village, 300m SW of Invergowrie railway station. The sandstone bluffs which break the former shoreline of the Tay to the S and W of Invergowrie have been the location of a series of important quarries from the Middle Ages until 1895 when quarrying ceased. Many of Dundee's buildings were constructed of Kingoodie stone, including, it is believed, the Old Steeple.

There are a series of quarry workings extending along the old shoreline to the W of the bridge carrying the Invergowrie-Kingoodie road over the Dundee-Perth railway line. The deeper quarry pits at most are now flooded and overgrown, but Kingoodie village itself, developed as accommodation for the quarriers, still has the remains of the pier from which the cut stone was shipped. The largest of the quarries lies to the E of the bridge over the railway, and is itself crossed by a 'bridge' carrying the railway line across its flooded depths. When it was drained in the early 1980s for repair work to be undertaken on the bridge piers, the old quarry buildings were revealed to be still intact below the waters. Immediately to its S, built from stone from the quarry, is a substantial wharf, possibly of later 18th-century date.

6. Turin Hill, Aberlemno NO 514 537

The N flanks of Turin Hill are pockmarked by numerous shallow pits. In two of them can be seen the remains of mill-stones which broke in the process of quarrying, and it is believed that the remaining pits represent the quarry-holes from which stones were successfully removed. There are no records of a substantial industry in mill-stone quarrying in this district.

TOURISM AND TRANSPORT

An Epilogue

The early 19th-century enthusiasm for the 'wild and romantic' aspects of Scottish landscape and culture, inspired largely by the writings of Sir Walter Scott, directed the eye of the aficionado towards the wild and rugged grandeur of the Highlands. As a result, to a great extent the eastern lowlands of Scotland, sandwiched between the popular Highlands and the Borders, missed out on the first rush of tourists seeking the 'wild' Scotland whose very antithesis was to be seen in the rolling agricultural lands of Angus and the Mearns. This preference was to be reinforced in the middle of the century through Queen Victoria's fixation with all things Highland, and her selection of Deeside for the location of her holiday home. As the ultimate arbiter of good taste, her preference literally set the royal seal of approval on the Highlands.

Holidaying of this type was, of course, a mainly upper class affair, far beyond the pockets of the lower middle and working classes of the larger towns and cities. This genteel holidaying saw the commercial development of villages such as Banchory – which had the added benefit of being in royally-endorsed Deeside – and Stonehaven, particularly in the period from 1860–1900. In these places, wealthy middle-class families could build summer villas, or local speculators would build houses for letting during the summer months. This fashion is now reflected in the large numbers of substantial baronial villas now converted into small hotels or guest houses. Changing tastes, however, saw this kind of holiday enter a long decline after World War I, especially as the upper classes began to go abroad. The one great survivor was at the top end of the scale. The enthusiasm throughout the later Victorian and Edwardian periods for sporting holidays and outdoor activities, encouraged by the pastimes of Edward VII and George V, saw the development of sporting estates along the Highland fringe in N Angus and across the ridge of the Mounth in Kincardineshire. The shooting register at *Fasque House* is a somewhat gruesome, if fascinating, record of the pre-World War I sporting obsession: on one day alone in 1905, the laird and seven of his friends shot over 3000 pheasants!

A transformation began in the later 1850s and 1860s with the development of the rail network through the region. Angus had, in fact, been at the forefront of railway-mania, the line from Dundee to Newtyle having been opened as early as 1831, making it one of the earliest passenger lines in Scotland. Although it had served a primary purpose of bringing in the agricultural produce of Strathmore to feed the expanding urban population of Dundee, it quickly developed a recreational function and remained popular until well into this century. The cheap transport which the railways offered quickly created a new phenomenon – holiday tourism. Whereas the development of holidaying in the Highlands had been largely an aristocratic and middle class affair, the railways served a wider public and put many parts of the country into the reach of the urban working classes.

The rapid development of the Clyde Coast resorts as the recreation ground for the urban masses of Glasgow in the late 19th and early 20th centuries was paralleled on a smaller scale along the east coast. Small fishing villages, like Broughty Ferry at the mouth of the Tay to the E of Dundee, which lay within easy reach of the city and was popular with rich and poor alike, experienced a rapid transformation into summer holiday destinations. Whilst the jute-lords and commercial barons of the city favoured it as the location for their out-of-town fantasy castles, to generations of working-class Dundonians it was the nearest escape to the seaside, brought nearer still by the arrival of the railway in 1848. The expanding rail network round Dundee opened up the city's hinterland in the same way, allowing day-excursions or longer holidays to such exotic locations as Kirriemuir or Liff. The Tay Rail Bridge, first opened in 1878, had a similar effect for NE Fife, encouraging the growth of the small villages along the S side of the Tay opposite Dundee, but it was the ferry links from the city – the Fifies – which had a deeper emotional hold for generations of Dundonians escaping the urban grime for the North Sea freshness of St. Andrews or Tayport.

BIBLIOGRAPHY AND FURTHER READING

Adams, D.G., *Bothy Nichts and Days: Farm Bothy Life in Angus and the Mearns* (Edinburgh, 1992).

Adams, D.G., *Celtic and Medieval Religious Houses in Angus* (Brechin, 1984).

Coutts, H., *Ancient Monuments of Tayside* (Dundee Museums, 1970).

Fawcett, R., *Scottish Medieval Churches* (HMSO, 1985).

Fawcett, R., *Scottish Abbeys and Priories* (London, 1994).

Hanson, W.S., *Agricola and the Conquest of the North* (London, 1987).

Henshall, A., *The Chambered Tombs of Scotland*, volume I (Edinburgh, 1963).

Laing, L. and Laing, J., *The Picts and the Scots* (Stroud, 1993).

Ritchie, G. and Ritchie, A., *Scotland: Archaeology and Early History* (Edinburgh, 1991).

Shepherd, I.A.G., *Exploring Scotland's Heritage: Grampian* (HMSO, 1986).

Tabraham, C., *Scottish Castles and Fortifications* (HMSO, 1986).

Walker, B. and Ritchie, G., *Exploring Scotland's Heritage: Fife and Tayside* (HMSO, 1987).

Walker, D. and McKean C., *Dundee: An Illustrated Architectural Guide* (RIAS, 1984).

Wickham-Jones, C.R., *Scotland's First Settlers* (London, 1994).